THE FATE OF HOLOCAUST MEMORIES

THE FATE OF HOLOCAUST MEMORIES

Transmission and Family Dialogues

CHAYA H. ROTH

with the voices of
Hannah Diller
and
Gitta Fajerstein

The Fate of Holocaust Memories: Transmission and Family Dialogues
Copyright © 2008 by Chaya H. Roth

First paperback edition, 2013
Published by Chaya Roth, Chicago, IL
crothphd@sbcglobal.net

ISBN-13: 978-0615796369
ISBN-10: 0615796362

Originally published in 2008 by Palgrave Macmillan, New York, NY

The Library of Congress has catalogued the Palgrave Macmillan edition as follows:

Roth, Chaya H.
   The fate of Holocaust memories: transmission and family dialogues / Chaya
H. Roth; with the voices of Hannah Diller and Gitta Fajerstein-Walchirk.
     p.cm.
   Includes bibliographical references and index
   ISBN 0-230-60607-5
   1. Diller, Hannah Kantorowicz Horowitz, 1908–Interviews. 2. Jews–Germany
–Berlin–Biography. 3. Jews, Polish–Germany–Berlin–Biography. 4. Holo-
caust, Jewish (1939–1945)–Personal narratives. 5. Holocaust survivors–
Biography. 6. Berlin (Germany)–Biography. 7. Roth, Chaya H. I. Title

DS134.42.D55 R68 2008
940.53/18092 B

                                                              2008004036

Printed in the United States of America

Dedicated to the memory of
Aron Jakob Horowitz
and
Hannah Kantorowicz Horowitz Diller.
May their names be remembered
for a blessing, courage, and love.

TABLE OF CONTENTS

LIST OF PHOTOS AND LETTERS

ACKNOWLEDGMENTS

This book has been in the making for a long time. I was almost eight, in August 1942, when I made myself a promise to write down what I saw happening before me. Decades later, when our children were born, I decided that in order to remember what I saw, I must tell it to our children so they will remember. But I was not up to the task. I simply did not know, understand, or remember enough. This book began as a collection of memories culled from my family members, woven into family dialogues concerning episodes during World War II and the Holocaust.

Nothing happens to anyone without the help of another; and so there are the family members, friends, and valued colleagues whom I wish to thank for their unconditional support and just hard fraught help.

To my closest I express my everlasting gratitude.

To Hannah Diller, my mother, without whom my sister and I would not have survived; who always told me the truth and made me feel that I was smart enough to understand the dangers we were facing.

To my dear sister Gitta Fajerstein, who was but nine years old when the persecutions began, in whose care I was entrusted whenever my mother was absent. She was very brave and responsible, watched over me lovingly, and always knew where to find me when I was lost. In our taped dialogues we checked our memories one with the other, and with our mother's.

To Ari Roth, Gefen Roth, and Miriam Raider-Roth, artist,

scholar, and professor, who listened, challenged, reflected my be-wilderment and dread, and encouraged me to disentangle what I was trying to embark on. With their uniquely honed skills, each held my feet to the fire when my nerve faltered. Each took time to improve on my writing, helped me to organize my thoughts, and critiqued various parts of the manuscript. Each surely knows the extent of their inimitable contributions to this work. This I know for sure: without them there would have been no book.

To Walter Roth, my friend, companion and beloved spouse, who liked what I did, revised, queried, and questioned but never hovered over me, never felt that it was for his sake that I had to suc-ceed in this or any other task—to him I owe every good thing that life has given me.

To Kate Schecter, Mark Raider, and Stephen Zeldes, my dear "new" nuclear family members, esteemed scholars and professors, who, without wanting to intrude, were exceedingly helpful whenever I needed their advice.

To Isabel and Sophie Roth, Miko and Tema Zeldes-Roth, and Jonah, Emma, and Talia Raider-Roth, the smartest, most beauti-ful, and caring human beings, my grandchildren, who make me proud and bestow their abundant love on Wally and me. They were involved in this project almost from the beginning; they produced questionnaires, asked questions, and helped find the priest Don Brondello whom we all honored as a Righteous Among the Nations in Cuneo, in 2004. Without them and their wonderful parents, there would be no listeners to hear our endless stories. Without them there would be no future. With them the possibilities are endless.

To Gitta's and Sam's children, Dan Fajerstein, Ron Fajer-stein, and RB, and all their children, specifically, to Sasha, Sam, and Jacob Fajerstein, who participated in the family project, who were inquisitive, thoughtful, helpful, respectful, and loving throughout, I give my unlimited love and thankfulness. Profound thanks to Ra-chel, Arielle, and Adina Bier and their parents, Michael and RB; to

Ron, who participated in the interviews; and to Ron and Kyla for their participation in the dedication and honoring of Don Francesco Brondello as a Righteous Among the Nations, and in honoring Andreina Blua and her daughter Anna Marabotto for their great courage in letting us stay in their *cava* in the mountains above Valdieri, in the most dangerous days of the German occupation, September 1943 to April, 1944.

I am grateful to Oscar Walchirk who read the manuscript and was kind and encouraging throughout its production.

Profound thanks to Helen Dittmer, my loving family, who read the manuscript from beginning to end and provided generous feedback and was almost as concerned as I with the many deadlines that hovered over me, and to Lowell and Mark for their quiet and meaningful support.

To Herb and Elsa Roth who were warm, supportive, and understanding throughout these many years, I am deeply grateful.

To my esteemed colleagues:

Peter Hayes, who unstintingly read the manuscript over and over until he was as satisfied with the punctuation as with its content and historical accuracy, my gratitude is boundless. He remains my source of unlimited and significant historical information and has been my role model for many years.

John K. Roth, whom I knew only from afar through his careful work on the Holocaust and who responded with an open heart to my request that he read the manuscript. He provided pointed observations throughout, offered immense help, and gave me more support than I ever could have dared to hope for.

Christopher Browning, who in spite of his loaded schedule read the manuscript cover to cover, commented encouragingly on what was innovative about the manuscript, questioned spelling, and as the biggest favor of all told me succinctly what parts I might consider omitting. Such assistance is the most precious gift of all.

To Susan Zuccotti, whose work on the history of the Holocaust in France, Italy, and the Vatican during World War II influenced me deeply, I am most grateful. Her latest book on Holocaust Odysseys brings together many stories of survivors who crossed the Alps in flight of the Nazis' ferocious pursuits. Susan Zuccotti has shown each of us child survivors the utmost dedication and wholehearted help. Her instructions as to how to proceed about nominating the now-aging padre, Don Francesco Brondello, as a Righteous Among the Nations on behalf of my family and many Jews hiding out in the mountains around Valdieri, was most useful and speeded up considerably the process with Yad Vashem. And if this were not sufficient, Susan Zuccotti, as a loyal and trusted mentor, took it upon herself to show me where I had to improve on my research and my writing of this manuscript.

To Phyllis Lassner, who read through the many parts of the manuscript, my profound thanks for taking time out of her own busy scholarly work to engage in thoughtful discussions and provide resource materials, thereby enlarging generously on my knowledge.

To Zev Weiss, founder and director of the Holocaust Educational Foundation, whose work introduced me to the best of Holocaust scholars, and shared with me much of his own widespread knowledge on the Holocaust, my gratitude knows no limit.

To my friend and colleague social scientist, Laurie Wakschlag and her husband Milt, who were thrilled by my work, read through it, raised questions and made most helpful comments that prompted deeper thinking on my part, I carry unlimited gratitude.

To Raya Schapiro, my dearest friend, physician, and colleague, who departed too soon, before this work was completed. She was my best friend and toughest critic, and my most loving one too.

To Bennett L. Leventhal, dear friend, physician, scientist, and colleague of long-standing, whose excitement knew no bounds when he read the first finished draft of the manuscript and whose interest did not waver throughout its preparation, I give my loving thankfulness.

To Alberto Cavaglion, historian and archivist of the Resistance and contemporary history, I owe deep gratitude for his help finding the necessary papers describing Don Brondello's activities in Italy during the War, 1943–1944, and for his friendship throughout.

To Enzo Cavaglion, long-standing head of the Jewish community in Cuneo, and Resistance fighter in his younger years, my heartfelt gratitude for all his efforts in bringing the community together to honor Don Brondello.

To Sandro and Piera Cappellaro, Gigi Ferraro, and Marcella Risso, activists, intellectuals, and historians of the state of Cuneo, who have opened their hearts to my family and have shown how serious research in vivo can enliven the scholarly life of an entire community such as Saluzzo, and beyond. They, together with the Cavaglions, and many others, dignitaries and citizens, have organized the Remembrance March of the Jews from Saint-Martin-Vésubie over the Alps, through the passes of the Ciriegia and the Finestre for the past eleven years in order to keep alive the memories of the flight of Jews from France into Italy in September 1943.

To my closest friends, Roz and Bernie Ebstein who unhesitatingly knew that this was the right thing for me to do, encouraged me to keep up the work, and responded from beginning to end with trust and affirmation.

To Joan and Irv White, our dearest friends, who stood by me, encouraging me to persevere in spite of the stumbling blocks I found.

To Ira Glick, Susan Glick, and Linda Siegel, what better friends than those who roll up their sleeves and actually try to provide guidance in the course of this project?

To Olga Weiss, Ava Schieber, and Isaac Levendel, dear friends and child survivors, each surely knows the extent of their support and encouragement they gave in developing this work, and how often they rescued me from solitude in the process of reminiscing. To Marcia Gilman for her most insightful comments throughout, and Danya Tzur for her unwavering and unlimited support and editorial comments.

To Elaine Fox and her husband Alan, who have known our stories and remembered incidents that no one except my mother knew. Elaine is the energetic constructive editor of the anthology *Out of Chaos: Hidden Children Remember the Holocaust*, ed. Elaine Saphier Fox, introd. Phyllis Lassner, Northwestern University Press, 2013.

To Jerry and Leona Schecter, our family, who joined us on the trip to Cuneo to honor Don Francesco Brondello and whose editorial eyes never missed a false beat in this manuscript, I extend more thanks than they can ever know.

To Raffi and Irit Shacham, and Annegret Wenz, who joined us from Israel and Germany in Cuneo.

To David and Liz Raider, our family, who knew of the project and queried with interest and approbation throughout, thereby offering a helpful shoulder in the work.

To Nancy and Jack Zeldes, our family, I reserve very special thanks, for without Nancy's contact I would not have arrived at the doorstep of Palgrave Macmillan.

To Jason Johnson, whose knowledge of history and the English language enabled me to trust his assistance on this manuscript.

To Colleen Russell, for her contributions to the preparation of the paperback edition.

To Matthew Miller, for his work on the cover design and photo editing for the paperback edition.

To Susan Rosenberg, my assistant, who is one of the most helpful editors I have met, my heartfelt thanks. She taught me what caring and careful editing actually is.

And last, but really first, to Judy Kaufteil, my childhood friend from Antwerp (1948), who kept my diary and all my letters written during my adolescence for all these years, I express my everlasting gratitude.

MAP: ESCAPE ACROSS EUROPE 1939–1945

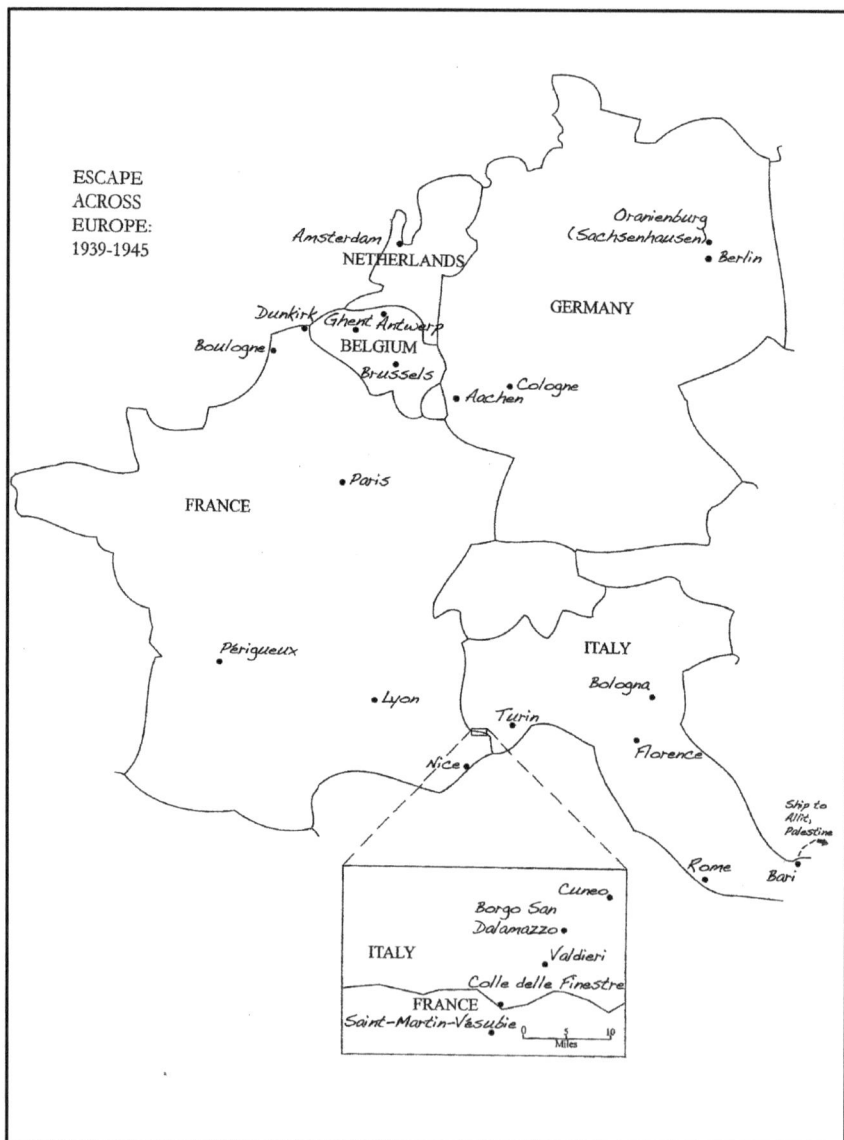

ESCAPE
ACROSS
EUROPE:
1939-1945

Amsterdam
NETHERLANDS

Oranienburg
(Sachsenhausen)
• Berlin

GERMANY

Dunkirk / Ghent • Antwerp
Boulogne • BELGIUM
• Brussels

• Cologne
• Aachen

• Paris

FRANCE

• Périgueux

ITALY

• Bologna

• Lyon
Turin

Nice •

• Florence

Ship to
Alise,
Palestine

Rome • • Bari

Cuneo •
Borgo San
Dalamazzo •

ITALY

• Valdieri

Colle delle Finestre

FRANCE
Saint-Martin-Vesubie

0   5   10
Miles

INTRODUCTION

Many years ago I committed to tell our family's story. We were in hiding then in the south of France, on August 26, 1942. As the youngest, at almost eight years old, I knew a number of essentials about our family's history but more was expected of me should we be caught in a roundup of Jews. That date, and my misfortune of being hauled off during a massive roundup in Nice, southern France, and later released, were grounds for my vow. Today, as an aging parent, grandparent, and a child survivor[1] of the Holocaust, I still wrestle with memories of my years of running, hiding, impersonating what I was not, and facing situations that threatened our family's life and mine. Though I have seen quieter times in recent decades, embraced the fruits of my extended family's postwar achievements, and experienced much personal joy and success, I still ache with aspects of my painful past and wonder "What have I passed on to my children about those chaotic war years and how will they remember what they had been told?"

"Will the memories I so insistently shared with them fade from their consciousness in time, and possibly from my own?" This concern clearly covers a deeper restlessness, the ultimate perhaps that demands, "What will live on after my death?" I hear the echo of Hayim Nachman Bialik, our famous Jewish poet who long ago voiced a similar apprehension in his verse, "After My Death."[2]

> After my death, say this about me
> There was a man and see he is no more.

He died before his time, that man.
His life's song in midpoint came to a halt.
A pity! There was one more song in him,
And now that song is gone,
Forever gone

I want to say, "Hold on, my task is not done!" I need to know whether my accounts of the war will lead to a remembrance that my children will be able to transmit to theirs, and they to their future children, as yet unborn, albeit with greater knowledge than I conveyed to mine. Even so, even when transmission of narratives does occur, no family tale is ever complete, nor can any person accurately reflect the stories of another. Family experiences during the Holocaust do not stand up to scrutiny or to comparison with the non-persecuted families. That is why my only option here is to be explicit about what I saw during the war, and to tell things my family and I remember, thereby bringing to the fore the unique voices of the few.

This manuscript then, tells my family's story. It reveals how we—our mother Hannah, my sister Gitta, and I—committed to pass on our memories of World War II and the *Shoah*.[3] We[4] insisted on telling what went on from the beginning of the war with the Nazi invasion of Poland in September 1939 until our liberation in Rome, in June 1944. Unlike many survivors who had been in hiding or living on the run, and did not speak much after they were liberated, hoping to move on with life without dwelling on the painful and troubling past, our family did speak about our attempts to make it through those years. Some survivors we knew who did not share their experiences with their children may have held back, possibly because they did not want to frighten their young ones and hoped to protect them from relentless anxieties; or perhaps they hoped to assure their children that the present, postwar times were not fraught with dangers such as existed during the Holocaust; perhaps they wanted to emphasize instead that they were living in a safer world now than their parents had. The scholarly literature on the effects of transmission is vast. I will only attend to its details as it pertains to our story, for mine is a task of description, not of explanation or deep hypothetical interpretations of the workings of the unconscious mind. My aim is that of recounting aspects of our family's experiences as we told our children and they told theirs.

Hannah, Gitta, and I spoke often about what happened to us. We tried to remember the dangers, threats, and near misses we had faced that seemed insurmountable; and recalled how we were saved with the help of others and how we saved ourselves. From the 1960s on, and throughout the next four decades, the tempo of our narratives intensified, especially after our children were born. Our narratives highlighted our fears of being picked up and deported, and the children knew that we were never free of fear; but they also knew that almost every experience we tackled ended in relief and not in demise (with a few terrible exceptions); to be sure, they also knew that during the war we were never safe for long, and even when we were out of harm's way it seemed but for brief moments in time. We shared with our children the realization that we were lucky to be alive, at times using our own resources and at other times with the help of a number of non-Jewish individuals that we had met during those difficult years, who were compassionate, daring, and exceptionally helpful on our behalf.

Because my internal world had never been secure, not during and not after the war, from the 1960s on, living in a safe world was not something I aspired to transmit. In short, I didn't believe that a safe world was something we could reasonably expect to attain. But trying to keep the children safe, as if to prepare them for the next onslaught and talking to them about the importance of learning to fall back on their own resources were clear goals of mine. When an episode about the war came to mind, I would say to my children, "This is what I want you to know." With this tone I implied that I expected them to remember the details of a story not only for the moment but for the long run and for safekeeping. The critical points for me were "to not forget" and to tell them what I knew to the extent that I did, so they would follow suit and tell their own children someday. In short, we shared Holocaust memories in family conversations and tape-recorded them over four decades. The major account here is based on the memories of events and the notes of these recordings. However, to cite Gary Kenyon,[5] "events are not objective facts.... [E]ach survivor's story... is composed both of facts as remembered by the survivor and the story created around the event. The story is a unit containing both [elements]." So, when I fixate on telling the facts without interpretations (as in letting the facts speak for themselves), it is useful to remember that there are no facts without the story that the teller has composed in order to make sense of those "facts."

About Memory

What is memory then, and what is the truth of a memory when one person tells it to another? Is memory "truth," "hearsay," or "fantasy"? Can a child's memory be trusted about events that happen from ages five through eleven? Can an adult's memory of events that occurred four or six decades ago be trusted? What is memory?

Psychologist Mark L. Howe,[6] in his book *The Fate of Early Memories,* speaks of memory as sensory, perceptual, attentional, motoric, and neural mechanisms that support the cortical and subcortical structures in the brain. From this vantage point memory's functions encode, store, and retrieve pertinent information from the environment as well as from the person's inner experience.

The retrieval processes necessary to memorize and retain information are laid down early in life. Research has shown that cortical structures can encode information from infancy on, but those infantile memories tend to disappear rapidly unless they are subjected over time to repeated reminders and elaborations of the encoded and stored events. In other words, one would not expect infants to remember events from birth on, even though they have the capacity to encode information. However from infancy on, some stressful and traumatic events can be held onto provided the stressors that brought them about in the beginning occurred repeatedly and frequently over extended periods of time.

Traumatized adults and children who suffered abuse, brutality, violence, devastation, and dehumanizing conditions cannot help but repeat or reenact sometimes the events to which they were subjected; but some horrifying memories can only be dealt with through dissociation. Dissociated painful experiences appear to have been "forgotten"; they split the memory of the trauma from consciousness, thereby making it possible for the individual to function normally in all realms except the one connected to the trauma. The literature abounds with writings on the retrieval, or lack thereof, of painful and traumatic experiences. Moskovitz and Krell[7] see dissociated, repressed, or suppressed memories as adaptations to survival. "Whatever the memories, much is repressed as too fearful for recall, or suppressed by well-meaning caretakers wishing the child to forget." Jane Marks[8] recalls a child survivor's words: "So much of my childhood between the ages of four and nine is blank...."

The problem for many survivors, and child survivors in particular, is how not to forget what they wish to remember. For me, as a young child between the ages of five and ten during the war, the central issue was to be credible. Too often I was told that I had forgotten what happened; as a result I developed a fear that if I did not commit to memory what had happened, my memory gaps would become larger than they already were. Robert Krell,[9] himself a child survivor of the Holocaust, speaks about such predicaments with young children. My commitment was to ensure that I remember correctly the events of my youth. Some particularly painful events I was able to repeat word for word, time and time again. Others, I had suppressed or dissociated. Others still, I needed to hear from my elders. And later, when I spoke to children and adults, I tried to explain how those ordeals had affected me. In short, what I wanted to avoid at all cost was to accidentally alter or distort the past.

As might be expected, as mother and daughters, Hannah, Gitta, and I differed in our approaches to sharing experiences; but somewhere deep down, what united us was the fear that forgetting might dull or efface even those memories we felt very sure of. To avoid distortion or surfacing with memory gaps, we sought to validate our memories with each other; and in later years, our children revisited the stories we had told and challenged what they did not understand, asking for explanations. An example of such verification in later years was the following: "But you told us that your father died of a heart attack! Then you told us that he picked up a young boy who fainted after standing a long time next to him at *Appell* (roll call), and he cried out *'Shema Israel!'* (Hear, Oh Israel!) Did you change the story now, or did you discover something new?" challenged my son. This confrontation was his attempt to test the truth of what I had told him. And there was a third version, the last and most authentic one, that my mother told us late in her life.

I understood that my children needed to verify what I had told them. But being challenged by them sent tremors through me nevertheless. Did my children think that I made things up, or worse, that I had lied to them? And, if the children heard several versions of the same story, which would have been the true account? In fact, there were several versions of a number of stories, so that I myself did not know which fragments happened when. I was more undone than they knew; because in forgetting to tell or in telling three versions of a single event, they could suspect the veracity of other memories I had shared with them. And once doubt and disbelief set in, will that not lead to a trivialization, or worse, a negation of the past? I should have said to my son, citing Katherine Borland,[10] a scholar in comparative studies, "This is not what I said. I told you several versions about my father's death as I came to know each version over the years in talking with my mother. And so the 'truth' of my father's death came gradually to me, and by approximations, just as it has come to you."

Autobiographical memory is what this work is about. According to psychologist A.D. Baddeley,[11] autobiographical memory is "the capacity of people to recollect their lives," to remember those events that shaped their lives and to understand the significance of these events to them. One may also ask, "Can life events once forgotten be remembered? And can significant life events once remembered be forgotten again?"

Forgetting aspects of one's history that one wishes to remember is frustrating and problematic. However, under certain conditions, as will be shown, certain aspects of one's life that were thought to have been forgotten can be remembered. But distortions, lapses, and memory gaps do occur, and these may never be retrieved. That too, is in the nature of autobiographical memory.

About Transmission

The transgenerational effects of the Holocaust on the children remain controversial. The central issues of transmission deal with the question of transmission of psychopathology. According to Kellerman,[12] "a rich body of unique psychological knowledge with almost four hundred publications" exists regarding transgenerational transmission of the Holocaust. Chaitin[13] developed a theoretical framework basing her work in part on Bar-On's, delineating five areas for understanding the consequences of the Holocaust on the families of survivors. These areas are: "knowledge of the facts; understanding the reason for historical events; emotions towards the Holocaust; attitudes towards the consequences of the Holocaust; and present-day behavior." In our family, the telling of our experiences to our children from early childhood on did in fact comprise these five aspects. As can be seen in every chapter of this book, particularly in chapters six and seven, our approach to sharing memories and events of the Holocaust fell easily into these five areas. However, I believe if we are to understand the world as it exists today, it behooves us to bring to our children the experiences of joy, aesthetics, pleasure, and the giving back to society what we have been able to glean from it. In addition, essential for the sake of transmission is not only our focus on "what" content is transmitted but also "how" transmission occurs. How transmission is handled, namely the character of transmission itself, affects the nature of the content in essential ways. Sure to be included are how affect and values are transmitted. And one needs to have a long-range perspective on how transmission will be handled in the future.

It is generally accepted that parental attempts to share memories occur not only in planned ways but also in unplanned and unconscious ways.[14] Transmission of past events can occur at different levels of consciousness but we try to confine ourselves to the manifest content of the past.

In our family, Hannah spoke openly about our family's past and about what happened to her during the war. She shared with us not only what happened to her and how she understood those experiences but also what she learned from those experiences. Gitta and I did similarly with our children. What we, once-hidden children, told our children (second generation) and what the latter, now parents, tell their children (third generation) is the mainstay of this story.

The Details of the Story

The book is divided into three parts. In part I, Hannah's memoir begins with eighteen handwritten pages in which she speaks about her experiences in Germany when Hitler is appointed chancellor of the Third Reich on January 30, 1933. She next revisits her family background with a stirring account leading up to World War I, 1914, and the courtship in the 1920s with her beloved Aron Jakob. She tells the story of her grandfather *Rav* (Rabbi) Itsche Kupferstock, under whose watchful influence they raised their family and with whom Aron Jakob studied to obtain *smicheh* (rabbinical ordination).

Next Hannah, Gitta, and I reminisce about our numerous escapes and times in hiding: from Berlin in 1939; Antwerp, Dunkirk, Boulogne, and Brussels, 1940–1942; Nice and Vence, 1942–1943; Saint-Martin-Vésubie, 1943; Valdieri, 1943–1944; Rome, 1944–1945; ending up in Israel (then Palestine), 1945–1946.

Part II illustrates the live telling of our experiences to our children, now grown. We traveled to Europe in 1982 to relive together incidents that had significantly marked Wally's and my early lives. We spoke about our experiences before and during the war, and our children, who had heard these stories in earlier years, participated in reconstructing the past even as they formulated new thoughts about the Holocaust. The aim of the trip was double: primarily we would transmit the experiences we had during the war and together we would learn the history of the Holocaust; but we also wanted to offset the somberness to which our children had been subjected with an infusion of the "good life" we had in Europe, when we were in our twenties and thirties and they were barely conceived. What I had in mind was to transmit and integrate our legacy, the bad and the good so to speak; and, therefore, discovering together works of art, stunning landscapes, delicious foods, music and dance of all kinds could not be omitted. Because in our minds, parental legacies, if they were to be accepted and enjoyed, had to consist of a commingling of all that mattered in our family life.

Part III focuses on generational interviews. Members of the three generation, beginning with Hannah (in excerpted versions from her earlier audiotapes) speak about the meaning of their memories; in addition the second-generation children speak about what they hope to pass on to their children, and the third-generation children imagine what they intend to pass on to their future children, the fourth generation. The manuscript ends with a chapter dedicated to the story of my Uncle Fishel, who survived Auschwitz and the Holocaust, to whom I promised that this story would be part of our family book.

The Interview Phase

The interview phase of the family project began in March 2000; it explored aspects associated with memory and transmission of the Holocaust. It consisted of semiformal discussions conducted by a journalist interviewer, Susan Glick, trained by Survivors of the Shoah Visual History Foundation (now the USC Shoah Foundation Institute for Visual History and Education) to attend to the narratives of survivors and of second- and third-generation children of survivors. All family interviews were tape-recorded and transcribed.

The Participants

The survivors are Hannah, Gitta, and Chaya (myself). Hannah's first taping took place in 1976 when she was sixty-eight years old. Gitta, the first-born daughter, was seventy in the year 2000; and I was sixty-six. Gitta's husband, Sam, died of illness in 1985 at age sixty-two. In 2000, at the start of the interviews, Wally's and my children, the second generation, were Ari, age forty, Gefen, thirty-eight, and Miriam, thirty-five.[15] Dan, also second-generation, Gitta and Sam's son, was forty. Isabel, third generation, Ari and Kate's daughter, was eleven. Sasha, third generation, Dan and C.'s daughter, was twelve. As such, as of this writing, the voices of ten family members are heard in these chapters: Wally, Gefen, and Miriam in chapter six; Hannah, Gitta, Dan, Isabel, and Sasha in chapter seven; and Chaya and Ari in both chapters six and seven.

On Holocaust Generations

As survivors of the Holocaust, Gitta and I had always seen ourselves as (hidden) child survivors, second to our mother's generation, which would relegate our children to the third generation, and our grandchildren to the fourth generation. The literature, however, holds otherwise. All who survived the Holocaust are identified as "first generation survivors," whereas those who were born after the

Holocaust are known as members of the second generation. This created a conceptual dilemma for us. As child survivors, Gitta and I identified ourselves as carriers of our survivor-mother and our father's legacies. When in the interviews I asked our mother how she coped with the tragedies of the Holocaust, how she instructed us on how to manage dangerous situations, and why, in light of our past, it was our mission to maintain good values and ideals, her parental approaches to these issues became guidelines in our daily lives, both during the war and afterward. As such, both my sister and I incorporated our mother's teachings. Gitta and I saw ourselves as Hannah's second generation inheritors. Combining these generational functions into one conceptual category—that is, as one "survivor" generation—did not represent our experienced reality during the war.

Nevertheless, my sister's and my realities were not the only factors to consider in the method of counting survivor generations. Because children of survivors cited in the literature have grown to identify themselves as second generation, as have our own children, for the sake of clarity and consistency with the works of fellow students of the Holocaust, this work does identify adult and child survivors as one generation. Still I argue that the fusing of the parent and child identities into one generation glosses over many distinctions that need to be made between adult and child survivors of the Holocaust.

Suleiman,[16] tackling a similar issue, speaks about "the 1.5 generation who survived in Europe during the Holocaust and were too young to have been [present] during the Nazi persecution." Similarly, Hirsch[17] speaks about the "post memory generation of those who were children born in the immediate years after the war to Jews who survived the Holocaust in Europe." Both scholars attempt to reckon with how to identify the children of Jewish survivors who were in Europe during and immediately after the Holocaust. My initial view that my sister and I, who are hidden child survivors, are, therefore, second to our mother's generation, made excellent sense to me, but because it was inconsistent with the established scholarly nomenclature, and more importantly, with our second-generation children who had already identified themselves as the second generation, I think the issue as to who is a second-generation survivor can be dropped for the time being, until members of the third and fourth generations find it appropriate to clarify these concepts further.

Ultimately, from where I stand, the question that requires understanding is how transmission of the Holocaust happened in our family.

Did I think of transmission as a linear process in which information is deposited more or less according to the developmental age of the children and can then be recaptured more or less at will? Or is it a multilinear and multifaceted process in which memories are stored according to unpredictable timetables? In short, is transmission predictable, or is it haphazard? What follows is our family's attempt at unfolding this process.

SIGNIFICANT FIGURES

Hannah Kantorowicz Horowitz (Diller)	adult survivor; mother of Gitta and Chaya
Chaya Horowitz Roth	child survivor; sister of Gitta
Gitta Horowitz Fajerstein	child survivor; sister of Chaya
Aron Jakob Horowitz	husband of Hannah; father of Gitta and Chaya
Sarah Gittel Kantorowicz	mother of Hannah
Simon "Simmel" Kantorowicz	father of Hannah
Betty Kantorowicz	sister of Hannah
Cilly Kantorowicz	sister of Hannah
Yakov Shloime Kantorowicz	brother of Hannah
"Itsche" Diller	father of Aron Jakob
Serel Horowitz	mother of Aron Jakob
Mirjam Diller-Horowitz	sister of Aron Jakob
Chana Diller-Horowitz	sister of Aron Jakob
Yossele Diller-Horowitz	brother of Aron Jakob
Hersch Zvi Diller	brother of Aron Jakob
Rav Abraham Isaac "Itsche" Kupferstock	grandfather of Hannah
Hene Hinde Chaje Kupferstock	grandmother of Hannah
Mendl Kantorowicz	grandfather of Hannah
Rachel Fajge Kantorowicz	grandmother of Hannah
"Tante" Roizele Horowitz	aunt of Aron Jakob; mother of seven children
"Itsche" Horowitz	husband of Roizele, uncle of Aron Jakob; father of seven children
Fishel Horowitz	one of Roizele and Itsche's seven children
Mendl Horowitz	one of Roizele and Itsche's seven children
Sam Fajerstein	survivor; husband of Gitta
Walter Roth	first generation refugee-survivor; husband

of Chaya

Ari	second generation; son of Chaya and Walter
Gefen	second generation; daughter of Chaya and Walter
Miriam	second generation; daughter of Chaya and Walter
Ron	second generation; son of Gitta and Sam
RB	second generation; daughter of Gitta and Sam
Dan	second generation; son of Gitta and Sam
Sasha, Sam, and Jacob	third generation; children of Dan and C.
Miko and Tema	third generation; children of Gefen and Steve
Isabel and Sophie	third generation; children of Ari and Kate
Jonah, Emma, and Talia	third generation; children of Miriam and Mark
Rachel, Arielle, and Adina	third generation; children of RB and Michael
Luzer Dafner	second husband of Hannah
Willy Toronczyk (and wife Regina, son Freddy)	committee member representing the Jewish community in Nice
Mr. Lempl and son Michel'eke	friends who brought Michel'eke to Hannah's care
Moishe Fass and wife Hindze	friend offering Hannah economic advice
Benjamin Bestimmt	cantor at the Oranienburger Strasse Synagogue, Berlin
Andreina Blua and her daughter Anna Marabotto	Italian woman and her daughter who hid Hannah, Gitta, and Chaya for months in a *cava*
Don Francesco Brondello	Italian priest who rescued Hannah, Gitta, and Chaya

PART I

HANNAH AND HER FAMILY

CHAPTER ONE

HANNAH'S MEMOIR

When I decided to write my mother's life story, I invited her to spend the weekend with me in a little resort away from the city. I asked her, "Would you like me to write your life's story?"

"And you are going away only with me and no one else?" "Yes Mama," I said. "We are going away together." Hannah answered, "And what will you say in my story?" I told her, "I will listen to your words, record them, and let your words speak for themselves."

After our first night, Hannah greeted me warmly at breakfast and handed me a sheaf of yellow pages. "This is what I wrote for you," she said. "It's the beginning of my memoir. I wrote eighteen pages last night so you can start your book."

Memoir of Hannah Diller from 1933 until After the War

[The first eighteen pages were handwritten in German in October 1982 and translated by me (Chaya).]

For Us It Began in 1933

For us it began early in March 1933 when the Nazi *Sturmabteilung* (SA, Storm Troops) rose up in Berlin. They went on a rampage against the communists and the Jews. The SA committed unspeakable brutalities against young people. They savagely assaulted both

Jews and Christians whom they suspected of anti-Nazi activities; because many Jews were also leftists, the men of the SA were especially brutal with them, torturing Jews with sadistic relish. They came to our building, in March or April, I don't remember exactly, and took a young man from a Jewish Orthodox home to the Horst-Wessel Platz, a building that had served as a central meeting place for the communists. This building had now been converted to a roundup place for communists and Jews, for all who were threats to the Nazi Reich. Here they were interrogated and tortured, and I, with my own eyes, saw the results of these interrogations. I saw what these beasts were capable of.

The Tennenbaums were our neighbors. They lived on the first floor and we on the third. Their son was a handsome young man and he was a leftist. After his interrogation at the Horst-Wessel Platz, he was brought home bloody with broken bones. His mother almost carried him up the stairs. Fearing that the SA would soon return to her apartment, she asked us to let him stay in our home. When I first laid eyes on him I was horrified. Leaning on his mother's shoulder so that his feet barely touched the ground, he looked as though he had been beaten to a pulp. Blood was coming out of his mouth and nose. He was black and blue from the beatings he had endured, and his finger and toenails were torn off. To do this to a human being I could never have imagined!

Madame Tennenbaum asked to use our telephone to call the older son who had fled to Metz (France). She wanted him to return to Berlin and help in his brother's escape. She knew if they were to survive, the boys would have to get away from here. Not long after this ordeal the SA came to search our house. Though I had anticipated this search, I did not know what to do about it. They came in the middle of the night. The children awoke and cried, and the SA took my husband, Aron Jakob Horowitz—may he rest in peace—to police headquarters. But I did not let them take him without me; I insisted that I accompany him. I did not let Papa out of my sight. We left the children alone without anyone to watch over them. But I had no choice because it was our housekeeper Erna's night off. Not long after that night we lost her anyway because by 1935, Aryans were no longer permitted to work for Jewish people.

When we arrived at police headquarters, I stayed close to Papa. I was terrified that they would do to him what they had done to the Tennenbaum boy. I talked, explained, and begged they should let us go. I explained that Papa had never been politically involved, that he is an Orthodox Jew, an upright, hardworking man. I don't know what made them do it, but in the end they let us go.

Kristallnacht

November 9, 1938, began with fire and smoke; it was called *Kristallnacht* (The Night of Broken Glass). Our friend, Benjamin Bestimmt, was cantor at the Oranienburger Strasse Synagogue [an important Berlin synagogue that seated 3000 and had an organ and choir]; he called at 6:00 in the morning. He could barely speak. Sobbing like a baby, he said to me, *"Hanne'le, Hanne'le, mein shul brennt!"* (Hannah, Hannah, my synagogue is burning!) He alerted us that we should be prepared to hear that all the synagogues in Germany were in flames. And he was right; storefronts belonging to merchants we knew well were broken up, windows were shattered and merchandise was vandalized. Goods were thrown out and wrecked. Prayer books and *sefer Torahs* (Torah scrolls) were thrown into the street and torn to pieces. We stood behind shuttered windows and watched the vandalism and the fires from above; we heard shouting, screaming, and calumnies against the Jews. We could not believe what was happening.

I pleaded with Papa, "Now we have to do something. Please, Yanke'le, go to Antwerp where your family and cousins live and try to arrange for our escape to Belgium while we still can." And this time Papa listened. He took the train to Antwerp; it was still possible to do that in November 1938. He saw the family, his cousins, and he especially sought advice from Fishel, his first cousin who had visited us in Berlin numerous times. He also discussed with his brother Herman whether he would be able to make a living in Antwerp. Fishel and Herman both showed Papa the diamond center and were determined to help bring the children and me over. But Papa felt like a total stranger in Belgium. He did not want to stay there and learn a new profession. He did not like that country. He didn't care for the narrow houses, their living quarters, and he particularly disliked the steep stairs. But most importantly, I think, he could not see himself leaving my grandfather, Rav Itsche, who had been his teacher and like a second father to him. So, he came back home.

Upon reentering Germany, he told me, he wanted to kiss the ground on which he set foot. He said that Germany was a good country, in spite of the Nazi regime, and the regime itself would soon fall. I did not believe my eyes when I saw him, nor did I grasp his words. Didn't he see what was going on? He had refused the affidavit that my cousins had sent from New York in 1937, and now he refused to join his family in Antwerp. I was outraged!

September 1939: World War II Breaks Out

On September 1, 1939, the Germans invaded Poland. Two or three days later, England and France made good on their promise to protect Poland and declared war on Germany. I could still see the horrors and chaos of World War I and now I saw another upheaval coming over us. Again I implored Papa to leave at once, and join the family in Antwerp. Again he listened because he realized that something drastic had to be done. He took the children and together they went to Cologne. There, they had to wait for the smuggler to arrive whom Uncle Herman, Papa's brother, had sent from Belgium. But no one appeared. Papa waited for eight days in Cologne and the smuggler never came. Rumor had it that he had taken off with the money and fled. We were like sitting ducks. What could we do, sue a smuggler?

Meanwhile, the High Holidays were practically at our door-step and here was Papa in Cologne with our little girls, without his wife and without my grandfather. Finally, he concluded he had waited long enough. Now, he felt he had to hurry home before *Yom Tov* (Jewish holy day). So he returned to Berlin with the children as quickly as he could. I remember that day as if it were yesterday.

It was September 12, 1939, the night before *Erev* (eve of) Rosh Hashana. [The Jewish New Year would begin the next night.] I thought I would have an apoplectic attack when they came through the door. I cried out, "Yanke'le what are you doing here with the children? Why didn't you stay with the family in Antwerp?"

"Hanne'le," he said, "Don't get yourself all upset; I just had to come back home to you. The smuggler never came. I waited for him, but no one arrived. I thought, perhaps this was a sign that I should come home to be with you and the Rav."

Papa Is Arrested and Hauled Off to Sachsenhausen[1]

The next morning, at 6 am, there was a sharp knock at the door. Papa was dressed and ready to leave the house for *Sliches* (prayers of atonement said before the High Holidays) at my grandfather's *shul.* But when I opened the door I knew...two Gestapo men in black came to arrest Papa together with his cousin from Danzig who had come to spend the holidays with us. Why were they taking them? Where were they going? When will they return? To these questions there were no answers. The children were crying, and I was so scared I could not catch my breath. I did not want to believe that this was happening to us today, the day before the holidays. The two Gestapo men, each holding Papa under one arm, walked out. I think Papa turned around but I did not see him. Those *kholeres* (bandits) took both Papa and our cousin to Sachsenhausen, a concentration camp maybe twenty-five kilometers from Berlin. It was the same camp where my grandfather Itsche had gone to free his Hasidim the year before. Papa's cousin, who had a stateless passport, was let go after a couple of weeks. But my Yanke'le, because he had a Polish passport, was unable to save himself.[2]

How They Killed Papa

Papa was murdered on his way to the camp's *Appellplatz*[3] eight days after he arrived. At *Appell* (roll call), inmates were rushed out from their barracks early in the morning to stand while their names were called; sometimes they stood for hours, and in the evening they had to stand the same way until each person was called. The "Danzinger" (the cousin from Danzig) came to see me after he was set free and told me what had taken place. Early one morning, rushing out to *Appell*, Papa had stumbled. A Nazi guard kicked him for not walking fast enough. The jolt caused him to stumble and fall. When he fell, he cried out *Shema Israel!* (Hear O Israel; the *Shema* is the most important prayer in the Jewish prayer book and declares

Photo 1.1   Reconstruction of the *Appellplatz* at the Sachsenhausen concentration camp where Aron Jakob Horowitz was beaten to death, Oranienburg, Germany. This reconstruction was a Russian installation and no longer exists. Photo taken 1996.

the Oneness of God.) Hearing the Hebrew incantation, the guard hit him again. With each blow Papa cried out the *Shema*. And the blows kept coming. Papa was not a strong man, so after all those beatings his heart gave out.[4] He was only forty-one years old.

I found out about Papa's death when Annie Friedberg, the woman who was our *Spaziererin* (the woman who took the children on their daily walks), on her way to the house, intercepted a telegram from the police. It read: "On September 19, 1939, Israel Aron Jakob Horowitz died. Cause of death: heart attack."[5]

On September 21, I was summoned to receive Papa's body. When the Gestapo called me, I thought I was to identify the body. I took Gitta with me, who at age nine was old enough to understand, and also my grandfather Itsche came with us. Chaya'le stayed home with Fraulein Friedberg because at age five I thought she was too young to see all this.

As we entered the room into which the Gestapo had ushered us, I saw a box in the middle of the floor, a box so small it could not possibly hold the body of a grown man! The Nazis must have cut him up to pieces, I thought. There was no other explanation.[6]

The *Taharah*

My grandfather asked the Gestapo men to open the crate so he could do the ritual for the *taharah* (the ritual cleansing and preparations for the burial). The men refused, "You may not touch this box!" was the retort. I was convinced that their refusal meant that they were under strict orders to not reveal what had been done to Papa.

My grandfather paused. He considered what to do next. Then, he performed the most heartrending *mitzvah* (Jewish commandment) of his life. He waited, asked for a cup of water, and then said, *"Reboyne shel Oilem* (Master of the Universe), since I cannot fulfill the *mitzvah* of *taharah ke'din ve ke'da'at* (obligation of purification of the dead according to our law and religion), I will pour a drop of water on every nail that hammered this coffin shut to symbolize the washing of the body of Aron Jakob Horowitz, and that will have to suffice." My grandfather, cup in hand, poured a drop of water onto every nail that had been hammered into the wooden crate. There were many holes and drops of water, each accompanied by a prayer. The Gestapo stood by and watched; no one dared to rush him. My grandfather said as many prayers as were needed. Gitte'le and I were holding onto each other. We witnessed it all and we will never forget.

Photo 1.2   Aron Jakob Horowitz's grave (killed in September, 1939), Adas Yisroel Orthodox Jewish Cemetery, Berlin, 1996

The Burial

It was a cold and somber day. I could barely walk and Gitta almost fainted; someone had to hold her up as we were walking on the grounds of the cemetery. The Gestapo kept their eyes on us from the time of the *taharah* until the box was put into the ground in the Jewish cemetery of Adas Yisroel. At the gravesite, my grandfather said more prayers and he recited the *Kaddish* (the prayer that sanctifies the Almighty and is recited in remembrance of the dead). We remained standing and in silence we cried. The SS stood guard. Their concern was the crate; it had to remain shut.

The Aftermath

Returning home on that gray and dreadful day, my grandfather suffered a heart attack. The pain of losing Papa and the ordeal at the Gestapo had taken its toll. My grandfather had befriended Papa when he arrived from Galicia to Berlin in 1922, I think, because I met him at one of my grandparents' *sedarim* (celebration of the Passover seders).

Papa had come from a small *shtetl* (little village) called Linsk (now called Lesko). He had no profession, training, or worldly education when he arrived, but my grandfather took a liking to him and helped him obtain a profession and an education. He steered him to attend night school and study accounting. And together they studied the Talmud.[7] They studied every day and when Papa was ready to receive *smicheh* (to be ordained as a rabbi) he stood for his examination in accounting too. Papa was like a second son to my grandfather, my grandparents' only surviving child, my mother, died before I was married. And my grandfather was so proud of Papa. He called him an *illui,* a *talmid chacham* (an exceptional scholar).

God granted my grandfather another six months of life. During that time he helped with my preparations to leave Berlin. However, he only lived to see the escape of my children in November 1939, because he died on March 2, 1940, one month before my escape.

Preparations to Leave

From the day we buried Papa and onward, the Gestapo inspected our house daily. They began taking away objects from the apartment: pieces of furniture and some items from our cutting rooms—the cutting rooms were our factory's work rooms, where we cut, sewed and sold raincoats according to various patterns. My job was to cut the patterns and pass them along for production. The equipment in the cutting room was much sought after merchandise for the *Yekkes* (Germans), so they hauled off what they could. But one thing the Gestapo were not allowed to do: they were forbidden to touch or move me, because the doctor had left strict orders, *"Diese Frau duerfte man nicht beruehren!"* (This woman may not be touched!) I was bedridden from the day of Papa's funeral until my own escape. Overcome with panic and grief, all of a sudden I was unable to see; I probably was in shock and I thought I had a nervous breakdown. I also thought I had become blind. I laid flat on my back and spoke to no one; I could not swallow any food, and tears were streaming down my face day and night. Within a week or two, thank God, my eyesight returned. Grandfather Itsche helped a lot and together with some of his men, they packed boxes of whatever the *Yekkes* had not taken away already, and what I had not sent earlier to Belgium. I don't know how I would have managed without him or my grandmother because they took care of me and my children and provided everything.

My Children's Escape and Grandfather Itsche Dies

At the end of November 1939, with my grandparents' help, I was able to prepare the children's escape. I sent them with a smuggler through Amsterdam to Antwerp. My friend Lotti Jungerwirt found a smuggler who took them from Berlin to Antwerp and brought them to *Tante* (Aunt) Roizele's house.

My grandfather, already ill and heartbroken, died, as I said, in March 1940. Since I was physically ill and emotionally over-whelmed, I was not allowed to attend his funeral, but I stood by the window and watched the funeral procession go by from the Muenz-strasse, where my grandparents lived, through the Alte Schoenhauser Allee, where our home was. When the procession passed our house, I saw my grandmother's face looking upward and nodding, as if to say farewell.

Photo 1.3   Rav Abraham "Itsche" Kupferstock's grave (Rav Itsche died March 2, 1940), Adas Yisroel Orthodox Jewish Cemetery, Berlin, 1996

The man who had been so good to us and had guided Papa and me was no more. Throughout the war, and even afterwards, I thought of him and even spoke to him. When I was in a critical situation I addressed him. I'd say, *"Zeidishie* (diminutive for grandfather), after I delivered you from the Gestapo in Moabit,[8] you promised that you will always look after me, and you will never forsake me. So please, advise me now, tell me what to do." When I had the possibility to send the children from France to Switzerland, I asked him for advice, and he admonished, "Never separate from your children!" I tried to follow his advice; sometimes it was not possible to do that, but I always felt safer knowing that he was watching over me.

I too Leave Berlin

One month after my grandfather Itsche died, it was my turn to leave Berlin. My grandmother Hene Hinde Chaje and I both cried bitter tears when we separated. We both felt this would be our last goodbye. Later, I heard that in 1941 in a roundup of Jews in Berlin, she was taken to Theresienstadt and from there, *nebich* (poor woman), to a *Vernichtungslager* (an extermination camp).

My escape was dreadful. I left Berlin with two of Papa's friends. I paid for their trip because I wanted them to accompany me across the borders from Germany to Holland and then to Belgium, and I also paid for the smuggler. Once there, I would be free to join the children and Papa's family. The smuggler took us through Germany to Haarlem (Holland). But at the border in Haarlem, the Dutch police arrested us. They denied us entry into Holland and sent us back to Aachen, in Germany, and there, the Gestapo arrested us. After lengthy interrogations, the two young men were led away. I heard that the blond man committed suicide in despair. I don't know what happened to the other man. As for me, the Gestapo interrogated me for hours, wanting to know who brought me here, why I was leaving Germany, where were my husband and children, and where was I going? I was getting exasperated and angry but did not feel fear. I felt that I had lost so much already so I didn't care what happened to me. Agitated, I shouted at my interrogators, "I have had enough! Quit torturing me with your questions! If my answers don't satisfy you, then go ahead and shoot me!" They must have thought I was either hysterical or nuts because after this outburst they stopped harassing me.

Then, a young officer entered the room. He must have been from the Ober SS, gauging by his highly decorated uniform. He was extremely proper and well behaved. He took my hand, called me *Gnaedige Frau* (honorable lady) and told me that they did not want to hurt me, but wanted to catch some of the undercover people who illegally smuggle German citizens in and out of the country. He was well mannered, soft-spoken, and sounded kind. Offering me his arm, he asked me to follow him to the train station. There he purchased a one-way first-class ticket to Berlin and told me to go back to my hometown and never show my face in Aachen again. "After all," he said, "Germany is a good country and we are good people. I promise you that we will take good care of you."

Ticket in hand, I followed him to the train. He helped me up the couple of steps and, with a curtsy and the clicking of his heels, he saluted goodbye. I looked around and saw that my compartment was well appointed and respectable. It was first class. But my mind was made up. Under no circumstance will I return to Berlin. So I stayed on the train until we reached Koeln (Cologne) and there I tried to find another smuggler. Furtively, I surveyed my surroundings as I left the station and immediately went to see the woman with whom Papa had stayed when he tried to leave Berlin. The woman recognized my name and allowed me to stay with her, but only for one night, she said. The next morning I will have to leave her house, she said, because she was being watched. She directed me to another woman's house; that woman, she said, will hide me for another day or two. But when the two days were up, I was on the street again. So, I returned to the first woman. She did not let me in. "It has become very dangerous to harbor Jews," she said. I offered her my fur coat. It was the coat Papa and I had bought together the year before *Kristallnacht.*

My Second Attempt

Standing in the entrance hall, fur coat in hand, the woman decided she would take the risk of harboring me after all. She would let me wait in Cologne until Uncle Herman sent another smuggler to bring me over. When the smuggler finally arrived, he and I went back to Aachen, hoping that this time we would make it across the border.

This was no easy crossing. The smuggler took me to the outskirts of town and from there we were supposed to go to a designated house. But just as the smuggler and I entered that house, a strange woman came running in. Grabbing my hand she pulled me with her saying, "Come quickly, there is no time to waste. Someone has betrayed you!" The Gestapo was looking for us both, the smuggler and me. Someone must have seen us and reported us to the police. Still holding my hand, the woman went through the back of the house, opened a door that led to a cellar, and pushed me down the stairs. Then, she promptly shut the door behind her. I heard the turning of a key. Now I was locked up and the smuggler was gone. The cellar was pitch-black. Holding on to the banister, I took a few steps down. But before I could turn around I found myself knee deep in water. The water was ice cold and I did not know what to do. Unable to sit on the stairs because I did not want to get wet, I stood on one spot, at the bottom of the stairs, without moving. I stood there for a very long time. Through the cracks on the stairs above me I heard voices; they were speaking German. "They are not here," said the one. "But someone said they had seen them," said the other. The search went on. My heart was pounding and I was afraid to catch my breath. Then, there was silence.

After some hours, wet, freezing to death and hungry, I heard the turning of a key. It was ten o'clock in the morning when I entered that cellar, and at midnight I finally was helped out of there. A man's voice whispered, "Are you still there?" Irritated and exhausted, I said, "Of course I'm here, where else could I be?" That person, I believe, was the woman's husband. He came down, took hold of my hand, and helped me up the stairs and out of the water. He gave me a towel to wipe my skirt and feet and said, "Now we must hurry, we have a long way to go."

Holding my hand, he ran and I followed. Several times I fell but he was so strong he just grabbed me and picked me up, and then we were running again. When I looked up, I saw that the sky was bright and cloudless. Stars were glistening and I could see clearly the fields around us, as clearly as if it were daylight. I looked up and whispered to my grandfather, *"Zeidishie* where are you? You promised to come to my aid if ever I should need you. Look at this sky, anyone could see us if they were chasing us. Please, let it rain, let it rain buckets with thunder and heavy clouds above, so our enemies will neither see us, nor follow us." And, you won't believe this, no sooner had I finished my prayer then it began to rain. Not just rain, but a torrential thunderstorm came over us! Now, I knew that my grandfather had heard me and that I would be OK.

In this manner, wet through and through, running and falling, we finally arrived to the door of another house. The man who had led me there quickly opened the door and pushed me into a room. The room was black but from somewhere in back I saw the flicker of a flashlight. A new voice spoke to me. "Please," he said, "don't be afraid, I'm coming toward you." This new man came toward me and asked if I was cold. I told him my legs are stiff as ice and I was wet all over. He sat down, took my feet in his hands, and began rubbing them; then he put my icy feet inside his shirt, against his naked chest, so I could warm my feet. We sat there for a while until I was able to move my toes again. And then he explained that we would have to walk again. He gave me a slice of bread to eat and something warm to drink, and left the room. By now I had gotten used to the dark and I began to distinguish the living room furniture. The man said I should rest a while before going on the next trek. I was feeling a little better and more hopeful.

But he returned too soon. "Now we must go," he said, "there is no time to waste." We took to the fields again and walked. This hike was shorter than the previous one. Nevertheless, I stumbled plenty and had to be lifted up more times than I can remember. Finally, we arrived at a farmhouse where I was told to wait until the car he had ordered arrived. After a wait I did hear the hum of a car. Taking my arm, the smuggler walked me to the car. "Madame," he said, "your journey is almost over."

I saw the driver and I saw the car, and I saw a wide-open trunk. As we approached I noticed that inside the trunk lay a big suitcase, like a large footlocker. I wondered about the open trunk, but I did not have to wonder long. Without explanation this man who had rubbed my feet against his chest and had given me food and drink picked me up and put me into that footlocker! Without another word he closed the top over me. I thought I'd suffocate. "What are you doing to me? I can't breathe! I'm choking! Please let me out." I heard my smuggler's voice urging me to calm down. "Dear lady, please try to stay calm, you will breathe more easily if you calm down. There is no other way to get you out of here and into Belgium; the borders are patrolled and more dangerous than ever." And without further ado, he shut the car's trunk. The car began moving. The footlocker was like a coffin but I was alive. I told myself that if I were real quiet and didn't panic I would be able to breathe.

We drove on for a while. Then, after less than maybe twenty minutes, I'd say, the driver stopped the car. He opened the trunk, then the footlocker, and lifted me out of the car. "We have crossed the border," he said, "and we are in Belgium now." He invited me to come and sit next to him in the front seat. Such gratitude I have never felt. The smuggler was gone. And I was getting my first glimpse of Belgium, the country that would be my home for many years. We were driving along and there was not a soul on the road. Then we entered a quiet town called Verviers, and drove up an empty street. The car stopped in front of a rug dealer's store and a lady came down to greet me. She had expected us earlier she said, but, "I realized that you must have encountered some unexpected difficulties." One look at me and she knew that her assumption was correct. She led me upstairs. "Well," she said, "you look a sight. We can't leave you in this condition, can we? I'll have to get you some proper clothes."

I was still standing in the hallway when I heard the voice of a man who had just entered the house. I turned around and couldn't believe my eyes. Uncle Herman, my husband's younger brother, had come in; he looked so much like Papa, I began to cry. We hugged and he told me how happy he is to see me, and soon I would see my little girls. They are both well and very well behaved; and they are awaiting my arrival impatiently. Also, they go to a Jewish school that is a little too *frum* (Orthodox) for his taste.

Now I had to wash up and get into clean clothes. The Belgian lady gave me everything I needed, warm underclothes, a skirt, a sweater, stockings, and shoes. Dressing myself hurriedly I gathered my dirty clothes and fixed myself up to look as presentable as possible. For all the difficulties of this trip, I was immensely grateful and incredibly relieved that I had finally arrived. My heart was full and tears were edging up in my eyes as I hugged and thanked this kindhearted lady. Then, Uncle Herman asked the driver who had brought me here to drive us to Antwerp, to Tante Roizele's house on the Grote Beerstraat, 3.

CHAPTER TWO

HANNAH'S FAMILY[1]

Hannah: You're asking me when I saw the first signs of anti-Semitism in Berlin and you want me to tell you again about my family? OK, I'll tell you.

I remember exactly, it was in 1932. Papa and I wanted to go to the movies, which happened rarely because we both worked such long hours. We had a company called Berolina that manufactured raincoats. But that night we decided to go out. Walking along the Koenigstrasse we noticed a man who was following us. He started shouting, *"Faule Juden! Raus mit den Juden!"* (Rotten Jews! Out with the Jews!) No matter how fast we walked trying to get rid of him, he continued to shadow us bellowing insults. I thought to myself, "How does he know that we are Jews? Do we look so Jewish?" Papa never looked very Jewish; he was not poorly dressed, and he did not have a long nose. And I certainly never appeared to be Jewish. I have a round face, black eyes, light brown hair, and my profile has always been nice and straight. But this man wouldn't let up; he scared us. So Papa and I decided to skip the movies and we ran all the way home from Alexander Platz to the Brueder Strasse, our first apartment; that was quite a distance.

I worked for the Mitropa firm at the time and my job was to fashion uniforms that waiters wear in the better hotels into men's suits. My grandfather Itsche got us the order, and we were very grateful because business was very bad. That is how I learned to sew, and because I did we were able to eke out a living. Later when I had more work than I could handle, I gave my work to the prisoners in the Ploetzensee prison. Papa and I provided the merchandise, and the prisoners did the work. At that time, Papa was a traveling salesman selling goods, linens, tablecloths, and the like. I watched over Papa and made sure he was careful whenever he traveled. And when he came home I took care of him, *comme il faut* (as one is supposed to).

Photo 2.1   Hannah's passport photo (date unknown)

My Family

I was born at home on April 30, 1908, in Tomaczow Mazowiecki, a city not far from Lodz, Poland. Yes, yes, I was born at home because my mother refused to go to the hospital and would not allow a man-doctor to examine her, *"beshum oiffin nicht!"* (Under no circumstance!) Not in a million years! We were all born at home and a midwife delivered us. Do you know that my father held me in a blanket as he was trying to put me to sleep, and while he was rocking me—he must have fallen asleep—I slipped off his lap straight to the floor? Yes, I fell on my head when I was eight days old. I fell on my head! I guess it didn't hurt me and maybe it shook me up and helped me become smarter.

Well, I was the middle child of five. Betty was the youngest. She had a little boy; a wonderful child, smart and beautiful. Both died in the Warsaw Ghetto, when the ghetto was burning. Trying to escape the fire behind them they jumped from their apartment window to the street. Betty's husband was a flaming Zionist, but I don't know what happened to him. I don't know whether he died in the Warsaw Ghetto uprising or whether he was killed in some other way. His name was Max Hopfenberg. He was a very good man. But Betty and her little boy died in the fire or in their attempt to escape.

After me came a little boy who died of diphtheria in infancy. I don't think I really knew him. But the oldest child in our family, I do remember; his name was Yakov Shloime. He was handsome and a wonderful person. You can't believe how handsome he was! He was my "God," I idolized him; I loved him with all my might and I was his favorite. He didn't like my two sisters so much. I don't know why he loved me more than the others, but he did, maybe because I was the fairest of them all, and maybe because I was good-hearted. But we lost him when he was twenty-one. He died of pneumonia. When he died it was a catastrophe. I was heartbroken and so were we all. You can imagine, he was the only boy in our family and he was our shining star. After we lost him, only we, the three daughters, were left; that's all.

My sister Cilly was the oldest girl—five years older than I. She was the mean one. She had a habit of pinching me without anyone noticing until I was all black and blue, and yellow, too. But I was afraid to tell anyone. Had I told my mother what Cilly did to me, she would have gotten a beating, but I wasn't a snitch.

The family on my father's side were the Kantorowiczs. My father's father, Mendl Kantorowicz, was a wealthy man. We used to visit him on his farm and we stayed with him in the city too. Mendl Kantorowicz, my grandfather, was also called Biemen Shoichet because he was trained as a *shoichet* (one trained to slaughter animals according to Jewish ritual; Biemen may be a nickname or a middle name, short for Binyumin), but he soon gave that up and became a businessman. He did not want to be a *shoichet* because there was no prestige in this work. But people still called him Biemen Shoichet. The Kantorowiczs were a mean bunch. On that side of the family there were no rabbis, but there was wealth, lots of wealth. My grandfather Mendl Kantorowicz was the wealthiest man in Tomaczow Mazowiecki. When he walked down the street people used to say, "See, there goes Biemen Shoichet, *der Gvier* (the wealthy one)." He became rich when he started a business in manufacturing soap. There were two soap factories in the area. One belonged to us, and it was called Mitlo Troika. The other was Mitlo Yellen; the man who owned that business lived in Krakow. The men did business together, but were also competitors, and both managed to become very wealthy. My grandfather Mendl owned buildings too; homes as big as palaces and an enormous orchard.

In 1914, when World War I broke out, Mendl Kantorowicz built a shelter on the grounds of his orchard in Myslowice. I was six years old at the time and I remember that we fled to Myslowice and hid there. At that time the Germans were winning the war, as they always do in the beginning of any war, and we were scared. But we were more afraid of the Russians then. So we hid in my grandfather's shelter, and I remember going out to pull carrots from the fields; I peeled these carrots with shards of broken glass and ate them straight from the ground. The rest I brought back to the shelter.

While we were there, Mendl Kantorowicz's wife died, leav-

ing him with eight children. He remarried when he was seventy
years old and chose a young woman who was thirty years old, can
you imagine? She came from Skernewitze and her name was Rachel
Fajge. She was my father's stepmother; can you believe this? She
never had any children of her own but she loved us like a grandmother loves her grandchildren. She was kind and good-natured, and
I loved her very much too; and she thought I was special.

My mother, Sarah Gittel, had five brothers but none survived. She was very beautiful and highly intelligent and that is why
we named your sister after her. But my mother died at a very young
age. She was ill with rheumatoid arthritis and was confined to a
wheelchair in the last two years of her life. She was forty-two years
old when she died. She died three months before my engagement to
Papa.

My father, Israel Simmel, was a *shoichet* like his father. He
had *heteruhe smicheh* here (this means he was ordained as a rabbi),
and he was also a Torah scribe. In order to make a living, he developed a business in electrical appliances. My father and mother were
married when he was sixteen years old and she was fifteen. After my
mother died, my father did not want to see any other women. He remained a widower for six years. Then, one day, his father Mendl
Kantorowicz came to him and said, "You have to marry again. A
man cannot remain alone for such a long time." So they began looking for a suitable woman, and found a woman who was fourteen
years younger than he. This was a big mistake, because after one
year of marriage, my poor father had a stroke and died. Everyone
thought that he died of a stroke because he had not been with a
woman for a long time and the excitement of intimate relations with
such a young woman was the cause of the stroke.

In 1914, my great-grandmother, she was Mendl Kantorowicz's mother, died. In 1917 we moved to Berlin because of my
grandfather Itsche's special relationship with Hindenburg. Hindenburg invited him to come to Germany, so our family moved to Ber-

lin. For a Jew to be invited to Berlin was an unusual honor because Jews were not welcome there, especially not Jews from Poland—and especially not in 1917. But apparently Hindenburg, who later became president of the republic, wanted to show his appreciation to my grandfather for his service to the German government. It was a very big deal. I myself don't know the entire story because I was only eight years old at the time. But I do know that my grandfather Itsche was welcome at the President's Palace and visited him every New Year's Day. Cane in hand, wearing his *streimel* (fur hat) and black *kapotte* (long cape; the *streimel* and *kapotte* were both traditional clothing of ultra-Orthodox men), he would walk over to the palace to wish the president a "Happy New Year." My grandfather even wrote New Year's Day poems to Hindenburg. One of these poems I was able to save, it is dated New Year's Day, 1924. I think I gave it to you when I moved, yes?

"These are very bad economic times," my grandfather wrote, "but the German economy will improve and the German mark will become as valuable as the American dollar!" President von Hindenburg awarded my grandfather a lifelong pension and a "Letter of Protection." By the way, that pension and the Letter of Protection were sustained even after 1933 when the Nazis came to power and until the day he died, in March 1940.

To show you how unbelievable those days were, on *Kristallnacht,* when all the synagogues were burning and Jewish shop windows were shattered, my grandfather's *shtiebel* (small synagogue, *shul*) was protected by two SS men who stood guard at the entrance to the house and protected the second-floor apartment where his *shul* was located.

Yes, my grandfather was a Hasidic rabbi. He was from the Gerer Hasidim (a follower of the Hasidic sect of Ger). His father had also been a rabbi and his name was Mordechai Beresh Kupfersztock, the Great Rabbi of Warsaw, but I didn't know him.

My grandfather's letterhead read *"Grossrabiner von der*

Ostjuedishe Gemeinde in Berlin" (Chief Rabbi of the East European Community in Berlin). Despite his status, he was not a rabbi with a large synagogue; no, his *shul* was a *shtiebel* that consisted of two large rooms located in the front part of his apartment. One large room was for the women to pray, talk, eat, and socialize. The other was for the men to study, pray, and talk. It was a long room with an *aron kodesh* (a holy ark that houses the Torah scrolls) and in it were three *sefer Torahs* (Torah scrolls). A long table stood in the room around which the Hasidim studied and discussed *Gemarrah* (Talmud). *Rav* (Rabbi) Itsche's congregation consisted of about seventy Hasidim, not counting their wives and their numerous children. By Hasidic standards this was a large community.

When we arrived in Berlin my parents sent me to the Jewish school on the Brueder Strasse. Later, I went to the *Hoehere Toechterschule* (secondary school for young ladies) and graduated from high school.

You say my life is interesting? My life is poison, nothing but bitter poison, that's what it is.

How I Met Papa

Papa was twenty-four years old when I met him at my grandfather Itsche's house in 1922. We were at Itsche's *seder* (the Passover ceremonial meal). I was exactly fourteen. Grandfather Itsche and Grandmother Hene Hinde Chaje made big *sedarim* (the plural for seder).

You are named after her because when she was very young she became ill; and as was the practice, when someone was ill and people worried that she wouldn't recover, they added the name Chaje, meaning life, so that she would live.

Grandmother Hene Hinde Chaje lived, but after their only daughter [Hannah's mother] died, I became almost like a child to her, and Papa was the same, like a son to Itsche. On *Pesach* (Passover) my grandparents always invited about sixty to seventy guests to their *sedarim*; they opened their house to people who didn't have a home or strangers who were passing through. Papa was one of the young men who came to my grandfather's house. And as I told you, he studied with Rav Itsche and passed rabbinic examinations; but he was also the best chess player in his chess club. In fact, he won first prize in a citywide competition that was held in the cafe on the Kurfuerstendamm. There, he played on Sundays, but on Saturday nights he was with the Hasidim for *shaleshiedes* (the third meal of the Sabbath) and *melaweh malka* (the end of the Sabbath).

And when you were born on *Hoshana Rabba* (the seventh day of the harvest holiday *Sukkot*) he wasn't with me but in Rav Itsche's *shtiebel*!

Our Courtship

You ask how I met Papa. As I said, we were at the Pesach seder table; the men sat at one table and the women at the other. All of a sudden, I saw this handsome young man whom I had never seen before. I kept looking behind me toward the men's table. Finally, I turned to my mother. "Who is this young man over there?" I asked. "He has such beautiful eyes. I feel all funny inside just looking at him. He is so handsome!" My mother scolded me, "Behave yourself," she said, "and keep your head toward our table, not theirs." We sat at the table until seven o'clock in the morning; that's how long our *sedarim* were. You should know that we were not allowed to eat the *afikomen* (a small piece of matzo—unleavened bread— eaten at the end of the meal as dessert) until after midnight. So at midnight we ate the *afikomen*, and after that the men studied.

You see I know all these rules because...well...they used to call me the *Rebbetzin* at home after I married Papa. Now in Antwerp, they call me the *Tzedaikes* (a woman who performs acts of justice/kindness) because I help people in need; like some young men who come here to *handel* (to do business)—if they need a place to stay for a while they usually stay with us. Also, I visit the elderly in the *Altersheim* (home for the aged). And I have a special lady friend who lives all alone in Brussels; I visit her weekly by train from Antwerp to Brussels, and I spend the afternoon with her.

In Berlin, your papa used to visit us every Sunday. He would come over to our house that he called the *drei meidelech* house (the house of the three maidens). He was interested in us, in Cilly and Betty too, but mostly in me.

On my seventeenth birthday, Papa came for a visit. He sat down next to me and said, "Hanschen would you like to go out with me some time?" "Of course I do, but first you must invite me!" I said. We only spoke German at home. I didn't speak much Yiddish until I came to Antwerp, did you know that? Papa and I only spoke German unless we needed to speak with the grandparents. My father, Simmel Kantorowicz, spoke Yiddish with his father Mendl Kantorowicz because he had a business in Schwartzwald selling electrical items; he often spoke Yiddish with his father so people wouldn't understand what they were saying.

But let's get back to Papa and me. With my parents' approval, Papa took me out on a date. We went for a walk Unter Den Linden. There, on the right side was a cafe. We sat down and ordered a cup of tea. Then he said, "Hanschen, what would you say if we got married?" I couldn't believe my ears, but I knew he wasn't mocking me. Quickly, I blurted out a response, "Yes, I love you and I want to marry you right now, but first we have to ask my mother. Though I'm afraid she may not approve." I said, half in jest, "Do you remember on Pesach when my aunt visited us? She noticed that I was looking at you more than anyone else. She turned to my mother and said, 'Be careful, Sarah Gittel, do not let your daughter marry a man from Galicia!'" With my father's family, you should have heard their outcry. To marry a Galitzianer when you came from the western part of Poland was humiliating! In western Poland where I come from, the people were learned and wealthy business types, whereas in Galicia, they were all peasants.

Disregarding these admonitions, my mother and father both agreed that I could marry Papa because they liked him very much and because my grandfather Itsche, who was my mother's father, thought highly of him. Unfortunately, my mother became ill with a severe inflammation, rheumatic fever it was, but I think it was worse than that. Within weeks she was in a wheelchair and then they took her to the hospital. I stayed by her side day and night. Then they brought her to Lodz, and I stayed with her. My mother was in the hospital for three months. I sat at her bedside in the hospital and I did not leave her side until she died, in January 1929.

Papa and I Are Engaged

Papa and I were engaged a few weeks after my mother died. My grandfather Mendl Kantorowicz said to me, "Now you have to stay here in Lodz with your father. You cannot return to Berlin." Not return to Berlin? I would not hear of it. "And what will my other grandparents do? They had only one living daughter and now she died. How can I leave them alone? Papa and I are like son and daughter to them! Oh no!" I said, "That is impossible." But it was not easy to say "No" to my grandfather Mendl Kantorowicz. I wrote to Papa and told him my problem with Mendl Kantorowicz, and asked him to come help me.

On a Friday morning, I hear the doorbell and have the surprise of my life. My grandmother, Rachel Fajge says, "Hanne'le, go open the door because Salke (the maid) is too busy right now." Salke was cooking for *Shabbes* (Shabbat), geese and ducks, and what have you—more food than you can imagine. So I ran to the entrance, opened the door, and came to a halt. There was Papa! My eyes stared in disbelief and my mouth fell open, but no sound came out. I looked at Papa and stood without making a move. "May I come in?" he gently said. "What are you doing here?" I asked as if I were dumb. Didn't I write to him, didn't I beg him to come and rescue me? "Don't you want me here?" he said. "Yes, sure I do, but I didn't think you'd come!" I wanted to hug him and kiss him on the spot; I didn't know how to behave. But Papa knew, he took me in his arms and embraced me, then he kissed me gently on the head and I brought him into the house. I introduced him to my grandmother, *"Bubeshie. Bubeshie* (diminutive for grandmother), this is my friend Yankev, *der Galitzianer."* Not uttering a word, she looked at him. He too stood still and with his probing black eyes he looked at her; finally, he and my *Bubeshie* spoke to each other. "I like him, your Yankev from Galicia," she said, "I like what you like," and that was the end of that.

As I said, my grandmother didn't have children of her own but married Mendl Kantorowicz who had eight children. So I was like her child. Remember, Papa came to Lodz on Friday morning and on Saturday night we had an engagement party. Can you believe this? The entire family had arrived!

It reminds me of your wedding: Wally arrived in Antwerp on September 13, 1955, and two days later we put up the *chuppah* (wedding canopy) in our living room!

I Visit My In-laws in Galicia

After the engagement party Papa wanted to visit his parents. It would be a long journey. On Sunday morning we took the train to Krakow; then, we hired a carriage that took us to Linsk (now Lesko), his little village. What can I tell you? When we arrived to his parents' place we entered a little hovel. I cannot describe to you what their place looked like. They were very poor; they had barely enough food. The place was dirty and there were wood shavings on the floor instead of a real floor. I couldn't believe that Papa came from this environment. I met his family. Papa's mother was Serel Horowitz; his father was Itsche Diller. There were five living children: Papa (Aron Jakob) was the eldest, then came Mirjam, *Onkel* (Uncle) Her-

Letter from our father announcing our parents' engagement

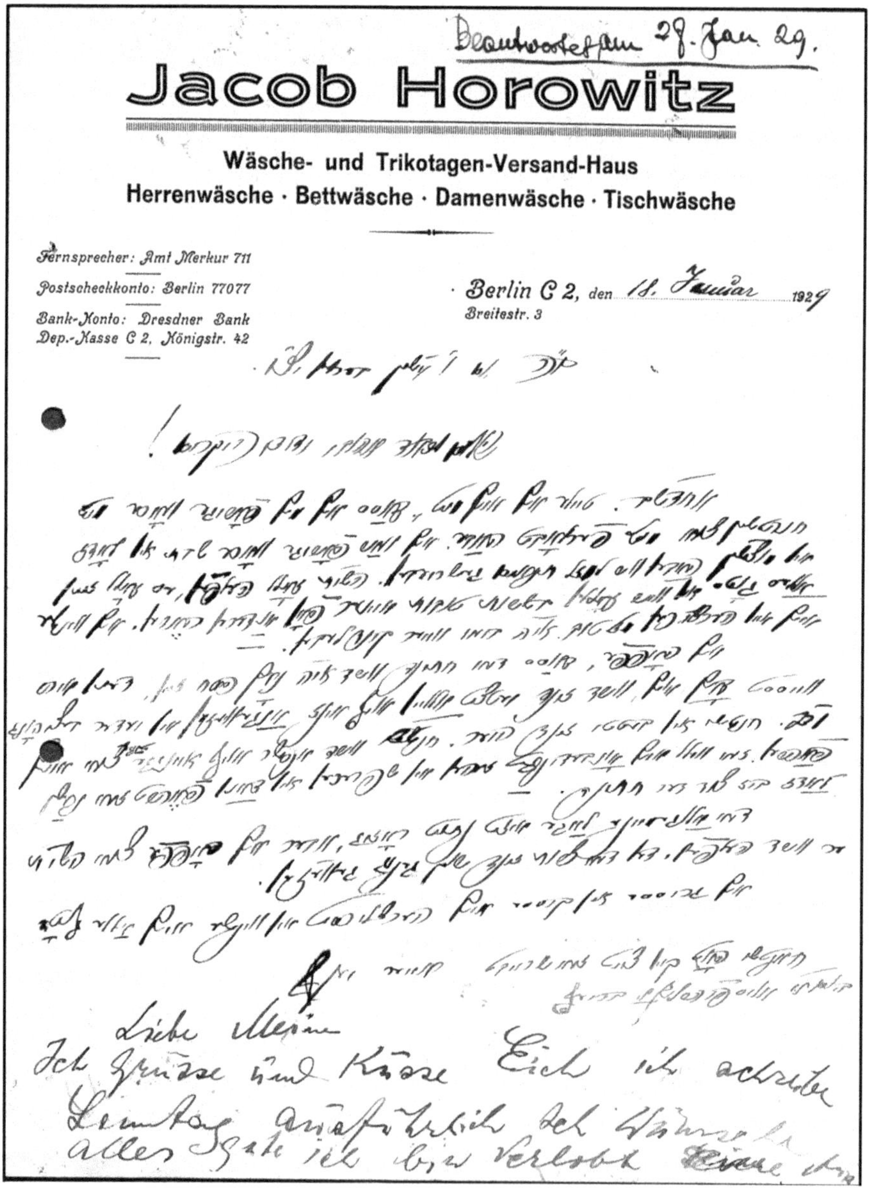

Beantwortet am 29. Jan. 29.

Jacob Horowitz

Wäsche- und Trikotagen-Versand-Haus
Herrenwäsche · Bettwäsche · Damenwäsche · Tischwäsche

Fernsprecher: Amt Merkur 711
Postscheckkonto: Berlin 77077
Bank-Konto: Dresdner Bank
Dep.-Kasse C 2, Königstr. 42

· Berlin C 2, den 18. Januar 1929
Breitestr. 3

[handwritten letter in Yiddish and German]

2.2 Jakob (Yakov) writes to a relative to announce his engagement to Hannah (Chancze). He thinks and hopes that the wedding will take place after Passover. Our father believes in G-d's help, but knows that the economic situation is dire. Our mother too is concerned and that is no doubt the reason for her brevity.

B"H (*Baruch Hashem,* praise G-d)
Friday [January 18, 1929], Berlin

My dear precious beloved one

After greetings of peace, I want to let you know that
last week it was my good fortune to get engaged to Chancze
(Hannah). Last week I spent the Sabbath in Lodz. May we
always share good news with each other. Let me convey my
sincere congratulations. *B'ezrat Hashem* (with G-d's help; G-d
willing) may it soon happen to your children.

I hope, *B'ezrat Hashem,* that the wedding will be after
Passover. You do know that until now I lived alone at 251.
Chancze and Betty were here. Chancze will, perhaps, visit you
for several days. She absolutely wants to see you and talk to
you, and then she will travel to Lodz [and stay there] until the
wedding.

In general, the situation is not rosy, but I pray to G-d,
B"Sh (*Baruch Shemo,* blessed be his Name), that He help us,
because we have had enough woes.

I sent my sincere regards and kisses and wishes for all
the best.

Chancze has no time to write a detailed letter.

Your, Yakov

[At the bottom of the page there is a brief note from Hannah in German]:

My Dear
I send you regards and kisses. I will write more details on
Saturday. I wish you all the best. I am engaged.

Translated from Yiddish and German by Khane-Faygl Turtletaub, PhD.

man, then your aunt Chana and finally Yossele. I learned that they also had twins, but both died in early childhood. I could not get over the poverty and the sawdust on the floors. I wanted to run away from there. But Papa's mother, Serel Horowitz, was a fine and very intelligent woman. She had a twinkle in her eye and she looked me over with an expression of satisfaction; I knew that she approved of me. And Papa really looked like her.

We did not stay there very long. I turned to Papa and whispered, "Do we have to stay here?" "No," he said, "We'll just stay a little while and then we'll leave."

From Linsk to Berlin and Back to Lodz

It was a long train ride back to Berlin, but we came home in time for me to revalidate my passport. When we arrived at my grandfather Itsche's, he said, "Now I have to separate you, because you are not married yet." For me, he put a bed in the hallway where the servant slept. And Papa he put somewhere else, but I wasn't supposed to know where. I thought to myself, "I will not stay in this house and sleep in the hallway!" So next morning I returned to Lodz with my other grandparents; I had three bedrooms. It was absolute luxury and such cleanliness you haven't seen. My grandmother had a cook, a cleaning woman, and someone who was there just to run errands. I received eleven boxes from my grandparents; silver, bedding, more silver, and blankets. All these and eighteen suitcases were sent to Berlin, and later to the Grote Beerstraat in Antwerp; and all the presents we received from my grandfather Itsche, we sent there as well. We even took some of those suitcases to Nice, but that's another story, I'm getting ahead of myself.

So, here I was in Lodz. Papa came to me after four months. He went to live at Tante Lubba's (Mendl Kantorowicz's sister), and I still lived with my grandparents, Mendl and Rachel Fajge. Then, we planned the wedding.

Photo 2.3   Hannah and Jakob's wedding, July 9, 1929

The Wedding Was Like a Dream

My grandfather Mendl gave me 100,000 marks, a lot of money then. Then he gave me a ring. From Papa, I received a beautiful *broche* (pin)—the one I gave you, remember? The wedding began at midnight but the *chuppah* (ceremony under the wedding canopy) took place at two o'clock in the morning. This means that Papa and I were married on July 9, 1929, one day after the date printed on the invitation. After the *chuppah* we finally ate. There was no singing because I was still in mourning for my mother. But there were many *drushes* (speeches on Talmudic themes). Finally, at seven o'clock in the morning, we ate breakfast. And only then did people go home.

Then Papa and I went to our room. First we talked. Your papa was a very gentle person and he did not want to frighten me, so he moved up to me very slowly. He told me how much he loved me and how lovely I looked. Then we hugged and he kissed me. But that night we did not make love. Only the next night did we make love. It was difficult at first, but finally we made it because Papa was gentle and I was responding to him.

But do you know what happened after the wedding? They cut off my hair, shaved it all off! You ask if I was upset? Yes, I was very upset, but *Bubbe* Rachel Fajge ordered a beautiful *sheitl* (wig worn after marriage) for me and then I felt better. Then my grandparents, the Kantorowiczs, blessed us both, *"Yivarechecha ve Yishmerecha,"* (May God bless you and keep you), and so on. On the third day after the wedding, we traveled to Berlin because my grandfather Itsche wanted to do the rest of the *sheva bruches* (the newlyweds are blessed with seven blessings and celebrated with food and drink for seven days). The last day was most beautiful of all. It was just like a second wedding. Afterwards, I had to go to the *mikveh* (ceremonial bathhouse); I hated that place because it was not very clean. When I came home from the *mikveh,* I made sure to wash myself again. Afterwards, every month, I had to go to the *mikveh.*

Life in Berlin: Our Children Are Born

We wanted to have children—Papa more than I. But I couldn't become pregnant. So I went to Poland to the Rav to ask for advice. I don't know what he said, but I think he reassured me that I was still very young and perhaps physically immature; therefore, I was not to worry. And indeed I became pregnant in 1930, but, like my mother, I was too shy to see a man-doctor. In Berlin, I did not know of a midwife, so it was not until my seventh month that I went to see a gynecologist for the first time. "Why didn't you come earlier?" the doctor said to me. "Because I was shy," I said. "But you weren't too shy to make a baby, were you? It's too late to examine you now. If I did, I could induce an early delivery and we can't take that risk. It could endanger both you and your child."

The labor was terrible. It was a long and very painful delivery. I labored for three days. But in the end I did it, and everything came out all right. Gitte'le came out, fully grown, with a full head of hair and she was very strong. Papa was very happy with his little girl, even though he would have preferred a little boy. But he loved his daughter with all his heart and we named her after my mother, Sarah Gittel. I was twenty years old when I became a mother for the first time.

Photo 2.4 Chaya, Hannah, and Gitta, Berlin, 1934

With you it was different. When I discovered that I was pregnant I wanted to die. I wanted to kill myself. I wanted to jump off the kitchen table hoping that I would lose the baby. This was no time to bring children into the world! Remember, it was 1934. I was close to delivery, in my eighth or ninth month. Everyone said I should quit working, that I might fall sitting on these high stools at the cutting table; but I had to finish an order, so I went into the cutting room and sat perched on one of our tall round stools. I was able to work, but suddenly you kicked so hard that I fell off the chair. I didn't go into labor that night, but soon thereafter my water broke and I was rushed to the hospital. You were in such a hurry to be born that they had to bind my legs to give the nurses and doctor time to

Letter from our father about Gitta's birth

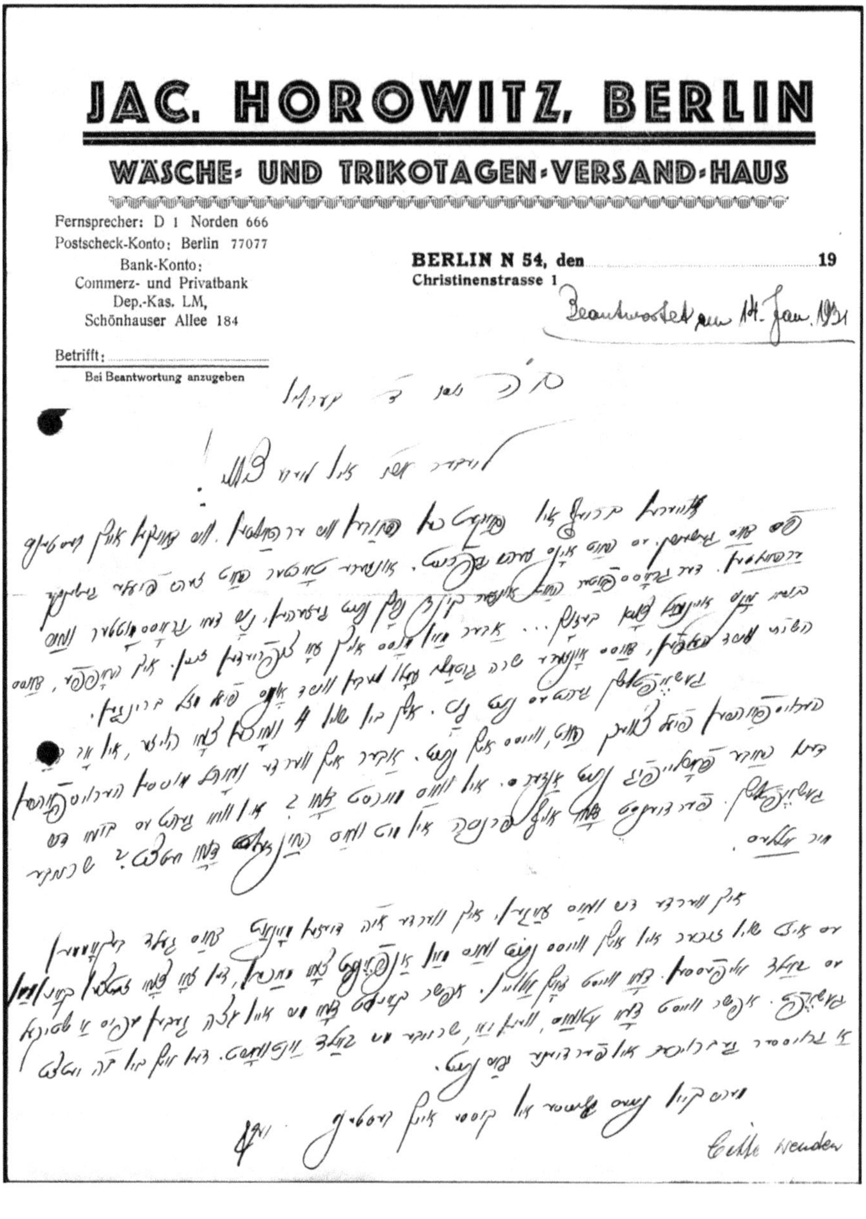

JAC. HOROWITZ, BERLIN

WÄSCHE- UND TRIKOTAGEN-VERSAND-HAUS

Fernsprecher: D 1 Norden 666
Postscheck-Konto: Berlin 77077

Bank-Konto:
Commerz- und Privatbank
Dep.-Kas. LM,
Schönhauser Allee 184

BERLIN N 54, den _____ **19**
Christinenstrasse 1

Betrifft: _____

Bei Beantwortung anzugeben

[Handwritten letter in Yiddish]

2.5 Jakob writes to Hannah's sister Cilly and Cilly's husband Aryeh thanking them for a gift for his new baby daughter, Sara Gitele (Gitta). He prays that Gitta will live and bring good fortune. He cannot express his happiness fully because of his enormous anxiety about his inability to provide for his family. He owes money and appears frightened about his debt.

B"H
Wednesday [January 14, 1931] Berlin

Dear Aryeh and Cilly

We received your letter and package. We thank you very much for the gift. It made us very happy. Our daughter received a lot of gifts. Our grandfather has not seen the child yet, but our grandmother did visit us once here. But we must be happy with this too. I pray that G-d, B"Sh, helps us, and that our Sara Gitele, long may she live, will bring us much good fortune.

Business is not going well. I have been at home now for four weeks and do not know if it even pays to travel [for merchandise], but I have to go, because right now I have no other choice. And how are you doing? And how is your business doing there? Are you making a living and what are you dealing in now? Write me about everything.

I will tell you something. With G-d's help, I will get the money this month. It is a certainty, but I don't know what they are going to be doing [with it]. But sitting around isn't good business. If you know of something, write to me immediately, because, thank G-d, I need a lot right now and am earning nothing.

There is no other news. I send you love and kisses and best wishes.

Yakov

Translated from Yiddish by Khane-Faygl Turtletaub, PhD.

deliver you. This time, I was sure to have a boy because you were so active and kicking when I carried you. Wherever I sat, you banged against my bones, my ribs, my stomach, wherever a baby can kick inside the womb. You are still like this today. I was disappointed that you were not a boy because I knew Papa wanted one; what man doesn't want to have at least one boy? But Papa was not like every man. He loved his first little girl so much that I knew he would love the second one just as well. And so he did.

My Father Dies

My father died six weeks after you were born. I was twenty-four at the time. The family intercepted the letters from Lodz because they did not want to upset me. They thought my milk would dry up. When I asked how my father is and why he does not write, they told me that he had injured his hand. Later Betty, my sister, wrote for him. Betty was a very good sister, but she and Papa had many arguments. I still have some letters from the 1920's from her to Papa and his letters to her. After my father died I was very upset that they didn't tell me about his illness.

My *bubbe*, Rachel Fajge, loved Papa. Every year she came to visit us. After her return from Marienbad, the spa, she'd always stop in Berlin. They were elegant Hasidim and when they came to Berlin they spoiled us with presents.

Rav Itsche and the Battle of Tannenberg

Chaya's Notes

Rav Itsche brought his family to Berlin in 1917, at Kaiser Wilhelm II's invitation. A charismatic personality, he moved as easily among his fellow Hasidim as he did in certain German political circles.

Rav Itsche's name is associated with Germany's early victory at the Battle of Tannenberg[2] on August 27, 1914, during the first year of World War I. It is said that he transmitted secret information to the German high command concerning the battle plans of Russian troops and their intended attack on the Germans at Tannenberg, a key city in East Prussia around which many battles were fought in the past.

According to Russian generals Rennenkampf and Samsonoff, the Russians lost this strategic battle because they were betrayed. Believing that their plan of attack was top secret, they expected to vanquish the German troops in a surprise attack. How these plans fell into the hands of the German generals, Hindenburg and Ludendorff, is variously reported in two versions. The official version was revealed in Hindenburg's book *Out of My Life* (1920).[3] On page six, Hindenburg describes how the Russian secret plan was inadvertently discovered, "...in the pocketbook of a dead Russian officer...." The Russian plan laid out a two-pronged attack by the Niemen and Narew troops to attack the German forces thereby leading to the fall of Tannenberg into Russian hands. This plan, now in German hands, led the generals to reposition their troops accordingly, and in a surprise attack against the Russians, the Germans won a decisive victory at Tannenberg. That victory, occurring when it did, was of great importance to the German high command, because it enabled them to concentrate their troops in the west, unencumbered by what could have been an eastern front that was now laid low.[4]

The second version that relates how the documents came into the hands of the German generals is Jerry Gerhard Bocian's[5] account. He was a Holocaust survivor who was born in Berlin in 1923. He lived in Germany until 1943, when he was deported to a work camp and later to Theresienstadt; he was liberated in May 1945. According to Bocian, his parents, Leo and Frieda Bocian, originally from Poland, moved to Muenzstrasse 25 and there became acquainted with the "Hasidic Rabbi from Warsaw" who lived in the same building on the second floor. Bocian himself was a young boy then and has no clear recollection of the Rav. But Bocian's parents, who revered the Rav, told their son many fascinating, almost unbelievable stories about this man, who lived in "those wild days of the First World War and the Weimar Republic...when almost anything was possible, even if unbelievable." (From a letter to Frau Krueger, 1992.[6])

Bocian's version of the Tannenberg victory is that Rav Itsche and some of his followers smuggled information from the battlefield to Field Marshal von Hindenburg. How they managed such a feat is unclear. But one of the stories Bocian told was that the Rav, who lived in Warsaw at the time and had a *shul* there as well, was in charge of the wellbeing of his followers and their families. Warsaw was in Russian hands then, and conscription into the Russian army was of the highest priority. In order to pursue their plans for expansion, the Russians drafted all able-bodied men into their forces. Orthodox Jewish men were not exempt. Anti-Semitism in the army was rampant: Orthodox men were not allowed to practice their faith; they were forced to eat non-kosher food and were subjected to taunts and ridicule. Therefore, many of the enlisted men deserted their posts. Among these deserters were three men who belonged to the Rav's flock. They were caught by the Russians and were executed by hanging. The Rav's sorrow and anger were such that he swore to avenge his men's deaths. Bocian wrote, "The papers containing Russian attack plans were obtained through the Rav's spying activities."[7]

How could these "spying activities" have taken place? And how does Bocian's story accord with Hindenburg's version in *Out of my Life?* In his book, Hindenburg does not specify who discovered the secret plans. How would these plans have come into the hands of the Rav? Did he and his followers go looking for such plans? Not likely. It is more probable that the Rav and his men came upon the officer's body on one of their not unusual outings into the fields. Whatever the circumstances, the Rav, or some of his followers, could have discovered the body of a Russian military man quite accidentally. And examining the body they could have found the valuable documents. The Rav may or may not have wondered of what use this find could be to him and his followers. No friend of the Russians, however, and stirred by his oath to avenge the deaths of his three men, the Rav decided to deliver the papers to someone in the German high command. How he got to Ludendorff or Hindenburg is another a mystery. But sometimes anger and looming danger can trigger grand plans in a man imbued with his "eminent descent" who holds a profound belief in his mission in life. In such a state of mind the Rav could have been capable of achieving unusual deeds.

With the victory at Tannenberg and the capitulation of the Russians, the Rav earned his reward. For this spying action he was invited by the Kaiser Wilhelm II to settle in Berlin in 1917 with his entire family and most of his Hasidic followers. In recompense for his help to the German government, the Rav was awarded a lifelong pension, and a *Freischutz,* a Letter of Protection, both of which were enforced for the remainder of his life.

One may wonder about the truth of this story but there is no denying that something unusual did happen around the battle plans of Tannenberg. Von Hindenburg's explanation that the information was found in the pocketbook of a dead Russian officer is not inconsistent with Bocian's tales of the Rav's unusual feats. And unless there is truth to this account, how could one explain such privileges granted a Rav, a Hasidic Jew from Poland, no less?

The Rav Visits the President's Palace

The Rav had a relationship with von Hindenburg, proof of which was found among Hannah's papers. She found a document among the papers that she had packed in a trunk and shipped from Berlin to Antwerp. A Christian family kept it safe until the end of the war. That document is a poem in the Rav's handwriting that he personally delivered to President Hindenburg. According to Bocian, "when Hindenburg became Reichspresident...the Hasidic Rabbi from Warsaw could be seen walking with his cane, his long black caftan and

round black hat to the President's palace, on the day of Hindenburg's birthday, past the Honor guards with their long glistening
bayonets to personally congratulate the President on his special
day."

The letter and poem below were not written for Hindenburg's birthday, but for the celebration of the New Year of 1924.

(GROSS RABBINER A.I. KUPFERSTOCK, From Warsaw
SPIRITUAL LEADER of the East European Community
In BERLIN
Muenzstr.25, front, #2.
Toward the New Year, 1924)
Hochgeehrte Herr,
Ganz [geehrter Herr],
Ich erlaube mir Ihnen zwischen all Ihren Freunde Meinem herzlichsten
Neu Jahr Wunsch auszusprechen.
Ich wuensche Ihnen und Ihrer Verwandschaft zum Neuen jahr Leben und
Gesundheit, viel Glueck und Freude, Amen.

(Your Honor,
I humbly allow myself to convey to you and all your friends, my
heartfelt wishes for a Happy New Year.
I wish you and your family good health, happiness and joy for this New
Year.
 Life, and Health, much good luck and happiness. Amen.)

Liebes Deutschland	(Dear Germany
1	
Es geht eine Neue Welt	A new world is upon us
Ihr werdet wieder stark	Once again will you be strong
habt schon gutes Geld	Your money is already good in
Reuben und Goldmark	Rubles as well as goldmarks
2	
Schlafett ruhig in eure Betten	Sleep soundly in your beds
Euer Geld bleibt immer Bar	Your possessions by your side
Alles werdet ihr retten	You will save everything
Mit euer eigenen Dollar	With your very own dollar
3	
Alles wird billiger sein	Everything will be less costly
Es gibt auch mehr kein Not	There is no more need or want

Alle beste Getraenke und Wein	The best of drinks including wine
Fleisch, Butter und Brot	Also meat, butter and bread
4	
Nur alle zusammen halten	We all must stand together
Das ist die Kraft der Velt	That is the strength of the world
Sich nicht in Parteien spalten	We must not split into parties
Wird das Land wieder aufgestellt	Then will this land be rebuilt!)

Mit vorzueglicher Hochachtung, Kupferstock
(With my highest respect, Kupferstock)

October 1938 to November 1938

After Hindenburg's death and advent of the beginning of the Third Reich, the Rav, who was among the *Schutzjuden* (the protected Jews), continued to receive his pension until the day he died. The Rav was also protected from hostilities and evacuation during the so-called *Polenaktion,* in October 1938, when many of his Hasidic followers, together with some 15,000 Polish Jews who had earlier settled in Berlin, were now shipped back to Poland.

"Many Jewish men, including some of the Rav's followers, were *verschlept* (rounded up) and taken to the concentration camp Sachsenhausen." Bocian wrote that in response to this roundup the Rav left his house, "and he rode to Oranienburg, Sachsenhausen, where he demanded to see the camp's commandant. After a lengthy wait, he was successful in his request, and his men were released the same day Rav Itsche arrived at the camp. The Rav and his Hasidim marched out of the camp as free men!"[8]

Hannah Saves Her Grandfather from Moabit

The Rav did not escape persecution all together. During the days of persecution in 1938, he was taken from his home to Moabit, the Gestapo prison.

Chaya to Hannah: Mama, this Moabit story is of special interest to us because it illustrates how the Rav's fearlessness was transmitted to you. He influenced not only your actions but also your attitude toward the Nazi authorities. You never admitted openly to being intimidated by them. Undaunted by their terrorizing actions, you behaved with a nerve that bordered on impudence and you devised numerous maneuvers that saved you, the family, and your children's lives. In your typical lively manner you told us how your grandfather, in spite of his protected status as a Jew, was picked up and taken to the Gestapo in Berlin.

No sooner had you been notified of his arrest, than you went to the Moabit prison insisting to see the commandant and demanding to know the reasons for their action: Didn't they know of his special status recognized by Hindenburg and even validated by the Third Reich? And couldn't they guess that your grandfather would go on a hunger strike if they kept him in prison because he ate only kosher food? After a number of telephone conversations validating the Rav's status, the Director in charge of Moabit sent the Rav home, a free man now and leaning on your arm!

CHAPTER THREE

HANNAH AND HER CHILDREN, 1940–1942[1]

Finally Antwerp

Hannah: I had never met Tante Roizele but I knew that she was an unusual woman, goodhearted and very wise. She had taken the children into an already large household, cared for them, sent them to school, and provided them with a large family of uncles, aunts, and second cousins who were more than willing to play many games and

Photo 3.1 Tante Roizele, Antwerp, 1930s

make them laugh. The children stayed with the family for four long months, not easy for children who had almost never been away from home and had lost their papa. Needless to say, we had a joyful reunion. Chaya'le did not let me out of her sight. She asked unending questions, "Where is Papa? Where is he now? Why didn't he come with you?" I had to explain over and over why Papa was not with me. She did not want to believe me and needed to hear over and over that her papa was not coming here because he was dead. Gradually, she stopped asking. Gitte'le was quieter, more reserved than her sister, but also very tender with me. She understood so much better than Chaya what was going on. She was, of course, almost four years older than her sister.

I must say I was overwhelmed. The Horowitz children, all young or middle aged, were fun-loving, warm, and noisy adults. They loved to tell jokes and play pranks with the children. This was a joyful household. I was deeply touched by their kindness. Tante Roizele said to me, "When your children arrived I was amazed to see how well behaved, quiet, and helpful they were. And I said to my own grown children, 'I want to meet the woman who has raised such fine children!' And now I see her; you are indeed everything I expected, and more!"

I was not well when I arrived. The physical hardships of the journey triggered a kidney infection. Tante Roizele, seeing the state I was in, put me to bed. My room was in the attic three flights up. It was a steep climb, just as Papa had said it was, but I was comfortable there. In order to see me, the girls had to run up and down those narrow stairs, and this was not a quiet affair. But I told myself, "Hanschen, don't be a fool. You have not come here for a rest."

Hannah, Gitta, and Chaya[2]

Hannah: Exactly twelve days after my arrival, we awoke to a sky black with German bombers. The *Yekkes* (Germans) invaded Belgium, the Netherlands, and France. It was May 10, 1940. The *Blitz-*

krieg had begun.

Gitta: The sky was the most beautiful blue and you could see the planes and you even saw the bombs falling from way up high. People came out of their houses, and everyone was looking toward the sky.

Hannah: We actually saw the bombs. It did not seem real. I was terrified because I knew the *Yekkes.* I said, "We can't stay here," and to myself I muttered, "We must leave this place immediately!" Other than the family, I had no connections here and I felt trapped. "We must get out of here," I said to Uncle Herman. Uncle had a friend whose name was Jacques, and this Jacques had a car; he too wanted to escape at all cost. He said to Uncle, "If you pay me for driving you, and for the *benzine* (gasoline), I will take you, your sister-in-law, and her two children. But, I must warn you, it will be very cramped in the car because I have my wife, my two children, my sister and my mother-in-law, and they will be traveling with us." We were four and they were six. How all ten of us would fit into that car, I could not imagine; because the car was not even a station wagon like you have today, it was just an ordinary car. But in the end we all fit in, and we left in that one car!

Die Vlucht—The Grand Escape

There have been many escapes in my life, but this one will always be called *Die Vlucht.* Leaving Antwerp on the main highway, we soon saw the condition of the roads. They were clogged with cars and all sorts of vehicles: small and large cars, *camionettes* (little buses), bicycles, motorcycles, and any possible thing on wheels. It was a real traffic jam. People were walking on the road with bundles and some had abandoned their suitcases.

Gitta: We could not move forward. Jacques took the road to La Panne and Pas de Calais along the beaches of Belgium and France. The Germans were bombing the coast and we had to abandon the car. People with carts, valises, and bundles were throwing things to the side of the road, because they could not carry those things. Every so often the planes would swoop down on the highway and we would run into the ditches. I remember a horrible thing: they told us if there were gas bombs, we should urinate on our handkerchiefs and put them over our faces. It was bedlam, sheer bedlam, and there were gas masks on the ground but no one was using them. The panic was unbelievable, and everyone thought this was going to be like World War I.

Hannah: We were running on the boardwalk of La Panne and every few seconds we threw ourselves down to the ground. And you, my *pitzele* (little one), you were crying and afraid that you would get lost. Your eyes were black as marbles and you were holding on tight. But Gitta was already a big girl, she understood that there was no other way; we had to run to save our lives. The bombing continued and it became impossible to stay on the boardwalk. We ran to a side street not too far from the boardwalk, and while running to avoid the bombings, I saw a basement apartment that seemed to be empty. I went down a couple of steps below the sidewalk level and discovered that there was no one there. But I saw rats and mice running for their lives. When I think about it today I still shudder. We had no choice; we had to spend the night there until the bombardment stopped. Do you remember I even found a can of *ananas* (pineapple) in the kitchen? With a makeshift tool that we used as a can opener, we opened the can and shared the fruit.

Gitta to Chaya: One way or another, Mother always managed to find food for us. How she did this I don't know to this day. She was always on the lookout and we were never starving. There were always crackers around or something. We were never without. Mother had enormous strength.

Hannah: The bombing resumed and continued throughout the night, but I was relieved because we were able to lie down there and rest. And we were together, the four of us, and that was what mattered. The following morning it was quiet in La Panne. When I opened the door and went up to the street, I saw that all the houses had been destroyed except for the one we were in.

Gitta to Hannah: And you looked up to the sky and thanked your grandfather Itsche for watching over us. "And that is why we are safe now," you said.

Chaya: Why did we decide to go to Dunkirk?

Hannah: I don't remember exactly; it must have been by word of mouth. The British were in Dunkirk with big ships and they were going to England.[3] So we wanted to go there; who knows what might happen.

Gitta: When we got there, the ships were anchored in the harbor and many soldiers were standing around. We thought they would be leaving soon, and Mother was hoping that they would take us with them. But they refused. There must have been thousands standing around just trying to get to London, but the British soldiers wouldn't take us. They took a lot of other people.

Hannah: I hoped that the British would take pity on us and save us. When I saw these friendly Allies I wanted to cry. Approaching first one, and then another officer, I tried to talk my way up to one of their ships. I explained our predicament: two small children, escaped from Berlin, husband killed by the Nazis. I pleaded, I begged, but the British refused. "Take the children at least, please," I said. Still, they refused; they were not allowed to take foreigners on board. The only civilians allowed on board were people with British passports. Priority, however, was given to the troops who had to get back to England to continue the fight against the Germans. That was their reply. That was very unfortunate for us. But in the end, it was for the best because the North Sea was mined and they, the British, could not possibly be responsible for us. I believe that they felt for us, because from aboard ship they bent over and handed us English tea biscuits and cans of *boula bess* (boiled beef). We were lucky, I guess because after they left, we heard that four British ships hit mines, exploded, and sank.

But where were we to go? We decided to go further into France. Then the unbelievable happened; I thought we were going back to the car and Jacques, but instead Jacques came up to me and said, "Hannah, I found a man who will help me and my wife, and our two children cross into Spain through the Pyrenees. I have to take that chance for my family." And he promised to return to pick us up later! This was beyond belief. It was the first time I encountered a Jewish thief and I was stunned. He wasn't really going to leave us, I thought. But he did. He took his wife and his children and they left. And his mother-in-law and sister he left with us! What was I to do? "Hannah," I said to myself, "this is very bad, but what are you going to do? Leave his family here? No, not I, not Hannah Falle!" (Hannah's middle name.)

June 1940: We Arrive in Paris

Chaya: We had to find a place to stay overnight and another mode of transportation. Somehow our mother managed it. With the help of a truck and a driver whom she was able to pay, we arrived at the outskirts of Boulogne, France.

Hannah: Next we went to Paris by train.

Chaya: It was our bad luck to arrive in Paris one day before the Germans entered Paris on June 14, 1940. I was holding my sister's hand when we saw a mass of green helmets marching on the street. I held on tight. I saw what I saw, but I do not recall hearing a sound: no clanging of boots, no singing, no airplanes overhead. And where did we sleep that first night of the 13th after we came into Paris? Leave it to our mother.

Hannah: I knew no one in Paris. In what direction do we turn? We walked around; I was afraid to go to a hotel. So we came to a *pletzele* (a plaza). I think maybe it was the Place Pigalle. A woman was standing against a lamppost. It was not difficult to guess her profession. I needed to know more. I walked up to her. "Madame," I said, "we are *en passage* (traveling through) and I am looking for a place to stay with my husband and my two children. Can you tell me where you work?" She pointed to a house across the street and said, "There, on the second floor." I went to the brothel and asked to speak to the Madame. When she came down, I told her that I was traveling through with my husband and two children and I needed a place to stay for one night or two. "I will pay," I said. She must have known we were strangers looking for refuge, but she didn't ask. The Madame gave us one room for the four of us; it was on the top floor. We entered and saw mirrors covering the four walls as well as the ceiling. You girls began to ask questions, "Why are there mirrors on the walls? Why are they on the ceiling?" Gitta asked about the people coming in and out. Who were they? So I told you, "These are friends who come to visit each other." The next morning Gitta saw the maids were carrying stacks of clean towels. She asked me why they were carrying all these bundles. "I don't know," I said, "maybe they had many guests last night." Uncle Herman was quiet; we were both trying to remain serious, but despite our situation we thought this one was unreal and comical!

We stayed in that house for a couple of days. I paid the Madame for food and milk because I was afraid to go out. But then we did have to leave. The Madame showed me a hotel nearby and I took a room in this small hotel, not far from the brothel, and I went out to look for food. I found a couple of stores on the street where I bought bread and meat; and I also bought a little cooker that used *benzine* and I cooked us a meal on that thing.

In the meantime Mendl arrived; he was Erni's husband and Papa's cousin from Antwerp. I don't know how he got to us, but he did. Mendl was hungry, so I took him in and he was so happy about the food. I had bought some *jambon* (ham) and Chaya said, "What kind of meat is this, Mommy?" "Oh, this is *kalbfleisch* (veal)." It was the first time I had given you *treif* (non-kosher meat) to eat. But you persisted, "Mommy," you said, "this meat tastes different than veal." "Well, I don't know about that," I said, "it does look a little different than usual but that is probably because the meat is sliced very thin." (I knew Yanke'le and my grandfather would forgive me, after all to save a life....)

Matters soon got worse. The Germans arrived and requisitioned all the hotels for their own use. The hotel owner asked us to leave; he was frightened, but we were terrified. Still, I went to a little real-estate office—I don't remember exactly how I got there—and asked them to help me find some lodgings. They found a *Schloss* (stately manor home). The *Schloss* was out of town, near Boulogne, and we would have to walk, but it was an okay place, they said.

We set out, taking our baggage, and walked to the outskirts of Paris. We walked and walked. While I was happy to get away from the *Yekkes,* we didn't know where we were going. We walked to the countryside with our baggage. [There must have been some transport for part of the way from Paris to Boulogne, though none of us recalled this in our later conversations.] Close to the outskirts of Boulogne, we came to a hill. I saw trees and bushes. We walked up the hill and around the incline and then we saw the *Schloss*. It was like a real castle with white brick walls and round turrets on top. The place looked deserted. We went in, and at first it looked like a good place to park ourselves. We had more space than we needed because we were [only] six people now. We settled down. I left the two of you to look around and check out the rooms and see where everyone would be sleeping, and then I went to find food.

I always did better when I went out alone. I walked a while and soon found a farm. The farmer sold me eggs, butter, meat, and bread. The farmer was friendly since I was spending a lot of money, so he gave me extra bread for the children. I bought what I needed and went back to the family. We shared what we had with Jacques' sister and mother-in-law, but I wasn't happy about it. I could not forgive him for leaving us.

We stayed in that place a few days, maybe a week. But I knew we could not stay there long because the rats and mice I had seen when we came showed up at night, and I was afraid to sleep for fear that we would be bitten. My fear got worse the more food we had. And so, we began to talk about leaving. But where does one go? Go further into France where we had no connections whatsoever, or go back to Antwerp? And how do we return to Belgium without a car or driver, and with no gasoline?

I walked back to Boulogne and I went to city hall, to the administration, to see what I could find out. Jacques' sister said, "I'm going with you." At first I accepted her offer, but along the way I thought it over and said to her, "I don't think going with you will work. Let me go alone, I will feel more comfortable talking alone." I went to see the chief at city hall. I think he was a major—a person of some rank—an important Nazi. I spoke to him in *Hochdeutsch* (in educated German) and told him of our plight. "We are six people including two children; we came here from Belgium and now we want to return to Antwerp, but we don't know how to get back home."

The Nazi commandant asked, "Why did you leave?" I answered, "I was afraid of the bombings and I wanted to save my family." He looked at me, quite astonished, and said, "But *Geehrte Frau* (lady, with all due respect), you are asking for something that is unheard of!"

"I am from Germany," I said, "You can see and hear that; and you are from the Wehrmacht (armed forces). I know the Wehrmacht are good people, so please, be *menschlich* (humane) and help us out. I wouldn't ask you but it is absolutely necessary! I need to buy enough *benzine* to get us back to Belgium, and I need a permit for that. I have a car and a driver already (recommended to me by the farmer who sold us our food), I only need the *benzine*."

The major then wrote out a permission slip for so and so many liters *benzine*. Then he sent me to the police for another slip. The Gestapo met me there. I repeated my story and showed them the permission slip. They looked at me as if I were nuts. And maybe I was! But they took the slip I handed them and gave me another one and I left. I now had a permit to buy some liters of gasoline! Later, I met the driver and I gave him the slip. You can imagine he was astonished. He bought the *benzine*; he bought even more than he needed. As a result I did not have to pay him for driving us; he said that he had made money enough on the *benzine*. He was an honest man and I made money on our deal too!

Our car turned out to be a *camionette*, we all fit in and had a capable driver too. Together we got back to Antwerp, in spite of the bombed-out roads and gaping holes. We dropped off Jacques' mother-in-law and sister and made our way back to Tante Roizele's. When she saw us she was gleaming with joy and took us in, heart and soul!

Back in Antwerp

But we couldn't stay there for long; that much was clear. There were too many people in that one house. I had to find us an apartment close by. That way we could see the family and we would have a place of our own. Over the Tante's objections, I found an apartment on a quiet street nearby, on the Memlinck Straat, 16. It was a lovely well-furnished place and the second floor had a little balcony. It had two rooms, a kitchen, a bathroom, a corridor, and also a courtyard where we sat when the weather was good.

I put a table and chairs there, and we drank *café* and I baked cakes; and Uncle brought his friends and they played cards. They came over frequently. And I sent you children to the *Orthodoxishe* (Orthodox) Jewish school, the Yessoide Torah.

We were now in early 1941. Uncle introduced me to his friends: Luzer, Rosenfeld, and Schiff. Mendl (Uncle's first cousin) and Erni, who had just been married, also came to eat, drink, and play cards. I made salads and all sorts of good things. Erni and I became fast friends and remained lifelong friends from then on. We stayed in Antwerp almost a year because, in spite of the *Yekkes* and new edicts coming out every day, the roundups and deportations had not yet begun.

Hannah and Luzer

Luzer Dafner was Uncle Herman's friend, and like him, a diamond cutter. They worked together in the same *zegerei* (small factory where industrial diamonds are cut). The factory was in a small building in which there were several machines consigned to the cutting, others to the polishing of diamonds. Many of the young men who came over from Galicia were taken in by the Horowitz family and were trained as diamond cutters there; only Papa had rejected that opportunity.

Luzer came over to the house frequently with Uncle Herman and he fell in love with me. He absolutely wanted to marry me but I was not in love with him. The only man in my life was Papa, and he always will be. Still, Luzer was persistent. I spoke to Tante Roizele and asked her advice. I did not love Luzer. "I could never love another man," I said to her. But Luzer was kind, very attentive to me, and also, he was not bad looking. He liked both of you too, especially you, Chaya'le, because you were always friendly and smiling.

I asked Tante Roizele, "What should I do?" Gravely, she replied: "More than one year has passed since your Yankev was killed, may he rest in peace. The situation with the war is menacing; for us Jews, the situation is even more ominous than for anyone else. And you, Hanne'le, are not in the best of health. Moreover, you have two little girls who need looking after. I advise you to seriously think about Luzer's proposition because this is no time for a woman to be alone with two little girls."

Luzer told me he loved me; he wanted to give me everything he had. He promised he would take care of the children. He said that I had taken over his heart entirely. He went to the Tante and spoke to her. She came to me and tried to convince me that I should marry Luzer and not even think about marrying Uncle Herman (Papa's brother). I had never thought of marrying Uncle Herman. My head was full of these men who visited me and who said that they wanted to marry me. The Tante kept telling me I have to marry Luzer because "he's dying to marry you, and he loves the children, in particular the little one who hangs on him." Fishel nagged at me, *Er hot mir gehackt a tcheinik* (he kept nagging me), meaning that this was the best thing for me to do. "Yankev would have wanted it so," he said.

Meanwhile, I developed a fever and had to go see a doctor. He examined me and after the physical said, "You are a very sick woman. The hardships you suffered during your escape from Berlin aggravated your condition. Your kidneys are damaged. Your life may be in danger if you don't take care of yourself immediately." He hospitalized me; this was before Pesach, 1941. I received good care in the hospital and my health improved, so I came home. Thinking about the children and their need for consistent care, and Tante Roizele's words, I agreed to marry Luzer.

A good Jewish man from Germany named Monderer befriended me when we came back from the *Vlucht*. He liked me for my spunk and gave Luzer and me our entire wedding and honeymoon as a present! We were married on May 14, 1941, in a little town outside Antwerp. I did not invite you to the wedding because I did not want to upset you. Also, I felt guilty for marrying Luzer. So I asked the Tante to keep you until we returned.

When Uncle Herman heard that I was to marry Luzer he was heartbroken. He cried all night before Luzer and I were married. I might have married Uncle instead of Luzer, but according to Jewish law, the brother of a husband who died is not allowed to marry his widow if she has children; however if the widow is childless he is expected to marry her.

Gitta to Chaya: Mother's marrying Luzer came as a big blow to me. I was truly devastated. First, because our father's memory was very much alive in my heart. I was really outraged. And I did not like Luzer as a person; I certainly did not want him to take our father's place. I was mourning for our father. I remember that whole experience quite vividly because it coincided with us having to go to Limburg (a town in Belgium)[4] where Jews who did not have Belgian citizenship were interned, supposedly for work duty. And in addition, Jews reporting to Limburg were supposed to sew the Jewish stars on their outer garments!

Photo 3.2 Gitta, Luzer Dafner, and Chaya, Antwerp, 1941

Hannah: That's right. After Luzer and I came back from our honeymoon, the police called at our house and brought papers ordering us to leave Antwerp immediately. We were to travel to Limburg and register there as workers for the German war effort. Limburg was full of Jews now. Jews had to register there and were assigned to labor duty; later they were sent to labor camps. I did not have to think twice about what I was going to do. We would not register for labor duty and we would not wear a Jewish star! So I brought you to the Tante again and took the train to Brussels. There, I acquired false papers for us all. Luzer had found an apartment in Schaarbeek (a suburb of Brussels), on the Wilhelm Kuennen Straat 46. He wanted to take the apartment in his name, but I said, "No! It has to be in my name."

We moved almost immediately. We did not know when we rented the apartment that our next-door neighbors were German soldiers from the Wehrmacht. What a discovery, imagine! But what were we to do? I thought awhile and decided that maybe this situation might work in our favor. Who would suspect a Jewish family choosing intentionally to go live next door to German soldiers from Wehrmacht? As it was, the Germans were neither good nor bad for us. They were gone during the day and drank a lot at night.

For Uncle Herman I found a studio not too far from our house, so we could all stay in touch and see each other. But Luzer was a difficult man. He was jealous of Uncle. I liked Uncle because he was Papa's brother; he was family and seeing him was a little like being home. We visited Uncle; I brought him meals and watched over him. But Luzer would not have it. We had horrible fights in the afternoons when we came home from Uncle's and Luzer wanted to know where we had been. Sometimes, I didn't want him to know where we had been because I wanted to avoid another fight. And that is why I asked you not to tell him when we visited Uncle. But one day it slipped out; you, Chaya'le, told him where we had been and he began to scream and yell at me so much so, that I was afraid he would hit me. The owner who lived on the first floor wondered what was happening in our house. Jokingly, I said to him, "Oh, it was merely a lovers' quarrel."

But our worst quarrel was yet to come. One day, needing to sell some diamonds because I was short of money, I went looking for them. I had hidden them in the basement behind a loose brick in the wall. To my dismay, I discovered that they were gone. When I saw that everything had disappeared, I broke out in a sweat. My first suspicion was Luzer. He must have taken them, though I did not know why he would have done such a thing. Not only were the diamonds missing but also all the jewelry, gold pieces, and the dollars I had; everything was gone! I was beside myself. Certain that he had taken my possessions, I immediately confronted him. He admitted to having taken everything. Why had he done such a thing, I asked? Very upset, he told me that I did not allow him to feel like a husband. Everything I did was without his consent. He wanted me to depend on him, and my having money deprived him of the feeling that he could provide for me. I explained that by his deed he had taken everything that Papa and I had worked so hard to acquire, and also what my family in Poland and Germany had given us over the years.

This was not a quiet debate; I screamed so loud, until I was hoarse. "I swear," I said, "I will leave you on the spot if you do not return my belongings instantly!" And that was when he slapped me in the face. He had a hard hand and he was strong. Assaulted by him I wanted no part of this man any more. I told him I had lost confidence in him. But I was frightened of his rage and I did not want to be hit again. So what was I to do? I retreated to your bedroom and stayed there for a long time.

The *Din Torah*

Later, after I had thought a while, I came out and told Luzer that we would have to see the rabbi in Antwerp for a *din Torah* (a judgment according to Jewish law). There was no other way. Luzer agreed and this is what we did. Luzer was no thief, but a jealous and angry man.

When I met the rabbi I told him all about myself. "I need the money he took from me to save our lives," I said. The rabbi called Luzer in and said, "These children are not yours. The money you took is what they inherited from their father. You are committing an *aveira* (a grave sin) by keeping it." The rabbi also explained to me that Luzer felt belittled by me, by my independence. God knows I always insisted, ever since I came to Belgium, that I had to make my own decisions. I decided when we should run, where we should live, what food and furnishings we bought, where we would go for false papers, where the children would go to school, and so on. These were big decisions and I trusted no one, not Luzer, not anyone. The rabbi talked to us and rendered his decision: Luzer had to return everything he had taken.

When we came home to Brussels, Luzer went to another room, and came back putting everything on the table. "Here is everything, it's yours," he said.

You're asking me how much money I had? I had more than I could count. Every week in Berlin, I went to a smuggler and brought him money to send to Belgium. Papa didn't know what I was doing, I just did it, and my grandfather Itsche helped. He knew about merchandise and how to convert it into money. During the war I had a lot of money. God, maybe two million German marks, and I used the money. We would not be here today if I had not used the money to live on and to pay people off to help us.

After Luzer gave back what he had taken, our domestic life became calmer. Luzer was very good to you, Chaya'le; this is absolutely true. Gitta did not like him much and was cold toward him, but you were nice and kind, and you sought him out. Also, he was good to me. He liked to give me cologne, pretty presents, candy. He wanted me to be beautiful. And I never met a man who was more handsome than Luzer. Not even Papa.

But, my two girls were not enough for Luzer; he wanted to have a baby of his own. I argued with him that this was no time to think about bringing children into the world. "We worry so about the children now," I said. "What would we do with a new baby?"

The Girls Go to School in Schaarbeek

I worried about you and your education. Whenever I felt we were a little bit safe, I looked for a school for you. And so it was now. I located a French-speaking public school that was in our neighborhood and registered you there. I knew it will not be easy to learn a new language, but I was convinced that you would learn fast. Gitta learned well from the beginning; she could read and write, and draw, and she began to speak a little French. But for you Chaya, learning was a struggle. You were unable to learn to read or write, and arithmetic was altogether out of the question! The teacher said you were a dreamer in class and you looked out the window much of the time instead of concentrating on your studies. But in a kind tone she added that you had a good memory for songs and poems and that the children in class liked you.

Gitta: It was easier for me. I don't really know why but I learned French quickly, and before the semester was over, I was first in class. It was hard to believe but I did it. But what was not easy was that we had to be so secretive about our lives. We knew we could not say who we were and what we did. Everything was a big lie.

Early in 1942 the Roundups Began

Hannah: We stayed in Brussels from May 1941 until, I don't know, maybe until February or March 1942. Things got very bad. Just as you were beginning to adapt to school and life in Schaarbeek, and our marriage became less stormy, the roundups of Jews in Belgium began full force. Early in 1942, Jews living in Belgium who were not naturalized Belgian citizens were taken to the concentration camps of Malines[5] and Breendonck.[6] People attempted to escape; some went to Belgian farmers in the country; some brought their children to the French-speaking parts of the countryside where they entered convents and boarding schools and where they passed as Christian children. All this cost enormous sums of money. Jews who could afford it tried to flee to Switzerland, Spain, or the south of France. Then came the new decree: All Jews officially registered in

Belgium had to wear the Jewish star on their outside coats. I too was given *magen Davids* (Jewish stars) by the Jewish community to sew on our coats. (There was a question as to the date when I received the yellow badges. But I know that I had them before Jews were mandated to wear them in May 1942, because we escaped from Belgium in March or April 1942 to the south of France.) One afternoon I remember sitting with a few coats on my lap, ready to start sewing those badges on our coats. Then, I was overcome by an incredible rage. "NO," I said "I will never permit such a thing, never!" I stood up with everything on my lap: stars, needles, whatever I had there, coats too, and everything flew to the floor. "What should we do with a Jewish star, walk into the arms of the Nazis?"[7]

We Leave Brussels and Head to the South of France[8]

Our family and friends were heading to the south of France. My cousins Ernie and Mendl were there already. There was no time to lose; I had purchased false papers earlier. My jewelry, rings, pins, necklaces, gold watches, I sewed into the linings of our coats. What *goldsticklech* (gold coins) I had, I covered with cloth and sewed on as buttons on our coats, just as I did in Berlin when we had our *fabrik* (raincoat factory). The Elbaums, whom I befriended in Brussels, left their leather-goods store and joined us on our journey. Mme. Elbaum became my constant helper and companion. Whatever I did, she did too; and wherever I went, she followed. She too sewed what jewels she possessed into the linings of her family's coats. Mr. and Mme. Elbaum were well off. They had a son, Bernard, whom they had adopted; he was a couple of years older than Gitta and he was strong. I thought he would be helpful with the many chores the young people would have to perform.

Now we also had diamonds. Where do you hide diamonds? I had no experience in these matters, but the men did. They bought condoms and carefully wrapped a few diamonds at a time into pre-folded special tissue papers, called *briefjes* (small envelopes in which the diamond dealers store diamonds with when they trade at the diamond center). These *brieffes*, they placed into the condoms. Each condom was then lubricated and inserted into the rear end of the adult men, Luzer, Uncle Herman, and Mr. Elbaum. But Bernard, Gitta, Mme. Elbaum, Chaya, and I were to watch out and hold on to our coats at all times because everything we owned was to pay for food, lodging, and paying off people who could hide us. It was a difficult night; hiding the money inside their bodies was no easy matter for the men. But everything got done. Then, we each had to study the information on our own identity card as well as everyone else's identity cards. We studied each other's false names, plus the names of the parents and the grandparents too. I worried mostly about you, Chaya'le. You were the youngest and I was afraid for you. I wanted to prepare you for a long interrogation. Because of your age I thought the border police, if they stopped us, would interrogate you the longest if they suspected anyone of us.

Gitta: I remember cramming these papers about our ancestry. But I remember you, Chaya, studied very hard too. From me everything was expected. Since I was the big girl I was supposed to know it all. But for you, Chaya, it was a different story. Everyone worried about you.

Hannah: Well, she was just a little girl of six and a half and you, Gitte'le, were already ten. Anyway, we packed as little as possible, leaving suitcases with our friend, Annie Bransdorfer, in Antwerp. Annie was not in danger yet because she was a Belgian citizen. Later, when the roundups intensified and Jews, regardless of citizenship were taken, Annie went into hiding and hid our belongings with a Christian family.

Finally, in the early morning of the following day, we went to the station in Brussels and boarded the train for Paris. Crossing the Belgian-French border was uneventful: the customs officers examined our papers and let us pass. But the border between the Free Zone and the Occupied Zone at Périgueux, in France, was a different matter. There we were stopped and told to get off the train.

Gitta: I remember we were brought to the police station and they interrogated each person separately. And I guess we each stuck to our stories, even you, Chaya. And they gave us candies and cajoled us, promising more sweets if we just told them what they wanted to hear. But they could not shake our story. And somehow or other, they let us go. To this day, I still shake at how scared I was.

Hannah: I remember how the police examined our papers very carefully. Then, after we were called in, one at a time, he took the youngest last. And she saved us all. I don't know what we would have done without you, Chaya. They started to speak German to you and you said, *"Je ne comprend pas ce que vous dites."* (I don't understand what you are saying.)

Hannah, Gitta, Chaya[9]

Chaya: How do you know that this is what happened? Since I went into the office by myself?

Hannah: You told me so when you came out. You had to study everyone's birth date and where they were born. You were born in Tongeren and your name was Helene Daveau, and Gitta's name was Gisele Daveau.

Gitta: Everyone was interrogated, but with Chaya the interrogation was the longest.

Hannah: Yes, we were worried plenty. I was scared for you, Chaya'le, and for us all. But finally, you came out with the officer and he was holding your hand. Turning to me he said, *"Alors, vous êtes catholiques?"* (So, you are Catholics?) I answered him, *"Mais oui, nous sommes catholiques."* (Of course we are Catholics.) Then, he said, *"Alors c'est bien, vous pouvez passer."* (Well then, all's well, you can pass.) You saved us all, Chaya! I thanked God, my grandfather, and my Yanke'le; I was sure they were watching over us. Free to go, we left the officer and the border patrol and returned to the train as calmly as possible. I said to you, "*Kinder* (children), don't say a word and let us *hoilechen* (walk away) from here."

We boarded the train and decided to split up; our train was going to Lyon and the others were going to Nice. The way to Lyon was easy, and once there we got off and went looking for a place to stay. I found a small flat, on the second floor, a couple of rooms, an old bathroom with rusty pipes all over, and the kitchen was not any better. I had been told that in Lyon there were smugglers who helped people to cross into Switzerland. I looked and tried to make connections but found none, except Shiye, an old relative from Antwerp. He said he had heard of a possibility to go over to Switzerland from Lyon. But when I inquired, I learned that this possibility was for families who had children between the ages of two and four. Chaya was too old. I realized then that there was no way to get out of France from Lyon. Our best chance was to get to Nice.

We Travel to Nice

Once more we took the train and I looked out for the conductor. I was more worried now than I had been earlier. So, before he came asking for tickets and papers, I quickly went to the W.C., just as I had done on the train from Périgueux to Paris. I told you children to stay in the compartment and pretend that you were asleep. Later, I gave the conductor a bar of chocolate, and for that, he gave us a compartment all to ourselves. The ride was long, several hours, but eventually we arrived in Nice. Here we knew people. As I told you, Erni had been in Nice since 1941. We went to see her, she took us in and gave us something to eat and drink. She gave me the name of a realtor who helped me to locate two apartments. I registered both apartments officially. One was on the rue du Congrès and the second one I don't remember; maybe it will come to me. Later I had a third apartment, but that was when we went into hiding. Now Luzer let me do whatever I wanted because he was very much in love with me, and he understood that I had to do what I thought was necessary.

A Terrible Thing

While we were in Lyon I began to feel nauseous, and within a week I was throwing up morning and night. I couldn't eat a thing; I knew that I must be pregnant. Luzer was a happy man and I was beside myself. We arrived in Nice in March 1942. I found a nice sunny apartment with big windows and two large rooms. The two of you stayed with us for a couple of weeks, but I was afraid that we would be caught. Nice was not as safe as people thought, I said to myself.

When I saw Erni I immediately told her about my predicament. It turned out that she too was pregnant and every bit as unhappy about it as I was! We both decided to see a doctor who would help with our abortions. I calculated that my pregnancy was probably a week earlier than hers; therefore, I would have the abortion first. The doctor we saw was very kind; he understood our situation and he explained how he would proceed. A wooden stake would be inserted into the uterus. "Let it stay there for two or three days and call me on the third," he said. On the third day, I called him and told him that I was not feeling well. This kind Jewish man rushed over to the house; before long, I had strong and painful contractions; and then, I delivered the fetus. My pains were very strong, but the baby had come out and I knew my body would recover.

While I labored Luzer sat in the apartment. He could not bear it; hands over ears, he cried his heart out. I could not calm him down. When I saw the baby, I too nearly died; the baby would have been a little boy! I cannot tell you what feelings of regret I had, and the guilt I felt was terrible. Those feelings never changed. After that, whenever something bad happened to us, I said to myself, "Hannah, this is happening to you because you aborted your little boy."

Luzer cried, tearing at his shirt; sitting on a chair, bent over, he was heaving, his upper body was moving up and down; and he recriminated at me, "For doing this to my baby, I will never forgive you!" He became mean again. I tried to console him. "Look," I said, "all the women are doing this. This is no time to bring a baby into the world. Where could we hide with a small baby? And what would happen to us and to the children if we were taken in a roundup? Then, we would never have a chance to save ourselves. Yes, I have done a terrible thing. But we have to move on."

I went looking for a boarding school for you and found one. The school was called L'Institut Massena pour Jeunes Filles; it was located on the avenue des Fleurs.

Gitta: C'etait une belle école. (It was a beautiful school.) It was grand and elegant. And we studied there; we even learned.

Hannah: Do you know what they said in Nice? "From where does this woman have so much money that she can allow herself to send her girls to such a school?"

Gitta: There were Jewish girls in the school and also French girls. Rich girls from broken homes, and daughters of government officials and foreign ambassadors. The upper crust.

Chaya: I remember drinking chamomile tea under a large willow tree with Madame la Directrice and other teachers. And on the table there were these little yellow flowers from the chamomile tree. We were offered piano lessons. I asked myself, "Why should I want to take piano lessons now?" I had acquired the mentality that learning was hard and was not meant for me at this point in my life. What was important was to be safe. But there we were, standing in this long narrow room, an upright piano against the wall; Madame La Directrice was scheduling piano lessons for Gitta and me.

Gitta: Learning was altogether unrealistic; we would be here and gone tomorrow, what difference did going to school make, and studying the piano?

Chaya: How did we learn French anyway, I wonder?

Hannah: You began learning French in Brussels and you were good students. And here, at the Institut Massena, Madame La Directrice told me that you, Chaya, were reciting *poésies* (poems) and singing songs to entertain the teachers after dinner.

August 26, 1942

Hannah: In the summer of July to August 1942, before the *grandes vacances* (summer vacation), I took you out of the school and we went to Vence. It was awfully hot in Nice and in Vence the weather would be cooler. But in Vence the Jews were under *residence forcée*; that meant that all Jews had to stay at one of two hotels, the Veranda Hotel or the Hotel Beau Séjour. I did not want to register anywhere, and I did not want to live where I was told; least of all, was I going to register officially with the Vichy police! You should know that whenever you have to register "officially," your life is at risk. Instead I went looking for another place and found a small hotel on a narrow street in the old town. It was called Hotel de Vence. It looked a lot better than those large hotels assigned to the Jews. It was a small and a comfortable place and we registered on our false papers.

One morning, after we had been there for ten or twelve days, I decided I had to go back to Nice because I needed money. "I must go to Nice to sell some merchandise," I said. "Oh, Mommy, let me go with you," Gitta said. "It's so boring here, there is nothing to do all day long."

I hoped to sell some diamonds to Moishe Fass; he was a good friend and also a relative and a diamond dealer. Moishe liked me and he always took my merchandise in exchange for money. I trusted him because he appraised my merchandise honestly. So Gitta and I left Vence and you, Chaya, stayed with Luzer.

La Grande Rafle: The Big Roundup

That trip was my downfall. Gitta and I left Vence on the day when *la grande rafle* (a major roundup of Jews by the Vichy authorities) took place in Nice; the date was August 26, 1942.

Luzer and you were picked up by the Vichy police and transported back to Nice, to a *caserne* (military barracks).[10] You were not quite eight then, Chaya. The men were separated from the women and children, and Luzer was sent to Drancy, and from Drancy to Schoppinitz.[11] I went to Willy (Toronczyk)[12] and begged him to help me because Willy was on the board of the Jewish Community in Nice. Willy said that he knew someone who will be able to free Luzer from Drancy for the sum of 10,000 francs. I gave him the money and kept 800 francs for our living expenses. But I never saw Luzer again, and I did not see my 10,000 francs either. Willy said the man escaped with the money. I didn't believe him; I think Willy took the money for himself. He and his wife, Regina, took money from us whenever they could. She even overcharged us for the bread she bought for all of us when we went into hiding. Still, Willy did find the apartment when we all went into hiding, on the rue Trachel 42 bis. But that is another story.

Chaya: How did Luzer die?

Gitta: We received one postcard from Drancy.[13]

Hannah: Salke Gaertner and Luzer were in Schoppinitz together, and Salke told me later, after the war, how Luzer died. He became ill with typhoid. He was sick already when he arrived in Schoppinitz. He was very weak and could not walk, "Better you shouldn't know, Hanne'le," Salke said to me.[14]

It was a sad day when I saw two men coming toward me on the boardwalk in Nice. First they asked me how I am feeling. Then they said these are bad times for the Jews and unfortunately there was nothing we could do about that. Gradually, they told me that they had been with Luzer in Schoppinitz and how sick he was. He'd said, "Tomorrow at this time I will not be here anymore. Please tell my wife she must go on living with her children, take care of herself, and have a goal in life." The following day he died.

When the men left, my hair stood on end and I actually turned gray on the spot. I did not believe these things happen, I thought turning gray as a result of shock was merely an expression. But when Erni saw me on the street, she said she did not recognize me; I was totally gray. She took me in her arms and brought me over to her house, and gently put me on the sofa. She put compresses on my forehead and gave me water to drink and urged me to sleep.

My greatest consolation, Chaya'le, was that you were saved! Because they took you together with Luzer from Vence to Nice. Then they separated you from Luzer and you started to cry without stop. After you cried, you told me that you screamed and yelled that the police were mistaken; that you are not Jewish and you are there in the barracks without your mother. You cried that your mother will be very upset because she does not know where you are and you have not come home yet.

You cried for a long time and the people standing around you were getting upset. Then a tall officer came out of his office, he bent over to talk to you and whispered that if you stopped crying he would take you home at the end of the day. And in fact, when the day was over, the officer kept his promise. He walked you out into a black Citroën and drove you to Luzer's French cousin's house. When he arrived in front of the house, he offered to walk you across the street; but you thanked him and said, "No, that would not be necessary."

When you walked up to the cousin's place, the door to her apartment was sealed. She was not there; Chaya, you stood there not knowing what to do next. You must have been frightened to death. But not knowing what else to do, you returned to the street. Just then, Gitta, who had been looking for you for hours, came around the corner!

Gitta: I was afraid to go upstairs to the cousin's apartment, but I knew she had a small child and Chaya had given her the doll that you *schlepped* (dragged) all the way from Germany! So I thought Chaya might have gone to her place.

Hannah: You were very clever and you saved our Chaya'le. When I saw you together, I thought it was a miracle from heaven. I thought it was my grandfather's and Yanke'le's doing. But first, when you brought her to me, I fainted.

CHAPTER FOUR

THE ITALIAN OCCUPATION, 1942–1943[1]

Chaya to Hannah: Mama, when we were hiding in Nice, how many people were we altogether? And what was it like living there?

The Apartment on rue Trachel

Hannah: The apartment was at rue Trachel 42 bis, on the third floor. We were four families and we all knew each other. Every family had one room. There was one small kitchen and one bathroom with toilet for all. Willy Toronczyk and his family had the largest bedroom because, after all, he found the apartment; also he was a member of the Jewish Committee in Nice and he knew what was going on more than we did. In a way, we felt safer having Willy with us because if anything were about to happen we would surely find out about it as soon as he did.

Well then, Willy and his family were three people: they were Willy, his wife Regina, and their son Freddy. The Elbaums were also three: Madame and Monsieur Elbaum, and their son Bernard. The Elbaums ran into two cousins from Brussels who needed a place to stay, so they joined us too. After we fled Nice we lost track of them; I don't really know what happened to them later. In our family we would have been five had Luzer lived. But after Luzer was taken and didn't return, I slept with you on the floor in an alcove in the hall; for Gitta I got a mattress, and Uncle Herman shared a room with the two cousins. In all, we were twelve people.

When everyone was installed in the apartment we received strict instructions from Willy: never turn on lights at night under any circumstances; never strike up matches or light candles; never flush the toilet during the day or use the water in kitchen or bathroom sinks; only after dark was it okay to resume some of our more normal life routines. But the green *jalousies* (wooden shutters) were never to be opened; they had to remain shut in every room for as long as we were hiding there.

Photo 4.1   The family in hiding in Nice, rue Trachel 42, August 1942

Chaya: And when did you move into that apartment?

Hannah: Gitta and I moved into the apartment on August 26, the day of *la grande rafle* (the big roundup in which Luzer was picked up). But this apartment had already been rented before that date. Willy T. had been advised to seek a hiding place for his family because some danger was brewing but nobody knew exactly what it was. Willy found this large apartment on rue Trachel and he brought his wife Regina and their son Freddy there. The apartment was located across the street from a Vichy police station. Again we would live under the nose of the enemy! But on the day of the roundup, when Gitta and I went to Nice, Willy bumped into us and practically whisked me away whispering, "Hannah, you must come with me, this is a terrible day; they are picking up Jews everywhere and no one is safe now." Gitta and I never returned to the old apartment. We followed Willy just as we were, no clothes, nothing. But a couple days later, I sent Gitte'le to pick up some clothes at our old apartment on rue de Congrès; that's when Gitta had a narrow escape with the Vichy *gendarmes* (policemen).

Gitta: Yes, you sent me to the apartment on rue du Congrès 11 to pick up a few pieces of clothing since we had nothing with us when we returned to Nice. But when I arrived at the apartment building, two Vichy policemen walked in behind me. I was frightened and didn't know what to do. So, instead of taking out my keys to open the door, I decided to ring the bell. One of the policemen asked me what I was doing there; I answered that I came to play with my girlfriend. Then, turning my back on them, I rang our bell. And since I knew there would be no answer, I turned around, shrugged my shoulders and said, "Oh, I guess no one is home." I left as if nothing unusual had happened, but my heart was pounding something terrible. When I came home I told you that it was getting dangerous on the street and we all must be very careful.

Hannah: Yes, Gitte'le, you were a brave girl! Even so, even when you were afraid, you and Freddy went to the market when we needed food and you bought whatever was available on any given day; sometimes you brought back fruit, or vegetables; other times you brought back *biscottes* (biscuits). Regina was in charge of purchasing the bread, but I could swear that she cheated us; she overcharged us for every single loaf of bread, I was sure of it! I was enraged at her; how could she do a thing like that?

Gitta: Once I stood in line and waited three hours just to buy those dry *biscottes.* But since that's all there was that day that's what

I stood in line for. Another time, I bought bunches of grapes because you could buy those things without stamps, and dragged them back to the house. Then, one day I was able to buy twenty bottles of wine; not that we drank so much wine, but I bought them because wine could be bought without stamps. I didn't carry all the bottles at one time. I took four or five bottles at a time and went back and forth from the market to the back of our apartment. Once I remember, Willy T. brought us a delicacy: he came home with one little can of tuna for all twelve of us, and everyone was allowed to have one lick! Well, eleven people because Chaya ate very little and refused to taste even a lick of tuna!

Chaya: Yes, I was a terrible eater and Mother worried that I'd be undernourished. But when you speak about shopping at the market, Gitta, where were the boys who were supposed to help you? Why didn't they carry some of those heavy packages?

Gitta: I guess it was too dangerous for the boys to go out, especially for Bernard who looked like a young man already. So, when it seemed unsafe for the boys, I went by myself. But I have to admit I was scared all the time. I expected a *gendarme* to come by, pull me out of line any moment; this constant fear inside me never left me as long as we were in that apartment on rue Trachel.

Hannah: The fear that Gitta had was terrible; and I was always distressed until she returned from the market. And when she didn't come back in time—I thought of the worst. It was the same fright I had when you, Chaya'le, were caught and taken with Luzer to the *caserne* (Hannah cries)....God knows what would have happened if Gitta hadn't found you on the street!

And after you came back to us, you developed a very nasty looking rash, Chaya. Your skin was red all over and you scratched the skin off your arms and legs. I didn't know what to do to help you; I was able to get some lotion to soothe the irritation but it didn't help much. I remember lying next to you night after night until you fell asleep—stroking your arms and back until the irritation subsided so you could fall asleep.

Chaya: Yes, I remember the rash; the looks of those bumps made me sick. When I scratched the skin away trying to get rid of the irritation, under the sore I saw four little red holes. I dreamt about this skin reaction, which I know was the result of malnourishment but saw it as my own revulsion against myself. I did not think about that at the time, but later I thought of it as my punishment for having told the Vichy policeman on the day of the big roundup where we were living. I had lost my head and gave away our secret address, telling him outright and showing him the hotel where we lived! These sores, since they appeared within days of my return to my family's undercover apartment, were sickening. Years later I thought they were the bodily reaction to the deed I had committed, my betrayal of Luzer. I reasoned the sores kept me from sleep and led me to suppress the memory of abandoning Luzer at the caserne Auvare. Still now, when I think of them, they remind me of the upheaval that lay buried inside me and came to the surface as my skin rash. Any clarification and understanding of what had gone on around me are only partial to this day, because I had blotted out from consciousness at least one or two days and have not recovered anything from this ordeal.

Chaya: Tell me, Mama, how long did we live in that apartment on rue Trachel?

Hannah: We lived there for three months and we did not stick our noses out the door, except for Gitta and Freddy sometimes, until the Italians arrived in November 1942. Then the Vichy regime left the southern zone,[2] [they left the Alpes-Maritimes] and the Italians occupied eight departments on the Cote d'Azur. [The Italians stayed in Nice from November 1942 until September 8, 1943]. No sooner were we free to leave the house then I sent you girls back to the Institut Massena. And Uncle and I, together with the Elbaums, stayed in the apartment on rue Trachel.

Chaya: I want to ask you a funny question. Why do I remember learning to speak Italian while sitting on the "john?"

Gitta: Not then, you didn't learn Italian then.

Hannah: I don't know about you practicing Italian, Chaya.

Chaya: Well, I have a definite memory of "talk time" and practicing Italian on the *toilette* (toilet). So, I figure that I must have tried to teach myself Italian after the Italians occupied Nice! Because I do have a clear memory of pretending to converse with Italian soldiers.

Chaya: Do you remember giving us swimming lessons?

Hannah: Yes, I remember it well. I gave you swimming lessons and you carried on terribly.

Chaya: For me they were disastrous lessons because I was so frightened of the water and terrified that I would drown. The teacher held me by a pole with a rope; he attached a belt around my waist and that belt was attached to the rope and the pole. As I entered the pool, I was shocked by the ice cold water. I couldn't have fallen into the water, but I panicked, screamed, and yelled, "Take me out the water! Please, take me out of here!" It felt like I was in the caserne Auvare again. But the people sitting around the pool were laughing at that me—this silly little girl who was afraid of the water. Eventually Mama, you felt sorry for me and told the teacher that he should stop the lesson and take me out of the water. I was terribly ashamed for being so frightened but I couldn't help it. Especially because Gitta—who could do everything better than I—was moving along so well. I could see she was learning to swim and the water didn't bother her at all. In the end, shame prompted me to resolve to learn to swim, and this time by myself.

The following day when we went to the seashore, I was determined: today I will learn to swim! I knew the moves because the teacher had shown them to me; and I had seen how Gitta had caught on. So, by holding on to the iron posts under the *brise-lames* (breakwater), and doing the breast stroke, letting go from one post and swimming toward the next one, I kept practicing my moves. I repeated these moves for as long as it took until I was actually swimming without holding on to any post. After a while, under the *brise-lames* and the protection provided by iron posts—just in case I needed to hold on—I realized I was swimming in the Mediterranean! The sea was warm, gentle, and inviting. I felt good and proud of myself, and I looked back in disbelief at yesterday's scene in that ice-cold God-forsaken pool!

Michel'eke

Hannah: When I brought you girls back to the Institut Massena, Mr. Lempl (an acquaintance from Antwerp) arrived with a terrible problem: his wife had a nervous breakdown after giving birth to a little baby boy, and he needed to find someone to care for the child. He asked me if I would do that. I did not think twice. Don't ask me why. I decided to take the child as if it were a sign of some kind. His name was Michel'eke and I gave him the best there was to be had.

Chaya: Why did you do this? Didn't you have enough worries at the time?

Hannah: In life, you can't always determine what will be put on your doorstep. Lempl was desperate, and I knew children. And the baby was a lovely baby boy...and you know I missed not having a little boy.... I went to people and asked them to help me provide for him because he was not well cared for. He came with dirty clothes; his mother was not normal and couldn't care for him. I received a little crib and put it in my room. The little boy loved me so, you cannot imagine. I taught him how to sit on the potty, how to make *kaka,* how to eat, and drink from a cup. I got a high chair that converted into a table. People trusted me and lent me their things, even sheets and little clothes. When I had errands to run people helped me and came to the apartment and watched over him.

But at the rate I was spending money, I decided to look for an opportunity to earn some extra cash. One of my friends suggested that I try contacting a *boutique de haute couture* (a high fashion boutique) where women who could afford designer dresses bought their clothes. One day, I presented myself to the owner of this boutique and explained my situation; I asked whether she could use extra clientele. I knew quite a few fashion-conscious Jewish women in Nice and would be able to recommend some prospective clients to her boutique. All I asked was that I receive a commission for each one of her sales to the customers I recommended. And so it was. I managed to earn some money from this contact, especially from the ladies who gambled at the casino; sometimes I made a small bundle on them.

Then, I went to my dentist who liked me and made him the same offer. For every patient I recommended to him I asked for a reasonable commission. I did not specify the amount; I thought I better leave it up to him since he knew my situation. I made a little profit there too. And that is how I could afford extra things for you girls and for Michel'eke.

Meanwhile, the baby was developing nicely. He stayed with me for nine months. I even took him along to Saint-Martin-Vésubie for the summer vacation where my cousin Hindze and I shared a big villa. Hindze was Moishe Fass' wife; he had always helped me sell some diamonds at a good price when I needed cash.

September 8, 1943: Italy Capitulates[3]

Hannah: When Italy capitulated to the Allies on September 8, 1943, the Jews in Saint-Martin-Vésubie went into a frenzy. There were so many Jews in Saint-Martin-Vésubie, maybe 2,000; most of us, I think, had come from Nice; some came from other parts in Western Europe. The news spread by word of mouth like wildfire. Then, the next piece of news came: the Jews in Saint-Martin-Vésubie were planning to escape through the Alps because the town lay at the foothills of the French Alps that led to Italy.

Why were we doing this? The Allies had already landed in

the south of Italy. Everyone hoped that if we crossed into Italy the Allies would be there! But that didn't happen. The Allies had a long and tough fight against the *Yekkes;* and the fighting in Italy, from south to north, would last another year and a half, more or less.

There was no time to lose. Lempl called me, "Please bring Michel'eke to Nice;" he was unable to pick him up because his wife was very sick and he did not dare leave her alone. I took a taxi and went to Nice, and with this same taxi I also took Hindze and her little girl Sabine, and I brought them to her husband, Moishe Fass. This time, Moishe asked me for money; he swore he would give it back to me after the war. I gave him 800 dollars! But this would be a gift, not a loan, because Moishe, *nebich* (poor man), was picked up on the street the next day, September 9, by the Gestapo. These *kholeres* (bandits) came down on men like furies; those who looked Jewish were dragged to the Hotel Excelsior and ordered to drop their pants, and for the Jews that was their end. Moishe was picked up and sent by cattle car to Birkenau-Auschwitz. And from there he never returned.

I was unable to go to the apartment, get clothes, shoes, or whatever else we might need. Willy T. bumped into me; he took ahold of me and said, "Chancze, run! There is no time to waste, get back to your children immediately!" When I came back to the villa in Saint-Martin-Vésubie, I took some pillowcases, one for each of us and for Uncle Herman, and I packed a piece of clothing, a dress, a pair of pants, a shirt, a brush, underwear, a sheet, a towel, whatever would fit. I took the bare essentials.

You might ask why we weren't prepared since I knew that something like this could happen. How could we cross the Alps in summer sandals and light summer dresses? It's just that when we left Nice for Saint-Martin-Vésubie for the *grand vacances* (summer vacation) in July, we didn't know that Italy would capitulate to the Allies. I thought we were coming back to Nice, and we were hoping that the Allies would be coming soon to France and liberate us! Everything happened so suddenly. It was said that the announcement [of the Italian capitulation to the Allies] was premature. Everyone was caught off guard. The Italians left in a hurry and the Jews wanted to follow them.

The Escape Across the Mountains

That is why the following day, on September 9, approximately 900 people with children and some older people went up the mountains. It was about four o'clock in the morning when we began the long trek. At first we walked, then we climbed; we climbed 3,200 meters! People carried their belongings in little pillowcases; the paths were so narrow that it would have been even more dangerous with suit-cases. We did not have a guide—at least none that I saw—but we followed each other. One person went to a *padre* (priest), another to a soldier, because a number of soldiers walked along with us; but most of the Italian soldiers ran away. It was bedlam. It was night when we reached the church of the Madonna and we all went to sleep in the church. People said that 350 men, women, and children returned to Saint-Martin-Vésubie that night.[4]

Gitta: The second night we slept outdoors. Young people were singing and dancing; I'm telling you, it felt like the liberation!

Chaya: I remember that night differently. We had come to a plateau and stretched out on the grass; I don't know how many peo-ple, but we were many. Again it was late at night, I remember look-ing up; the sky was dark and against it the stars were shining. There was stillness; the only sounds we heard were the buzz of the summer crickets. Then, a little boy's voice rose up: it made the sweetest pur-est sound. He began singing "Oyf'n Pripitchik", a Yiddish lullaby about children learning the Hebrew alphabet in *heder* (Hebrew school). First, he sang one song then another; and then, the entire community, flat on our backs, joined him in song. I will always treasure that night. We felt such a bond with each other there, and such hope....

Gitta: That night the Italian soldiers of the 4th Armata gave us soup; I was with my friend Leah Haberman. There were many young people singing and it felt like a real community.

Hannah: But later, before sunrise, we began walking again. We walked over stones and branches. We walked on narrow paths that were no more than one foot wide. Sometimes we thought we might trip and fall down the ravine; I remember them well, the ravines; they were to the right of the path and the mountain slopes were to the left.[5] Every few meters there were markers showing where a mountain climber had fallen to his death. It was terrifying for the parents who carried little children who couldn't walk.

But then the climb got worse; we had climbed quite a bit and we were all tired. You too, Chaya'le. There were children younger than you—you were a big girl already in comparison to them—so you continued to walk without complaint until we came to the next plateau and there, before our eyes arose a mountain of gigantic stones, like big boulders. These stones were of a different color than what we had seen so far; they were black and rust color, but mostly black. It was an ominous sight. I thought, "This is *gehenim* (hell)!" Someone said, "Be careful, don't dislodge even one stone or you'll set off an avalanche of stones rolling down on the people below you." I was worried. I was afraid for you, Chaya'le; you would not understand how careful you had to be. I walked behind you and admonished, "Be careful, walk slowly, I am right behind you!" One woman below me fell; they said that she was pregnant. I don't know what happened to her. I also heard that two women died on the way. But finally, with God's help, we made it to the top and reached the Italian border!

The descent into Italy was unforgettable; in front of us was a huge expanse of green and a short distance away a border guard stood with a rifle over his shoulder. I was prepared to show him our papers but the guard just waved his arm and without turning around he motioned us to pass.

Walking down the mountain was not as difficult as some said it would be. We were walking toward freedom; the Italians were no longer fighting on the side of the Germans and there were no Germans here. We came down into a small village named Valdieri. There was a large piazza in the middle of town and to the right stood a church. The Italian soldiers, some without uniforms, now in plain civilian dress, put us up in barracks. They gave us soup and bread. We were grateful and tired, and fell asleep almost immediately.

But in the middle of the night, maybe around one or two o'clock, I woke up in a sweat. I asked myself, "What am I doing here?" A *Vorgefühl* (premonition) came over me; I felt that we must leave this place immediately; there was no time to waste! I tiptoed to each of you and whispered, "We must leave now! I'm afraid this is a trap. The Germans could be here any time, and here we are, huddled together as if waiting to be picked up!" Mme. Elbaum did not want to move, she was tired. I said to her that if she did not want to join us, I would leave with my children and Uncle because I had a feeling we were not safe here. She understood and promptly got to her feet.

All seven of us ran back up the mountains. We ran back up, and how we ran I'll never know. It must have been the fear and the adrenaline because when I woke you up, you were still very tired, but as soon as I scared you to death saying the *Yekkes* are coming, all of a sudden you were able to run. When we were out of immediate sight from the barracks and into the mountain, we slowed down; we were out of breath but we continued walking. We walked for hours. We tried to find someone who might help us, but did not see a soul. I felt that we had no time to waste; we had to go up as far up as we could.

At one point, I looked down; it was five or six in the morning. I thought we had come a long way from Valdieri; but no, the town was below us and we heard gunshots. We had climbed quite a bit but this was no time to stop. I backed away and said, "We must move faster now and continue our climb." The entire day we heard gunshots—firearms. I knew the *Yekkes* had come! We walked for hours and did not know how far we had gotten. But at least, I hoped, we were out of reach.

We were exhausted, tired, and hungry. I saw a cabin with a balcony. "Let's go up and knock there," I said. A tall, grim-looking man with a mustache came out. I asked him whether we could stay in his cabin and rest awhile; I also asked if he could give us something to eat and milk for the children. He was outraged! He told me to take my kids and get away from here. I moved up closer to him and said in French again, "We are so tired, we came from Saint-Martin-Vésubie; maybe you could spare just a little milk for the children!" He practically pushed me out the door and shouted, "If you don't leave here immediately with your children, I'll shoot!" And he pointed his rifle at us. I thought this man could really hurt us; I grabbed both of you and we left—fast!

Later I noticed another cabin. First I saw the top, a roof sustained by wooden beams, then, a woman. She saw us and I approached; I told her our story and promised her that I would pay for everything. She understood, nodded, and showed us to a large balcony that was wide enough to house all seven. She did give us some food and kept us until morning; in the morning she told me we had to leave. She did not think we would be safe with her. I asked to pay for the night and gave her what she asked. It wasn't much.

We went on; Mme. Elbaum was giving up. You too, Chaya'le, were exhausted. We all needed a rest. Then, a man came our way. He seemed to have come out of nowhere; suddenly, he appeared climbing near us. I looked at him; he did not feel dangerous to me, or mean. I asked him if he knew of a place where our family could stay. We needed to rest, I explained, we needed food, we had escaped from Valdieri and I believed the Germans had come after us and occupied the town.

The man said, "Yes, they did!" He looked us over and he told us to wait. This man would be our rescuer, but I didn't know it then.

He left us saying, "Wait here." We waited and rested and after a while a woman arrived; her name was Andreina. She had a good face and seemed kind. I guessed she was about my age. She said her cousin had told her about us. I told her our story and asked if she knew of a place where we could hide and rest. I promised to pay, but we had to be safe, and we needed food.

The *Cava*

Andreina offered, "I will take you to my place. It is a good place. And it is safe." More climbing. I didn't know if we could hold out much longer. But just then, we saw Andreina's place. It was a little shelter made of stones. There was a door but no windows. Andreina called it her *cava* (a place where the shepherds sleep in spring and summer when herding their flock). Now that the summer was almost over the *cava* was empty and we would be able to hide there.

The entrance into the *cava* was low. It was dark inside; there were no windows, no light came from the outside. After we got used to the dark, I guessed this place was no larger than six-by-six feet. Across from the entrance, the wall and the ceiling were black, both were made of stone; I noticed ashes on the ground and a few pieces of burnt-out wood.

"How do they cook here?" I asked Andreina. She explained that the herdsmen cook on an open fire on the ground. There was no flue, nothing but ashes, pieces of burnt wood and a black wall and ceiling above.

Andreina assured us, "You will be able to keep warm here. But you will have to stoop down when you cook because without windows there is no place for the smoke to escape; when the fire is going, the smoke fills the space of the *cava* from ceiling to waist. Therefore, when you walk into the *cava* you all have to bend down to avoid getting smoke in your eyes and lungs."

I don't remember where we sat, maybe on large stones, but I do know that next to the *cava* there was a barn. Andreina said that this is where we would sleep; the barn was empty now since the herd had already been brought indoors for the winter. She brought us clean straw and a few blankets. She also brought food: bread, cheese, a few potatoes, and a couple of eggs. She was a good woman, I was grateful to her and I paid what she asked. Believe it or not, I learned to cook in that fireplace and we ate. The sleeping was difficult because, once again, there were mice and rats in the barn. Andreina gave us a shovel for protection, but also for shoveling away the snow that would accumulate in front of the door once winter set in.

Gitte'le had a friend, his name was Lorenzo; he liked her; he supplied us with cream, and nuts, and cheese. Once, Gitta became ill and she developed a high fever. There was a coffin in the barn for us to hide in should anyone come looking for us. We put Gitta into that coffin to keep her warm; after a while she recovered, thank God!

Once a month Andreina slaughtered a little lamb or a calf. She hung the carcass high up, but naturally in front of our eyes. There was no other place. I remember we became sick from looking at the meat, in particular you children. Once there was an avalanche, and luckily it stopped at the rear of the *cava*. Had it not stopped the entire *cava* would have been crushed with us underneath. We stayed in the mountains like this until the end of January 1944.

Gitta: I remember that before we left for Turin because we feared the *razzias* (raids by German soldiers to plunder and pick up Jews), we were in another place where they cut marble. It was a place higher than Andreina's and we slept there with many people. We were about twenty or twenty-five people. We stayed there for about two days. The Italian soldiers who had visited us below came up to reassure us, and we sang by the fire.

Hannah: I had a bad feeling about that place, another *Vorgefühl*. I said, "Please let's leave here and return to Andreina's." Mme. Elbaum, no sooner had I finished said, *"Ich vill mit."* (I want to come along.) We went down to Andreina's and huddled in the little black *cava*; I put some straw on the floor and that night we slept there.

At 6:30 in the morning Bernard came running. He shouted, "We've been robbed! The *Italiener* (they were said to be Italian deserters from Sicily) took everything, even the gold in people's teeth!"

Gitta: There was a woman who nursed her baby. I don't know what happened to her. Anyway, we had to leave there because it was no longer safe; the Germans and the Fascists were looking for Jews and partisans all over the mountains.

Chaya: Mama, when did we leave the mountains the first time?

Hannah: We left in January or February 1944. We went to Turin; at the station waiting for the train there was a little boy who shouted, *"Mame, Mame, geb mir a stickl Broit!!"* (Mama, Mama, give me a piece of bread.) Don't you remember? He kept repeating this, that poor child! A German soldier was walking back and forth along the waiting area. My heart was in my mouth! I had given Andreina my last watch so she would accompany us to the train and sit next to you girls, apart from me, so I felt a little bit safer.

We waited for a long time in the station and then we heard that the tracks had been bombed and that we had to return from where we came. I don't know how we got back to Valdieri. Do you? Anyhow, once in Valdieri, Andreina went to her house and we walked back up to the *cava*. But we didn't find anyone. Then, suddenly, Gitta recognized Bernard's whistle and she whistled back their familiar tune, and Bernard came to meet us and took Chaya and me up to the mountain where the men were. They had moved to Borgo San Dalmazzo after the other *cava* near the quarry had been robbed.

Gitta: Anna, Andreina's daughter, walked with us. Then she and I went back down to the village. I was going to pick up a few things for the family. But when it was time to get back I had to get directions how to find the new *cava* above Borgo (San Dalmazzo). I went to find Anna and asked her for directions. Anna showed me the way up where the men had moved, she said it wasn't too far and it was easy to get to. That was around three o'clock in the afternoon.

Gitta Faces the Mountains Alone

Gitta: I began the climb all by myself. After a while I started to worry. It had been a difficult day already and now I was getting nervous. I was afraid that I might not find the new place.

Hannah: I felt terrible, how could I have let you go by yourself on the mountains after such a day?

Gitta: I began following Anna's directions, but the climb took longer than Anna had said. I walked for a long time and realized that dusk was setting in. I continued up and began seeing crosses and markers—here this person fell, there another person. The sun disappeared behind the mountains and the sky grew dark. I was frightened but continued to walk. Suddenly I saw a little light in the distance; I thought I was close to the new *cava*. But the light disappeared and the earth under my feet turned to ice.

I realized I wasn't going to make it and decided that the only recourse was to go back down. But going down was worse than going up now because I had no traction at all and I was afraid to fall into a ravine. So I sat down and decided to slide down on the icy path on my bottom. I moved over to the side of the path and thought I would have more traction on the snow bank; in trying to move over, my shoe snapped. I lost it. I looked for the shoe groping on the ground here and there, and I found it! The shoe was broken—I was unable to put it back on so I held on to it and took off the other shoe. Now I was with my knee socks and without gloves. Holding on to both shoes I tried to slide all the way down. On my way down there were icy stones and I lost the traction. Now I was tired and totally lost; I lay back and rested a bit. Then I thought, "I will not be getting up if I stay here." I sat for a while and my body was getting numb; I realized that if I did not move now, I might freeze to death. I wanted to go to sleep. But I realized that if I let go now I would never get up again. So, I gave myself one last push and managed to slide down to the foot of that mountain. I was back in Borgo.

It was dark; I looked around and saw a light coming from a farmhouse.

I was scared now but what choice did I have? I went to that farmhouse and knocked on the door; a man opened up. He looked like a farmer. I told him that I was lost and needed help. He looked at me with compassion. Then I began to cry. The farmer showed me the way to the barn and let me sleep there with the cows. It was warm in the barn from the warmth of the cows and I fell asleep. In the morning the farmer came to me and said, "I will bring you to someone who can help you." He brought me to a Jewish woman who had a child with her. The woman fed me and looked at my hands; they were frostbitten. She rubbed my hands in hers; she rubbed my feet; tears were running down her face and mine.

(Gitta cries as she talks; Hannah is choked up.)

Hannah: Gitta darling, you don't have to continue talking. You are all upset and that's not good for you. Let's talk about something else. Bernard was looking for you and I was crazy with worry.

Gitta: The woman gave me warm milk from the cows, but I couldn't swallow that. Then she gave me some dark liquid to drink; it was either chicory coffee or dark tea. Then she took my shoe and said she knew someone who would fix it; this Jewish woman kept her word. She watched over me and made sure I was sufficiently recuperated before she let me leave. Finally, after a couple of days, I was ready to go.

Hannah: I was out of my mind until I saw you; just as I almost went crazy when Chaya was taken in Vence. Then I swore that I will never leave my children again! That is when I asked Andreina if she knew someone who could help us leave this place. It was March 1944. I knew we had to get out of there.

Andreina Finds a *Padre* in Valdieri

"Yes," said Andreina, she knew a *padre* in her church and she will ask him to come up to the *cava*. Do you remember the *padre*, Gitta?

Gitta: Yes, Mama, I remember you went to find a priest.

Hannah: And the *padre* came up to the *cava* from Valdieri and took our pictures. Within a day or two he returned with the false papers; he also brought warm clothes and shoes that the Italian soldiers had left behind. Gitta, you got a pair of shoes that were about a size 50! And you couldn't walk in them. I didn't have any shoes either, but for you I needed shoes so you won't get sick.

Chaya: I don't remember the priest.

I remember listening to Mother's tape and it is there that I heard her say that she asked Andreina to find a *padre*, and the *padre* came and helped.

Gitta: Yes, I remember.

Chaya: Also, I remember we had Pesach in the mountains and Mama made matzos and those matzos were black! Still, we all tasted the matzos and remembered it was Passover! To this day I can't believe that you were able to bake matzos in the *cava*, Mama!

Hannah: You think it was easy to bake matzos on next to nothing, on a little fire I could not control? But the cantor, the old man who joined us from another mountain, had a *luach* (Jewish calendar) and he told me it was Pesach. So we did what we could.

We Leave the Mountains and Go to Rome

After Pesach we left the mountains for a second time. The railroads were bombed out; we got as far as Bologna. I know we were alone, only the three of us. Onkel and the Elbaums must have come too but not with us. There were no trains and I was afraid to wait any longer, so I decided to hitchhike. I took out my black felt hat from my purse and put it on. I always carried it with me because it made me look a little bit elegant. I stood on the road by myself and told you girls to stay back to the side. I was afraid that if a driver saw a woman with two children he would not stop for us. Then we waited.

Gitta: Do you know I did not remember this part of our story until Chaya showed me the tape where you spoke about hitchhiking. But it did come back to me.

Hannah: Sure, it happens. After a wait, I saw a car in the distance. I raised my hand as the car approached, but it did not stop, thank God, because it turned out to be a German military car. Behind that car came a large truck and this one did come to a stop. I said to myself, "Hannah, this is your life, what are you going to do now?" The driver in the truck leaned over. "What can I do for you, *Genaedige Frau* (honored lady)?" he asked. I replied in my best German, "Would you be going to Rome? My children are tired, they can't walk anymore, the train tracks have been bombed out and we must get to Rome." I said. The driver took pity on us and said, "Well then, come on up, we'll see how far we can go." He told me to sit next to him. I took Chaya'le next to me, and Gitta had to go to the back of the truck to sit with the German soldiers who were sitting on large crates.

Yes, I was very upset. The driver started the truck and began to move. But as the truck began to roll, the car that had passed us moved in reverse and when it reached us, it came to a halt. An officer stepped out of the passenger's seat and came up to the driver. "What are you doing with these people?" he shouted, "You cannot take passengers on this truck! The back is full of important material [explosives]," and now he was swearing. Hearing this I opened the door of the cabin, what did I have to lose? I stepped down and went up to the officer.

I addressed him in *Hochdeutsch* (good German), "Will you please let us drive with your caravan; my children are so tired and we need to get to Rome." The German officer impatiently asked, "Who are you anyway?" I said we were Catholics, Hungarian refugees.

"Ach!" he said, "Ach! Hungarians, dogs and Jews, they're all alike!" I showed him my papers. He examined the papers and looked at me, "So you are Madame Anna Kantor and these are your daughters, Hella and Gisele?" He shook his head in disgust, turned around, and walked away.

Our driver and the soldiers were from the Wehrmacht and they must have felt sorry for us because as soon as the officer left, the driver motioned to me, "Come, get in, I'll bring you as close to Rome as I can."

Gitta: I remember the fear in the pit of my stomach. I thought I was sitting on a powder keg, and the truck kept jolting, stopping, and moving ahead. Except that by now we were so tired like *beteubt* (numb), I didn't care anymore; whatever will be, will be. But tell me Mama, when did we get on the train where I fell asleep standing up?

Hannah: The *camion* (truck) dropped us off; he could not bring his truck into Rome, instead he brought us to the train station in Florence. There were no trains, and because of the curfew we were not allowed to go anywhere from eight at night until six in the morning. That meant we had to sleep in the station. We couldn't go any further. I guess we fell asleep but I was in a panic. I woke up all of a sudden and started running around as if someone were chasing me. You must have thought I was crazy, but I think I had a nightmare. The panic was unbearable and I wanted to return to the men in the mountains at once. But I didn't, it didn't make sense. Instead Gitta went up to the ticket master and asked when the next train to Rome would arrive. The ticket master replied that there would be no trains because the tracks had been destroyed.

Gitta: I remember we slept two nights in the station in Florence.

Hannah: But I was afraid to sit around for such a long time so I asked you to take Chaya and go for a walk.

Chaya: I remember walking along a narrow street holding Gitta's hand. We were walking along the walls of a church when she decided to go into that church. She said it was safer to sit in the church pretending we were praying than being out on the street. Besides we were both very tired, it would do us good to rest a while.

Gitta: Yes, we stayed in that church and no one bothered us. Later we returned to the train station and slept near Mother. In the morning the loudspeaker announced a train was due to come and its destination was Rome. People were pushing to get on; it was an open train and it was packed with people.

Hannah: We were packed like sardines. Everyone was standing up. And when the train began to move, people began to nod off, standing up, one next to the other.

Gitta: I remember that someone held you, Chaya, but I stood up and fell asleep. To this day I don't understand how I could have fallen asleep standing up!

Rome and the Convents

Gitta: When we arrived in Rome, Mother brought us to a convent and we met the Mother Superior, Sister Maria Stanislava. She must have received the name of that convent from the priest in Valdieri who brought us the false papers. Sister Maria Stanislava took us in. There were about thirty other Jewish children there, she told Mother. But we did not stay there long.

Hannah: One day when I came to visit you, the Mother Superior told me that she had heard rumors that there would be a *rafle* (roundup), maybe the next day. There was no time to lose. The Mother Superior put me in contact with an archbishop from the Vatican. I don't know how I got there. I went to see him, and he made it possible for me to meet with the Swedish ambassador who gave me a paper that said that I was married to a Swedish businessman who was Protestant; because of the war he was missing and I lost track of him. He sent us to this ultra-Orthodox Catholic Convent of the Dorothean Sisters; he said they would take us in. He gave me a letter of introduction to this convent but he admonished me not to tell anyone that we are Jewish. I was supposed to say that your father is Protestant and I am here alone and I don't know where he is now. That is exactly what I said, and that is how you ended up in this convent that was just one block away from the Vatican.

Gitta: At the convent we had to behave like Catholic kids. We went to confession, to mass, attended services morning, noon, and night. When the bombs were flying we had to get up and pray on our knees for two or three hours. My knees were so swollen; it was horribly painful. I was already wearing the dress of a novice, a short black gown. It was a terrible time.

Chaya: I remember the chapel and the day Gitta almost fainted; two novices held her, each under one arm, and helped her out of the chapel. Her knees were incredibly swollen and sore and I was terribly frightened for her and for myself too. I looked down on my knees and was relieved to see that mine were only a little swollen.

One of my big problems was going to confession. I did not know what to do there, or what sins I should be confessing to. Also I had to lie, which was really a sin, no matter what religion I was supposed to belong to; when I was sinning was I Catholic or Jewish?

I had a little girlfriend with whom I traded "saints"—these were holy cards—like the kids trade baseball cards here. At first I had no cards to trade, but I think my little friend must have given me some, because we played and looked at the cards and exchanged them between us. I think she taught me a lot but I was also very confused. When I had to go to confession I asked her what sins she confessed to. She told me having a candy in my mouth during mass is a sin, and not saying all the prayers during mass is another sin.

With these two sins in my arsenal I was ready to meet the father confessor. I had seen the little wooden house; the confessional looked like a booth once you entered it. On the day of my first confession I sat on a little bench and faced a grilled window. I waited for the priest behind the grill to speak to me. Then I told him what I had done, what I learned to confess, and he told me to say so many "Ave Marias" and after that, so many "Pater Nostras." I had learned the prayers by rote; that was not hard to do, still, I felt all jittery inside.

The nuns were kind to me; they liked my recitations. When the time came to celebrate communion, the Mother Superior asked my mother if she would agree that I have communion like the other girls. My mother was taken aback; she must have thought that taking communion is like being baptized and converted to Catholicism. She thought quickly and then she explained to the Mother Superior that I already had my first communion. Then the Mother Superior asked whether my mother would agree to have me do my second communion; my mother replied that without her husband's consent she would not want her little girl to have a second communion. The Mother Superior relented, but she still wanted me to participate in the procession on their holy day.

As a result she thought of another task for me: I was to lead the communicants down the aisle to say mass, and then I would receive the wafer representing the body of Christ, just like all the other communicants. And she did not ask for my Mother's permission.

When the day of the celebration arrived, my hair was washed by one of the novices and set into curls with a hot curling iron by another. A third pulled a long blue silk dress over my head. The novices stood around me giggling, they were excited and enjoyed themselves. Then someone put a tiara on my hair and another attached a pair of huge white, feathered wings on my shoulders. At some point, I remember seeing the Mother Superior passing through the corridor; as she walked by, she quickly glanced sideways at the girls and at me. The slightest smile came across her face; she seemed satisfied and continued on her way.

I was instructed to walk slowly down the aisle. I do believe there was another angel at the head of the line across the aisle, but I am not sure. I was trembling, maybe the wings were too heavy, and maybe I worried about what was going to happen next. This ritual was going much further than I imagined it would. Was I going to be converted there at the altar? Kneeling in front of this holy man who might have been a bishop, I'd be receiving the wafer, "the body and blood of Christ."

When it was my turn to bow my head I received the wafer. It didn't taste like flesh or blood. I knew enough about symbols to know that the wafer merely symbolized Jesus Christ. The wafer was so thin it tasted like paper and quickly dissolved in my mouth. Then I thought to myself, "This is not so terrible, I am just pretending that I am a Catholic angel!"

When the ceremony was over, I ran up to my mother who sat in the balcony with many other parents. I don't know what she was thinking. But I embraced her forcefully and kissed her face all over, "Oh! Mama, don't worry about me; this was just like being in a play! On the outside I was a Catholic girl, but on the inside I was and will always be Jewish!"

Where was my sister, I wondered? She was not with my mother; she must have been with the big girls. I did not see her but I wondered what she thought of the whole thing.

June 4, 1944

The Allies liberated Rome.[6] The Germans retreated on the main avenue, Corso d'Italia, and the Allies came up later on the same Corso. Our mother picked us up from the convent very soon after liberation; I believe it was June 6. She brought us to the apartment where she and Onkel had been hiding, on a street at the outskirts of Rome. The name of the street was Via Bradano 5/6.

Before leaving the convent our mother told us that we should not reveal our true identity to the Mother Superior. She did not want her to know that we are Jewish.

Mother said, "Let's just tell her we are going on vacation for the summer like all the other children."

I asked, "But why, Mama? Are you still afraid?" "No," she said, "I don't want to offend the Mother Superior; I lied to her about so many things like the whole business with the communions, so I don't want her to feel that I made a fool of her."

On our way out of the convent Mother, Gitta, and I were walking on the narrow sidewalk. I hung back and was thinking about me. Who am I now? Walking up to them I said, "This, I want you to know, Mama and Gitta: from this day on, I will never have another false name; I will always be called Chaya, the name you and Papa gave me the day I was born."

CHAPTER FIVE

ERETZ-ISRAEL, 1945–1946

After Rome's Liberation

Chaya: After we left the convent, Mother brought us to the apartment that she shared with Uncle Herman on Via Bradano. It was a quiet street away from traffic and the sounds of the city. Mother enrolled us in two different schools: Gitta went to a *lycée français* (a French high school) and I went to an Italian public school. Gitta and I lived with Mother and Uncle Herman for approximately seven months (from fall 1944 to spring 1945). Gitta graduated first in her class; I made the honor roll in my school. Coming downstairs after class one day, I saw a framed roster with children's names on it who had received various awards. Actually, I did not know what to make of this honor. I don't think I applied myself in any special way at school, but somehow I had earned that distinction. "That's nice," I thought, but school achievement just wasn't part of my valued baggage. Not yet. When I told my family, they said, "Oh! That's nice." But none of those accolades that came my way—deserved or not—were as meaningful as, "Chaya'le, you saved the entire family!" Well, so much for that. I almost missed the fear, tension, and vigilance that kept me on my toes all those years—where were they, I was wondering.

I became friendly with a little girl, my next-door neighbor. We lived in the same apartment complex and we became fast friends. She taught me how to eat dark bread with olive oil and fresh garlic sprinkled on top; we would chase each other from her apartment through mine with that delicious fare until we landed either outside on the street or up on the roof. I hadn't felt so safe in a long time. My little friend taught me several popular Italian songs. The one I still remember tells the story of a little girl in whose shoe a little stone got stuck. The lyrics were as follows: "*Ho un sassolino nella scarpa, aye! Che mi fa tanto, tanto male, aye!*" (I have a little stone in my shoe, aye, that hurts me very, very much, aye!) I'll continue in English because I've forgotten the Italian words: "I'd move my foot up, I'd move it down, but I am unable to budge that stone around." We prepared a performance for our families on the roof of the building where we lived, and we sang the song while skipping and dancing to the words.

The years 1944 and 1945 must have been particularly meaningful for me, otherwise why would I remember these three unrelated events sixty-one years later: the honor roll, the garlic bread, and the performance on the roof? I believe the channel to my memory was the freedom I experienced with Mother, Gitta, Uncle Herman, and all those around me. The fact that for the first time someone knew my name, my real name this time, and knew that I was Jewish meant more than words can tell.

Our Voyage to Eretz-Israel Began When the Jewish Brigade Entered Rome

Gitta: One day, sometime in 1944, when the war in Europe was still raging, Mother saw a platoon of British soldiers marching down the Corso d'Italia. Suddenly, she pointed to the last few rows of marching soldiers; excitedly she whispered, "Look at these soldiers there, they are wearing an insignia on their sleeves with a *Magen David* (star of David)!" She ran up to the one closest to the outside row and in Yiddish she asked, "You are Jew? And from where are you?" The soldier stepped out of line and explained that he is from *Palestina*

(Palestine), the Jewish Homeland, and the soldiers of his platoon are members of the Jewish Brigade[1] coming from there; they are fighting with the British to help bring this bloody war to an end.

Mother knew that the war was far from over, but she was overcome with joy seeing those Jewish faces, all "Jewish soldiers." Who would have dreamt of such a thing? Jewish soldiers were now doing battle against the Nazis! We were proud for them and for us. After all the years of running, it looked like peace might finally come. Our hope was kindled, but it would still be another eleven months until peace came to Europe. During the war when we were in the mountains we had a little shortwave radio. Come to think of it, I don't know whether our radio ran on electricity or on batteries, but what I remember hearing most frequently were the whooshing sounds coming through, and the grown-ups used to try catching the news from the BBC, I think, as often as they could. Not only was the interference very strong but we had to be extra careful when we listened. Still, we managed to hear the news and knew more or less what was going on and where the battles were taking place. Now as we listened to the news on the radio without fear, it was clear that this war would last much longer than anyone expected.

Mother befriended a handful of Jewish soldiers through the young man she met when his platoon marched into Rome. She invited those whom she had gotten to know for Friday night dinners first to the apartment we were renting on Via Bradano. Later after we moved to a larger place, they came to Via Catanzaro 2.

Hannah: Yes, they all came and I cooked for them and they told many stories, especially about Eretz-Israel. They brought me stockings, coffee, and cigarettes, and other good things that I was able to exchange on the black market; what do you think, I could find butter, flour, eggs, meat, and whatever I needed on the street? I wanted to cook something good to eat for the boys because they had gone through some rough battles and there were many more battles to come. Bobby, who was one of them, was a driver for a British officer; he was especially nice to me. He did everything for me, whatever I needed he was able to "commandeer."[2] I was like a mother to him, that's how much he loved me, and in fact he called me "Mama." Bobby was able to bring me anything I needed because he went to the officers' mess and just *handelt* (traded) for what I asked. The soldiers loved my food and they licked their fingers from the cooking because they hadn't seen home cooked food for a very long time. And after you girls were already in Eretz-Israel and the war was won, Bobby helped me to get back to Belgium by putting me in a vat of salt. That's how he drove through the frontiers all the way to Belgium because the roads were not open to civilians yet, and at that time I had no papers at all!

Photo 5.1   Gitta, Asher (a member of the Jewish Brigade), and Chaya, Rome, February 2, 1945

Chaya: I remember Bobby, but the soldier I remember best of all was Rubin. He smoked a pipe and spoke with a strong British accent; I don't know where he came from, but he was very English. He wore a Magen David on his sleeve and was exceptionally friendly. He had a round face, a mustache, smiled easily, and he liked me very much. I still have a picture of him and me standing on the balcony of the Via Bradano apartment looking into each other's eyes. That picture I find a bit embarrassing. I was so sweet and nice, so coquettish that I felt I had overdone something.

Photo 5.2   Chaya wearing Rubin's Jewish Brigade beret, Rome, 1945

Then there was another man who befriended us—he was heavyset and older-looking than the other two, he was extremely gentle, had an open, broad face and a very deep voice. He worked for the Jewish Agency and Youth Aliyah[3] and was in charge of sending Jewish orphans to Eretz-Israel. His name was Aryeh Simon.

Gitta: Through our relationship with these soldiers from the Jewish Brigade we developed a deep connection with Israel that had not existed before. We always felt connected with Eretz-Israel through religion, but with these soldiers something new happened. We heard stories about the land, the early settlers, and the important work they had done and were doing now. This teacher who lived in Ben Shemen told our mother, "You've got to send your children to

Ben Shemen. It is the best educational institution in Eretz-Israel."

Chaya: And he was right. Shimon Peres' children went to school there and Moshe Sharet (his name was Moshe Shertok then) had his children there too. There were more children of the Israeli upper middle class who lived and studied in Ben Shemen because the director, Dr. Lehman, brought the most advanced educational methods to the village that emphasized self-determination within a strong educational and agricultural curriculum.

Gitta: In Italy they were preparing a transport of orphans to leave from Bari to go to Israel (then Palestine); that was around March or April 1945. Intense fighting was going on in the rest of Europe and nobody knew when the war would be over. I mean things were so chaotic. Mother and Uncle Herman wanted to wait until the end of the war and go back to Belgium to see who was left alive and what they could salvage from the things they both had left. So Mother decided, with the support of this *shaliach* (emissary) whose name was Aryeh Simon, to send Chaya and me on one of the first Youth Aliyah ships that left from Bari. And I, of course, would be in charge of my little sister.

Chaya: Many years later, I discovered that this same Aryeh Simon had won the Israel Prize for his work on behalf of children from the *Shoah* and for finding them a home in Eretz-Israel. The amazing coincidence was that he was my *madrich* (counselor) at the children's village in Ben Shemen.

Gitta: We went to Bari and stayed there in a kind of refugee camp that was quite horrible.

Chaya: I remember a huge hotel or spa up in the hills south of Rome; it was called Fiuggi Fonte. I believe I wrote a card from there, but I don't know if I ever sent it. I remember it was pretty bad—dirty, noisy—I'm sure there were mice and rats there as well. We both must have been upset about our situation. Why after all these years on the run were we here now, without our mother and Uncle Herman?

Gitta: Well, we did go to Bari after Fiuggi and got on a ship [the *Princess Kathleen*] that was meant to transport soldiers. When you went down to the hull of the ship there was this enormous hall and countless hammocks hanging from the ceiling. Everybody got seasick and we were all throwing up.[4] The stench was horrible! Eventually we came into Haifa, and we were immediately taken to Atlit, a transit camp run by the British. There were barracks and huge tents. The food, the barracks, the latrines and the washing installations all felt like a concentration camp. We were never beaten or anything, but it was pretty bad. We had never been in a camp before, and now we were in one after all these years!

Then one day, an entire group of *shlichim* (emissaries) came to interrogate us. They asked many questions, our names, backgrounds, were we religious at home? Did we light Shabbat candles? They wanted to establish what kibbutz or children's village to match us up with. I remembered the teacher from Ben Shemen who had said to Mother that we should go to Ben Shemen. So, when our turn came, I said we both wanted to go to Ben Shemen.

We celebrated Pesach in Atlit. It was the first time after many years that we celebrated Pesach.

Chaya: Except when Mother baked matzos in the mountains on an open fire!

Gitta: I remember it very vividly. We sang songs. The Israelis wore shirts and ties because they tried to make the holiday as festive and nice as possible.

Ben Shemen—Trauma and Adjustment

Gitta: After the Passover holiday, we were prepared to leave Atlit and were divided into groups. Chaya and I went with a group of children and adolescents by truck to Ben Shemen. This was a wonderful place and it was our salvation. We had a year and a half of wholesome living in Ben Shemen. I was put in the *Kvutzat Noar* (adolescent group) and you, Chaya, were placed in the *Kfar Yeladim* (children's village), but you and I were in the same location. Even though we did not live real close to each other, we saw each other frequently.

Photo 5.3   Chaya and Gitta in Ben Shemen, Eretz-Israel, 1946

Ben Shemen was good for us. I worked in agriculture and studied. I did other things too, like weaving and standing guard at night. We received many letters from Mother, maybe two or three a week. We wrote a lot too, but she wanted us to come back. She didn't want us to stay. I really didn't want to leave Israel at that point, even though we both missed her. But she didn't want us to remain there, she missed us too.

Chaya: I missed Mother a lot. I was homesick for her—to be with her, listen to her stories and make me feel safe; that was all I yearned for.

You know, I don't remember leaving Mother, or saying goodbye to her in Rome. It was just like it had been in Berlin, I didn't remember leaving her then either. There was no choice back then, but now there was no reason that I could see why we had to separate and go to Palestine! But Mother argued that she never left me alone because, after all, I always had my sister to look after me. Yes, I always had my sister with me. I don't know how Gitta liked having me around to watch over me, to explain things to, and to console me. I took her presence for granted and thought that though I was a burden to her, I also took her mind off her misery because there were times when she was just as lonely as I was.

Still, leaving Mother in Rome was difficult. Peacetime had come to Rome, and life was living with your family, and with Uncle now acting like our father, and I was going to school there too. Leaving Mother in peacetime seemed an awful thing to do. I don't remember how I took it. I don't remember crying, protesting, yelling something like, "this is not fair!" No. Maybe Mother explained things to me, she always had before, why we must separate; maybe it was just as hard for her to leave us. She relied so heavily on Gitta to take care of me, that she must have felt reassured. We had another uncle and aunt in Eretz-Israel on my mother's family side; it was her sister, Aunt Cilly, and Cilly's husband, Uncle Aryeh. They had moved to Palestine in the early 1930s and lived in Tel Aviv. Mother wrote to them and promised to send them money to help look after Gitta and me; she asked them to buy us whatever we needed. That's what Mother told me later when Gitta and I returned to Belgium after the war.

I wrote to Mother every day during those first months in Ben Shemen. I told her how much I missed her, how much I loved her, how I dreamt that she was coming to the port of Haifa by boat and I came to meet her when she arrived. I recognized her from afar and we waved to each other. Then I woke up.

Usually after I wrote my letter I would go to Gitta's room in her part of the village and bring the letter to her. Sometimes when Gitta was not in her room I'd leave the letter on her bed. Then one day, I don't remember if it was summer, winter, or spring, I came with another letter. Gitta was not there but one of her friends told me to wait for her because she would be back soon. So, I sat on her bed and waited. Looking down at the side table next to her bed, I saw a shoebox. Nosy, I looked into the shoebox and saw a stack of letters. Now I was curious and wanted to see what all these letters were. I looked in and discovered my letters, the ones I had written to Mother and thought Gitta had mailed! Maybe not all the letters I had written to Mother were in the box, but very many were. I was shocked! How could she? I wrote to my mother daily and was certain that Gitta had mailed those letters. Maybe I was scared Gitta would get mad at me because I snooped in her things. Or maybe she'd get mad at me and then, I don't know, maybe she wouldn't let me come to her room again. The long and short of it was that I felt betrayed and I was afraid that if she knew the extent of my anger, she'd retaliate. So I kept quiet and neither told her what I'd discovered nor made a scene. I wanted to ask her why she had stashed my letters in a shoebox instead of mailing them. Much later, many years later in fact, I asked her why in the world didn't she send those letters or tell me that she did not send them. Then, she explained:

Gitta: I didn't have the money to send so many letters every week! Uncle Aryeh, Mother's brother-in-law, who was supposed to have given us money for little expenditures, such as stamps and candy in Ben Shemen's little candy store, neglected to do that and I was too proud to ask. Mother insisted that she sent money to Aryeh and Cilly just for such expenditures as well as for larger ones, such as shoes or dresses that we might need. But they hardly ever did this and I did not like Aryeh very much, so I didn't ask.

Chaya: I understood about wanting things and being too proud to ask for them. First I didn't ask Gitta about the letters because I was too proud to ask. I imagined that she'd think my letters weren't all that important. After all, they were the letters of an eleven-year-old crybaby who kept on writing that she misses her mommy! Second, I understood about being too proud to ask for money from Uncle Aryeh or Aunt Cilly, be it for stamps or, God forbid, candy—an unthinkable indulgence—because they were not the indulging types, and I never entered the little candy store in Ben Shemen. Why would I? I was there many times, but never went inside. I didn't have the money, so why go there? So, I understood Gitta's pride, but I could not forgive her for not telling me why she had not sent the letters but put them in a shoebox instead.

Gitta: I knew you were having a very hard time but there was nothing I could do about it. We both had to deal with the programs we were involved in and there were many adjustments both of us had to make. And wouldn't you agree with me that those twenty-one months we were in Ben Shemen gave us the most wholesome living experiences since the start of the war?

Chaya: Sure, I agree. And when Mother recalled us back to Belgium, neither one of us wanted to return. More importantly, when we did come back and saw what was going on in Antwerp with the survivors and their children, we saw the difference between the life we had left behind and what we were expected to adapt to: namely to a conventional, petit bourgeois type of city living that differed blatantly from the free environment we had left in Ben Shemen where exploration, study and friendships were encouraged; where we were surrounded by culture, readings, theater, music, dance performances, each associated with the specific topics we were learning in class. The Jewish holidays were celebrated like so many tableaux in which the main actors were the children themselves. I have not experienced anything like it in my entire adult life!

But when I first arrived in Ben Shemen the shock was too much for me. First came the separation from Mother, then the separation from Gitta.

Now I felt really alone. I don't know what it was like for you, Gitta. Maybe you looked forward to having some freedom away from me; not having to worry about me all the time (Was I safe? Was I unhappy? How could you help me?)

For me that arrival in Ben Shemen was painful. Was it a truck or a bus that brought us there? I don't know. My first memory of that place was the girls' showers. The water was warm, I think; I washed my hair and then my head was doused with gasoline to rid me of the lice that infected all the new arrivals. The gasoline did it! It jettisoned me out of my blank confusion. We all had white turbaned towels around our heads. I had not been singled out; all the girls and the boys stood around like I did, and some were laughing. We received new clothes, underwear and short shorts that I liked. They are still my favorite kind. There must have been tops to go with the shorts, but those left no impression. Standing around I saw where we were: Gitta was gone. Thinking back now, I'm sure she worried about me because she knew me well, and I guess she too must have felt the separation. Adapting to her new group could not have been easy for her, I just knew that, because I observed her at times from a distance and saw things she did not talk about. Regarding me, she was probably told that she could visit me again, and she probably did, maybe that evening or the very next day.

White towel around my hair, scalp stinging from the gasoline, the smell creeping up into my nostrils, I looked up. We were standing in a large dusty courtyard; an old gnarled carob tree stood in the middle providing shade for the entire square-like space, but it didn't cover us. We, the newcomers, were standing in the sun together with the yellow, gold, orange, and red Mediterranean flowers that grew along all four low ranch-like buildings. These were built with heavy, unevenly cut bricks that I would come to recognize as

Jerusalem stone. Behind us were the showers and a two-storied brick building that housed the teachers who were living here and would become my teachers. On the other side of the yard, behind the carob tree were two more two-storied brick buildings. These would be our school. A large iron gate separated the two buildings. On the left side of the school buildings, looking toward the showers where I stood, was a long row of one-storied rooms: these were the children's rooms. On the right side of the square were another row of low-slung buildings, but they were made of wood. These were the day-workers' quarters. The white dust covering the ground came from the fine, white gravel that would offer us the opportunity to thoroughly wash the stone floors of our rooms with water plus gasoline, of course, at least twice a week. What else but gasoline to disinfect against all sorts of crawling critters that roamed around our quarters? That's why the flowers, of which there were so many, were not as outstanding as they could have been, because their vivid colors were covered during most seasons with the same white dust that spread uniformly all over the square.

Only in the winter did the dust settle, but by then the weather was too cold to provide the pleasure of seeing what was growing outside.

We had been given new clothes and were shown to our rooms. They were pleasant rooms: whitewashed walls, light-colored stone tile floors that were cool in the summer and freezing cold on winter nights. A narrow bed stood against the wall, a little side table by the bed, and maybe a place to store our clothes; I don't remember if we had a closet to hang our clothes in. I say "we" because each girl had a roommate. My first roommate's parents lived in the city. To have parents nearby was a status symbol. Maybe this is where my troubles began to show. Belonging to no one, I felt poor. I was ashamed that I had no family to visit except my uncle and aunt.

After our first deep hair cleansing, I can think of none other than the daily combing with a fine-toothed comb to rid my strands of hair of the lice eggs that were still trying to grow in my hair. I'm not sure whether we were sprayed, as needed, with additional white powder, DDT maybe? After a while I became adept at combing my hair regularly with those small combs and quickly removed those now-rarely found eggs.

When it was time to go in for dinner I joined my group in the dining room at long narrow tables. My place was somewhere in the middle. I sat and was served, but didn't eat. I can't say I remember what sort of food was offered that evening. I know I didn't eat. Not that night, and not for a long time to come. I probably ate bread and drank something. But my group counselor Amos began to worry. He came to sit by my side, coaxed me to eat, and even tried to feed me, but to no avail.

The days' menus did not vary much. With breakfast came hot cereal (*dayissa* they called it); I know the name now: it was hot cream of wheat. And some kids really seemed to like it; today, I make it daily for my husband, especially when the weather is cold. So it couldn't have been too bad. But for me it was. Then we were served *lakerda*: a salty fish, probably a marinated cod, said to be good for one's health, like cod-liver oil. I remember nothing else. It was revolting in taste and smell! Amos, my counselor, sat next to me day after day prodding me to eat, feeding me, especially at noon when the hot meal was served. He threatened he would sit with me until I finished my food, even if it took all afternoon. I don't know how we resolved this impasse. We both sat. He had better things to do than sit next to me. I was ashamed to be sitting there with him prodding me on. Somehow the standoff was resolved, but I don't remember how.

I don't remember eating any good food until I tasted the fruit of the carob tree. Hard and brown, the shape of a flat banana; sweet when you bit into it and let it linger on your tongue; the shiny brown pits inside the fruit were like evenly shaped dark brown beads that you could actually collect. The kids played around the carob tree and liked to suck on those dark brown pieces and the look of that fruit was appealing. And so I became familiar with my new home.

Amos still worried about me. He had just had a baby, he and his wife Greta. They were our house parents, and now they had a baby of their own. One day, early in my stay, Amos suggested I visit Greta who wanted to show me their new baby. Shyly, I knocked at their door. Greta was there, sitting in an easy chair, feeding the baby from a bottle; I believe it was a bottle and not the breast. She let me look at the baby, but I don't know that I was interested. She told me to look around on the bookshelves because she had an entire collection of little metal figurines made by the house of Bezalel in Jerusalem. These figurines were beautiful, no larger than two inches tall, carved, and engraved into kings and ladies-in-waiting, Arab women, and exotic warriors—there were so many. I don't recall the various shapes and sizes, but I knew these figurines were not mine, so what was the point of standing there and looking? I think Greta wanted me to come and sit next to her, and perhaps tell her why I am the way I am. But I was unable to engage, it hurt too much to be in that room. My visit did not last long; I thanked her and left. I did not return to Greta's house again.

I began school, *Kita Hey* (fifth grade). I enjoyed learning now. Hebrew came fast; history too, and best of all was Hebrew literature. We read poems by Rachel, Bialik, Alterman; we sang songs; I began reading adventure stories in Hebrew about Ivan the Terrible, maybe a Hebrew translation by Pushkin. I learned geography about the land of Palestine, Eretz-Israel. We constructed a huge three-dimensional map, in relief, with papier-mâché, and we painted the rivers, mountains, forests, deserts, and seas. Our teacher was Dr. Lehman's wife; she was tall and dark-haired, older than our counselors; she was serious and imposing, but not scary, because she was a terrific teacher. Whatever she taught was so interesting that the object of the lesson never remained flat for long—and my curiosity grew the more she taught.

Then, a bunch of new kids arrived from Bulgaria and the displaced persons camps. In our group was a boy whose name was Yossi Habibi. He was not a refugee like us. He was, I believe, Yemenite though he had red freckles and blond hair. Yossi liked me and sent me little notes; he wanted to walk with me from class to wherever I wanted to go. But I didn't want him to be with me all the time; still, I was glad that someone liked me well enough to follow me so. Then the new kids arrived; they were like a blast of raw energy in our midst. There was Israel from Bulgaria: he was blond, had blue eyes, a big wide face, and he was loud and very sure of himself; he played the trumpet. I admired him immediately, but he was not interested in me; I was much too quiet and shy. I don't think he even knew that I existed! Then, there was Yitzhak: a very small, thin boy with brown curly hair. He was special because he had a talent for playing the violin and on holidays when the children's orchestra played, he always played the solo part. But even more impressive was his talent for directing the orchestra. Once he picked up the baton, he never returned to playing the violin, at least not with our orchestra. I don't know where he came from, but from his looks I'd guess he came either from one of the Eastern European countries or from Germany.

Why don't I know? Because no one ever asked where one came from. Children and even the grownups just didn't make conversation like this. They didn't need to know about your past, they just wanted to be in the present, and they wanted to know what you were thinking, doing, studying, eating, and the like. And that suited me just fine.

Until Yehudit arrived: a young girl with black, curly hair, about my age, although I was taller than she. She had dark eyes and very pale skin. She was an orphan who lost both parents in the Warsaw Ghetto. She spent the rest of the war years in a concentration camp. And she became my second roommate. I think my first roommate was asked to move out; her name was Sarah Chapchik: a good-natured girl who seemed so very much at ease with herself that we didn't make a good fit. And our *madrich*, Amos, must have sensed that Sarah being my roommate was too difficult for me since she had parents in the city and she went home regularly to visit them. Sarah even invited me to her house once, but I refused.

So Yehudit became my roommate, and from the moment she entered our room and I showed her around a little, she began talking and so did I; we never stopped telling each other things. I told her about me and she told me about her. There was no comparison between what she went through and what happened to me during the war. She told me how she was smuggled out of the Warsaw Ghetto and was separated from her parents and never saw them again. She had been in a camp; I didn't know enough to ask which camp it was. She saw torture and abuse, and she spoke a great deal about what she saw. In the evenings, after the lights were turned off she began to talk; she spoke for a long time. I was an avid listener and the longer I listened, the more alive I became. Yehudit shook me out of my shell and made me feel that it was good to be alive. I believe she felt the same. We were best friends. Then, I told Yossi that I liked him very much, but I could not be "best friends" with him. I was very busy now and had a lot of work for school.

School was very important now; my class in Hebrew literature and the class assignment that each student select a Hebrew writer and develop the themes of that author's works suited me well. I elected to work on Rachel, the Hebrew poet who was one of the early settlers to help dry out the Hulah Valley; she became ill, first with malaria, then she was hospitalized for a very long time. From her hospital room she wrote her most beautiful poems, and then she died. She died of tuberculosis; she was buried in a small cemetery on the banks of Lake Kineret. Her poetry was mostly sad and many of her poems were put to melody by famous songwriters and became folksongs. I loved Rachel! I wanted to become a poet like her. And indeed, I received a diary from my sister Gitta. In that diary I wrote little poems that spoke of my initial pain: first, of my mother, how much I longed for her and how I ached in her absence; next, I wrote about life in Eretz-Israel. About the *Struma*,[5] a boat of refugees that exploded at sea, and the fast day that was held across the land in memory of the drowned, and about the beauty of the land. I had Rachel in mind, of course.

In Ben Shemen the children learned all sorts of things, from music and singing to sewing and swimming. Now swimming I had mastered in Nice after the frightful ordeal in the icy pool. But here we were training for a swim meet and learned to dive off the side of the pool——"race diving." I had taught myself the breaststroke and was not going to flunk this time. But I had never learned to dive, even if it was low and flat diving. Yossi offered to train with me; he was a good swimmer and I was happy to learn from him. When the day of the Maccabia (meets and competitions in many sports, held by Israel's national sports organization) arrived, I participated in one of the races and won the race, dive and all! I received a little green medal to wear on my shirt. It meant a lot to me. And so did all those who touched my life there in Ben Shemen.

Aryeh Simon and Amos, who cared so much and did not know how to reach me at first; geography with the creative Mme. Lehman; Israel who played the trumpet and Yitzhak the musician; boys who came from hell taking on life with enormous energy; Yossi, who wanted to be my boyfriend but accepted friendship just the same; Sarah Chapchik, gentle and kind, whose well-being I did not tolerate easily; Yehudit who had seen the nightmares of the *Shoah* and had no one to call her own—she and I were paired off and we were inseparable; Rachel, Rachel my idol, whose courage and poems and songs I breathed. And then came the swim meet and the Maccabia—winning but one race was enough for me. I had made it! I was now a child of Eretz-Israel!

With summer, the *Shavuot* (harvest) festival was immense: a real pageant with fruit and vegetables from the orchards and gardens that the youth units had nurtured and grown; a parade of dancers in brilliant costumes with hoes and rakes. When the parade was over the music and dance performances began. First was the concert: this was no band, as most children's bands seem to be. No, this was an orchestra directed first by our one-armed music teacher and conductor, Hanan Eisenstadt, and then by Yitzhak, the diminutive stunning boy who conducted Haydn, Mozart, and Bach.

Gitta and I did not leave Ben Shemen until the winter of 1946. We saw Ben Gurion marching past our closed gates, a prisoner of the British. War was coming to Palestine; it was in the air. But for Gitta and me it was a sad farewell. Mother had tried to bring us back to her, and finally she succeeded. She'd written to Camille Huysmans, the mayor of Antwerp, engaging his help to provide the permits allowing us to return to Belgium. Neither Gitta nor I were ready for this departure. I had finally begun to absorb all that Ben Shemen so grandly offered and I felt part of this land now. I was not ready to leave. But the longing for my mother, though it had subsided, was only submerged. Deep down, I still needed to be with her.

And Gitta felt similarly. She finally had forged friendships with her own kind, and more than I, was part of the productive enterprise that brought forth fruit from the land. As she said, she had a wholesome nineteen months here, and now she had to leave it all to go where, toward what future?

The fall saw my entrance into *Kita Vav*, sixth grade. This was going to be a challenging year with math, a heavier literature schedule, and *Tanach* (Bible). But what I cherished most was my beginning classes in Arabic! I'd be good at that, there was no doubt. So, we began the year and it was good. When November arrived with our mother's announcement that we would shortly return to her, we had little time to prepare. The names I knew and mentioned here I have never forgotten. The farewell party with pictures and names, and good words written on pages, just like children have here in their yearbooks was my first and last great school experience.

PART II

TRANSMISSION

CHAPTER SIX

THE SUMMER OF 1982:
REVISITING THE PAST[1]

We Share and Repeat Memories
with Our Children, Now Young Adults

When our children were young adults, we decided to revisit our past, taking a trip with them across a few countries in Western Europe. Our goal included learning the history of World War II and what happened to the Jews in Western Europe where we had lived. We took along some history books, a few notebooks, and audiotapes for recording conversations. Still, since this would be our first family trip to Europe, we wanted to share and enjoy its beautiful parts: the arts, music, architecture; the landscapes, foods, and its people. This journey, then, would represent a kaleidoscope of our passions: to be with each other, learn together, share life as it was now, and remember the past.

So, in 1982 during summer vacation, we took our family to Europe to retrace with our children the experiences that shaped the early years of our lives. Our plan was to go to Germany where Wally (Walter), my husband, was born. Then we visited France and Italy to where my mother Hannah, sister Gitta, and I fled during the war. Belgium was not part of this itinerary because the children had each been there to visit their grandparents when they were quite young. And Berlin, the city where Gitta and I were born, was not part of this itinerary either. We were not ready for a visit to Berlin, which would only take place in 1994.

Our three children, now grown and on the threshold of young adulthood, were drawn to sharing this journey with us. Ari, at twenty-one, had completed four years of college; Gefen, at twenty, had finished her third year of college, and Miriam, at seventeen, was to enter her senior year of high school. Ari and Gefen had each spent one year at Hebrew University. Gefen's year in Israel was just ending; her return from Israel was to coincide with her arrival at Schipol, the airport in Amsterdam.

This journey was no chance event. We had talked about going back to Europe for some time. The children had been exposed to our childhood stories for many years. They knew their father's recollections of his hometown, his memories of leaving his village in 1938, and his journey on the ship *New York* from Bremerhaven to New York. Among his memorable experiences on the ship, he remembers his vile seasickness and the radio broadcast of the incredible return match between the German heavyweight boxing champion Max Schmeling, and the acclaimed American, Joe Louis. Joe Louis won that match, so there was jubilation on board the ship, but also fear. The Jewish refugees feared that the Nazi crew who saw them as sympathizers with Joe Louis would harass them. In truth, the Jews on board could barely suppress their pleasure at this black American's victory. The Nazi crew was disgruntled and angry, muttered "foul play" and blamed the Jews.

In Wally's mind the pain of leaving Germany, where he left his beloved grandparents, family, and friends, was inextricably combined with a sense of relief at being on board this ship that would liberate him and his closest kin, bringing them to safer shores, the United States.

Our children had heard about my experiences during the war, including my mother's and sister's stories about how we fled Berlin in 1939 and came to Antwerp, and then to Brussels. How with false papers, we lived as Christians and then fled to Dunkirk in 1940 in the hopes that the retreating British would take us with them to safety. Having failed at that attempt, our children knew about our maze-like escape to the south of France. Finally, they were mesmerized by our escape across the Alps into Italy when the Italians declared an armistice with the Allies on September 8, 1943. Then, when all was safe and the war was almost over, they knew that my sister and I were separated from our mother, who remained in Rome for the remainder of the war, while we sailed from Bari to Eretz-Israel in April 1945, under the auspices of Youth Aliyah. We stayed in Ben Shemen, an agricultural village for children, until October 1946, a total of eighteen months.

The children knew what mattered to us and they had a good sense of where they came from. They had learned Jewish history in their Orthodox Jewish day school; they had gone to study and work in Israel; they belonged to Reform Jewish youth groups and summer camps. Moreover, they had studied European history in high school and college. Their Jewish education was, as they playfully liked to call it, "Re-Conserva-Dox" (an acronym for Reform, Conservative, and Orthodox). In addition, their political and social beliefs were an amalgam of labor Zionism and liberal Americanism. These positive influences notwithstanding, I knew that I intentionally conveyed to my children certain alienating attitudes. I reminded them more often than I care to remember that they were not like other American kids, they should not take their well-being for granted because they were, and always would be, children of refugees and survivors.

I wonder now what the purpose was of these admonitions. Did I mean to keep my children off-balance in order to instill in them the same feelings that preyed on me of not quite knowing where I belonged? Did I want to deprive them of feeling grounded in the country in which they were born and whose citizens we all were? In truth, I did not want them to forget their identity, just as I was not allowed to forget mine: I was the child of a survivor and I was a child survivor as well; as such, they were the children of survivors and had to carry the responsibility of remembering from where they came. Moreover, from earliest of times, I needed to tell them who I was and where I came from, for with them I felt safe, and I hoped that this feeling of togetherness in sharing stories with one another would be reciprocated.

Eventually my children set me straight. One day, after one of my tirades, my oldest, looking at me very seriously, confronted me, "You know, Mom, you may feel like a refugee because you are one, but we were born here and we are Americans, and so are you, but we belong here and we are not outsiders even if you feel that you are."

The security I shook from under them Wally managed to repair because, being a child who left Germany just in time, he wholeheartedly wanted to feel that he was an American Jew. He was a significant member of the Jewish community; chairman of a Jewish day school's board; president of another organization; vice-president of a third, and a leading partner in his law firm. So there was no alienation on that side of our parenting partnership. As for myself, as a trained psychologist, I initiated research in psychotherapy at a university, taught psychotherapy and worked at it. I was also an active member of a number of Holocaust projects.

Though this generalization may be too simplistic, I believe that our children received many good values from us. Still, there is no denying that with all the good stuff, both Wally and I also have handed down our share of problems and pains.

In short, the purpose of our 1982 trip was to help integrate with our children what we had handed down over the years and what they were discovering on their own. Wally and I were all too aware that all three of the children, now young adults, would soon leave home. This trip, therefore, was a celebration of our early family years, of what we had imparted to them, and still hoped to discover with them before each embarked on their road to adulthood. The European trip, while aimed as a vehicle of transmission with the stated goal of acquainting the children with the places where we grew up during the Nazi persecutions, was also meant to be enjoyable: we would continue to share our family's passions, appreciation of life and art, and esthetics, and of the delicacies that Europe had to offer.

We decided to keep individual diaries and to tape-record our conversations. What follows is based on my diary of our journey and the family's tape-recorded conversations.

Tuesday, July 27, 1982

We leave Chicago at 5 pm. We are four upon leaving the United States, but will shortly be five after our arrival at Schipol. Our plane is crowded. The kosher food is less than edible. (Whenever I order a kosher meal on an airplane I feel exposed as if I were announcing: "I am a Jew." I could have ordered vegetarian. But I know, of course, the issue is not the food ....)

The flight is fine and without hitches. We arrive in Amsterdam at 8:45 am, walk over to an adjoining gate and await our daughter Gefen's arrival. Suddenly she appears. She is radiant! Tan from the Israeli sun with her multicolored Indian blouse, she appears like a freshly painted watercolor. She races toward us, and lands into four heartfelt embraces. It is a joyous reunion, with each admiring the other, how they have grown: all three look beautiful, handsome and exotic. We experience ripples of excitement and perhaps also fear. What will this journey be like?

Predictably our first excursion, even before registering at our hotel, is a canal boat ride. "It is the best way to see this city," says Wally. He seizes any pretext to arrange a sightseeing boat ride! And I admit it is a great ride through scenic canals, churches, and houses. Next we stroll to Dam Square and find a restaurant that is open and specializes in cheeses, crusty breads, chocolate milk, and mounds of great Dutch chocolates. Wally and Miriam, our resident chocoholics, don't mind standing in line for such delicacies. Personally, I could stand in line for a piece of crusty bread and Gouda cheese.

Only after tasting a bit of Amsterdam do we arrive at our hotel: our room is clean, spacious, and pleasant, maybe overpriced given that there are no shower curtains around the bathtub. And so, we make it through our first day in Europe and agree that despite so much togetherness during this vacation, we each will preserve our unique characteristics and recognizable foibles. Before retiring, the kids acknowledge that they miss their special friends: Ari misses K., Gefen misses S., and Miriam misses B. And Wally worries how we will get around tomorrow without a car, as it won't be ready for pickup until tomorrow or the day after.

Wednesday, July 28, 1982

Should we visit the city by taxi, train, or tram? Gefen and Miriam have no need for a car; they prefer walking. And Ari, like many young men who love trains and trolleys, is looking forward to riding the trams. So we do both: we walk and take the tram.

Our destination is the Anne Frank House. It is a museum now. It maintains the Annex, the attic where the Frank family lived in hiding from July 9, 1942 until August 4, 1944. The original Anne Frank diary is on display here. The museum serves as a documentation center about anti-Semitism and other racist ideologies.

The deportations from Westerbork to Auschwitz and Bergen-Belsen, the photographs and the writings are our main concerns at this time. Leaving the Anne Frank House, we walk to the memorial dedicated to the Dutch Jews deported in 1942. The first transports occurred in 1941, and the largest transports in 1942. From a Jewish population of 140,552 in 1940, 110,000 were deported in 1941 and 1942, and of those only six thousand returned.[2] Powerful facts.

Friday, July 30, 1982

The day begins with minor aches and pains and worries about the car. Will it be ready? Will it work? Will it be sufficiently roomy?

Why such worry, I wonder? I think, no, it's not the car, it's something else. The car is just fine. It's comfortable, clean, and roomy. We drive to Alkmaar, a small village outside Amsterdam, to Den Haag, the capital, and to Scheveningen, a world famous seaside resort. We picnic on the beach, play in the sand, romp around, and laugh—so far, so good. I try not to think about tomorrow, but I do.

Saturday, July 31, 1982
From Holland to Germany

Today is the tomorrow I've been thinking about. Leaving Amsterdam is not easy. I've not been to Germany since we left in 1939. Forty-three years have passed and now this: our first autobahn experience. I think of those great roads Hitler was so proud of. Surprisingly, the countryside is peaceful, vast expanses of green in different shades; such fertile land, such tranquility. I am ill. We stop at a filling station; I cannot step out of the car. I hear the station attendants' voices, the sound of their language triggers waves of nausea. I am unable to drink or swallow a thing. But the kids, yes, the kids! They present me with reality and they poke fun at me too, they mimic the manner and speech of the Germans around us. "Mom," they say, "these people are a new generation. They are not the Nazis of World War II."

(In the car, Miriam tapes our conversation)

Chaya: Yes, I know.

Miriam: We arrive in Roth-Wolfshausen in the afternoon. Before going to the hotel, Dad shows us the River Lahn and we sit on its banks, looking at the water.

Ari: (begins to sing) "Al Naharot Bavel" (On the banks of the rivers in Babylon we sat and we cried upon leaving the land of Zion.)

Welcome to the land of Germany, study of contrasts. Here we will be reading selections of Elie Wiesel's *Night*[3] while driving through the fallow countryside of present-day Germany 1982. "The camp looked as though it had suffered an epidemic, empty and dead; there were just a few ill clad prisoners walking about between the blocks" (45).

"Bread, soup—these were my whole life. I was a body. Perhaps less than that even: a starved stomach. The stomach alone was aware of the passage of time" (50).

And today, driving on the road to Wolfshausen we see beautiful fields, lush waving grain, rye, caraway seed growing in the distance, rolling hills, green trees, hard to believe.

Gefen: The air is foul; it smells so bad here.

Wally: It's just the animals, you know.

Miriam: Tell us about your family, Daddy.

Wally: They were all transported to Theresienstadt. The people who stayed were gathered in certain villages but most of them stayed in Roth until September of 1942. If you read the history books you will find that this was true in Berlin too. In the book *The Last Jews in Berlin*[4] they describe when the last Jews were transported. It was after the Nazis had their conference at Wannsee in January 1942, where they decided on the Final Solution: the total destruction of the Jews. On September 20, 1942, our family was transported to Theresienstadt.

Miriam: Where is Theresienstadt?

Wally: In Czechoslovakia. It was supposed to be a model camp to show the world that the Jews were not mistreated as the outside world had begun to hear. As it turned out toward the end of the war, Theresienstadt became a funneling place for Auschwitz. They kept this fact from the outside world. But they allowed a theater, an orchestra, and a school to be put up, and Rabbi Leo Baeck, who was the Chief Rabbi of Berlin, was the head of the camp's community there.

Miriam: He lived through the war?

Wally: Yes, he came to our synagogue Habonim in Chicago and he also came to Jerusalem.

Ari: I saw him there.

Gefen: Who appointed him head of the community?

Wally: The Nazis did. And Leo Baeck withheld everything from the Jews about what was going on in the camps.[5]

Gefen: There was a lot of criticism of Leo Baeck because he kept silent.

Wally: His answer to this was, "What good would it have done to let these people know that they were going to their death?"

Gefen: There were a lot of people like that. In Bialystok, that guy Barasz. He also knew what was going on, right, Dad?

[Efraim Barasz was in charge of the first *Judenrat* (Jewish council) in Bialystok. Though informed about the mass murder of Jews by the *Einsatzgruppen* (Nazi mobile killing troops) he believed that collaboration with the Nazis would benefit the Jewish population in the ghetto. In the end, he and his family, and the members of the *Judenrat*, and twenty five thousand Jews in the ghetto were deported on different transports in August and September 1943; some were sent on trains to Treblinka and others to Majdanek.[6]]

Wally: Yes, he did. By hindsight it was a big mistake. The people should have been told everything, and then they would have responded with all the panic they naturally would have felt. But the heads of the Jewish communities thought that they were sparing the people by keeping their community functions going, making it possible for them to live life as best they could.

Miriam: But to say that is hindsight.

Wally: That's true. Hannah Arendt said it too, and people condemned her for it.[7]

On the Way to Amoeneburg, Hessen

Wally: This is Amoeneburg. Konrad Adenauer came from around here; he was chancellor of Germany after the war.

Ari: Der Alte, der Alte.

Wally: The princes of this area lived on the highest parts of the hills. They did it for security reasons. During the Thirty Years War this area of Hessen was destroyed. Looks a little bit like Har Tavor (Mount Tabor), doesn't it?

(I find Wally's association of the German landscape to Israel jarring. Though the history he cites, without thinking twice, gives me great pleasure.)

Miriam: Where would you say our ancestors lived?

Wally: It would be the Judenstrasse.

A German family is walking below the fortress.

Chaya: In Nice, I once saw a family walking along the street below us. We were in hiding then and we were not allowed to leave the house; I was jealous of that Christian family. They were free, but I wasn't part of that world. They belonged and I didn't.

Wally: I too felt excluded, just like Mommy. This explains a lot about our behavior in groups today. It's always a little like we don't belong, and that happens even with our good friends. "You are a lost generation," Rabbi Wechsberg, our rabbi from Habonim, used to say. "You are German-Jewish refugees and that's what you always will be." He explained that we were uprooted at such an early age that we did not have time to build a solid base for ourselves: not in Germany and not in the United States. Though in some ways, it made adaptation to the United States easier, but in other ways we felt uprooted.

Chaya: Miriam asked whether as children we thought there was a justifiable reason why we were excluded and persecuted by the Nazis.

Wally: The only thing about that is that my dad always felt that I wasn't picked on at all in our village. He thought that I was perfectly happy, always. And that was clearly not true.

Chaya: Adults often think that little children don't suffer much because the grownups who are responsible for them do the best they can to protect them. They are so worried for their kids' safety that they cannot imagine that the children have worries or anxieties in spite of their parents' best intentions to safeguard them from harm.

Wally: Dad used to say to me, "You were always laughing and singing," and believe it or not, I did have a good voice at the time, but I was very much afraid and also I was very sad often.

Ari: So what happened? To your voice, I mean?

Wally: I tell you, ask people in the village, I used to ride on the wagon and sing!

Gefen: (teasing) Maybe the people in the village wouldn't know whether you sang on tune or not!

Chaya: This is a bit farfetched but could it be that you lost your pitch after you left Germany because you may not have wanted to speak German after you left? And with the loss of language and everything else you left behind, could it be that you also lost your ability to sing?

Wally: I wanted so desperately to participate with the other kids. But what happened was this: my birthday was on April 18; Hitler's birthday was on the twentieth, on that day they used to have big parades celebrating his birthday. I remember once I was so upset because nobody celebrated my birthday, nothing. But on the twentieth, I remember the people from our street were standing together when a marching band came by, and they wore Nazi uniforms. Everyone raised his arm in the "Heil Hitler" salute. I raised my arm too just like everybody else, but Dad slapped my hand down and said, *"Das tun mir nit!"* (We don't do that!) And I didn't know why. Herb (Wally's brother) says he read the newspapers already and listened to the radio, but I didn't.

Ari: What a confused little child you must have been. But don't forget Herb was five years older than you.

Wally: I was in a very ambiguous position being the youngest child (laughs).

Miriam: The youngest child always has that, believe me, I know! Do you think that Jewish children during the war came to believe that there was something wrong with them because they were persecuted and had to hide their Jewishness? Mom said that she didn't feel that.

Wally: Maybe if you came from an assimilated background you felt there was something wrong with you because the assimilated Jews always felt that there were no differences between them and the Christians. But when you came from a religious home, you had more of a base and you knew all along that being Jewish you were different.

We leave Amoeneburg and return to our car. Gefen drives back into Roth and up to the hotel. The Hotel Bellevue is situated on top of a hill and on the outside there is a pleasant garden and a stone terrace. Looking toward the horizon, the green and yellow parcels of land remind Wally of Israel, again. "It is just like Ma'aleh [Hahamisha]," he says. (Ma'aleh Hahamisha is the kibbutz in the Judean hills where Wally worked for over a year in 1952–1953.) The earth here is reddish-brown, and the smell of the pine trees is everywhere. Yes, just like Israel indeed.

We register, bring up our bags, and are ready to explore Wally's world. He will need to lean on us some as he revisits his village. We drive through the village but not into it. Wally is not ready yet. Instead, he guides us up the road to the Jewish cemetery and the forest nearby. A fence surrounds the cemetery. The gate is locked, but we enter anyway, climbing over the fence. It is shady and cool here. Not a sound is heard. A cool breeze touches us; we are standing on the Geyersberg, the hill on which the cemetery is situated.

The Cemetery on the Geyersberg

We look around on the ground and at the tombstones. Slowly we become accustomed to the markings on the headstones and look for familiar names, but it is impossible to make out the markings or the letters on the stones—they are too faint and unrecognizable. The cemetery is neglected; the tombstones lean sideways, in odd directions. Some are broken and some are disintegrating. Creeping moss threatens to cover everything. The earth here is also red, and our sandaled feet step on dry pine needles.

Chaya: Be careful, you don't want to get hurt here.

Wally searches for his mother's grave. We cover the perimeter of this small space. We read what is legible, but don't find Selma Stern Roth's gravestone. We look for his great-grandfather, grandmother, uncles, but we do not recognize any of them. Wally's mother's headstone is not here. It is gone. Something will have to be done about the missing headstone.

Climbing over the fence, we leave the cemetery. Wally points to the forest before us.

Wally: This is where I came as a young boy after my mother died; it was very comforting here.

Into the Clearing

We walk through the wheat fields into the woods. It was hot in the valley, but here in the shade of the forest we feel cool and unexpectedly serene. Wally tells us about Erdman, his dearly loved dachshund who was his constant companion. Erdman accompanied him everywhere. Wherever he went for a walk, in the garden, or in his house, Erdman was with him. After Wally's mother died, Erdman became especially close to him. When they went up the Geyersberg and into the forest, Wally and Erdman sat on the ground under their favorite tree and Erdman lay so close to him that Wally could feel the warmth of his body and the pounding of his heart.

Wally: Up above, beyond the trees, under the puffy white clouds, I imagined seeing my mother, thinking she was watching over me. That's what my grandfather said when I asked him where my mother went.

These were peaceful hours for Wally and Erdman. Wally composed poems and songs for none other than Erdman, his mother, and himself. We each find a tree to lean against, and Wally resumes his story. When he speaks about his mother, we sense that he must have been her favorite child. He deeply regrets not having been allowed to attend her funeral. There was no closure for him. I commiserate, because I too had to stay home on the day of my father's funeral.

Gefen: What do you remember about the time before you left Germany, Daddy?

Wally: Did I tell you about the day I had to give up Erdman? Dad had said that because we could not take him with us on the boat, he had to find a good family to take care of him. And he found one, but they lived in another village. The day Erdman and I parted was too painful for words, so I ran into the house. Then Dad took Erdman away. But Erdman was a very smart dog and he did not accept Dad's decision. On the day he arrived at his new owners' place, he lay silently at the door's threshold, and in the evening he just ran away. He ran all the way home—that was some distance! But then Dad took him back to his owners. It hurt to let him go again, but we had to, we had no choice.

Miriam: Were you ever persecuted as a Jew?

Wally: Not that much, but I did have unpleasant encounters with German anti-Semites. I believe I told you about the time when we were still allowed to go to the general school and how I was accosted by some big guys whom I did not recognize. They must have been from another village. They taunted me and called me "dirty Jew." Then they took my new pencil box and broke every pencil in it. After that they broke the box and threw it away. And you probably remember the story I told you about my teacher who offered a prize to any child in our class who finished first on his math exam. Since I was good at math then, I worked fast and finished first. I went up to the teacher and gave him my exam paper. He looked at it and said, "This exam is not for your kind of people," and with a snicker he crumpled my paper and threw it in the wastebasket.

This was when we were still going to school with the Gentile kids. After about 1936 none of the Jewish kids were allowed to go to the village school, so for a time we had a Jewish teacher who came from another town to teach us at home. But by then, thank God—and thanks to Grandma Toni's relatives in the United States—we had received an affidavit and were already preparing to emigrate from Germany.

Ari: Weren't the Nuremberg Laws written in 1933 when Hitler came to power?

Wally: No, they didn't appear right away. Don't forget, when Hitler came to power he had a lot of opposition. He just barely won a close election.

A lot of murders and dreadful brutality happened before he was able to consolidate his power. And a lot of non-Jews were killed too. They were leaders of the socialist and communist movements. The German people didn't yield to Hitler right away. A lot of things happened. A lot of good people were killed. You know the Germans lost close to 15 million people in the war. The first Nuremberg Laws were enacted in 1935. They were edicts: Jews and Gentiles may not intermarry; Gentiles are not allowed to work for Jews; Jews are forbidden to practice their professions; Jews are forbidden to be teachers, or judges; Gentiles are not allowed to buy goods from Jews; Jewish children are not allowed to go to school with German children, and so on.

Ari: Mom, it's your turn to talk, now. Tell us about Luzer.

Ari is aware that Luzer's being a member of our family has been a touchy subject in the extended family; still, in our nuclear family we did speak about difficult relationships.

Wally: Mommy's stories will come later when we get to France; Luzer is part of that story when they were in Nice. So you'll have to wait until we get there.

We leave the forest, pick up the car near the cemetery, and drive to the village over the bridge of the River Lahn. The streets are paved now.

Wally's Old House

We look for Wally's house but he does not recognize it. Looking further, we see a house with the date 1774 engraved on the front brick that marks the foundation. This is it. Wally recognizes his old house! We knock and are received by a man who looks us over suspiciously. He must have known by now that a family of strangers had come to town; nothing goes unnoticed in a small village. Wally explains who we are, assures the man that he merely wants to look at the house to show his wife and children where he once lived. The owner grudgingly approves. We wander through the house; it has been remodeled since the old days. The owner shows Wally a large knife that had been used for slaughtering and sausage making in the old days. Wally recognizes his dad's knife! Then, as we are about to leave, Wally sees an old Phillips radio in the corner of the entrance hall and whispers, "This is our radio, I'm pretty sure. This is where we used to hear the news and Hitler's bellowing speeches." He wants to look around to see what other objects from the old days he might find. But just then the owner's son arrives. He offers to show us the barn, the yard, and the rusty old pump that is still functioning. We take turns at working the pump and taste the cool water from the well. No one speaks for a time.

The Jewish Synagogue

We drive along a street that parallels Wally's old house and I notice a small, gray building with a pitched roof. This house has not seen any remodeling, judging by its state. But my eyes move toward the windows that are framed by arches. "Look at these windows," I say, "they are arched at the top just like you'd see in a synagogue. Could it be, Wally?"

We stop the car and try to enter. The neighbor next door, guessing at our intention, comes over, unlocks the door, and shows us in.

The neighbor explains, "This building was the old synagogue; over the past forty-two years it has been used as a place to
store grain, that is why it is still standing. They had to keep the place
dry so the grain wouldn't rot."

The place is dirty and dusty. But through the grimy paper we
detect pieces of the original paper on the ceiling and we even see
some white and blue stars through the accumulated dirt. The children notice the upstairs balcony that must have been the *ezrat
nashim* (separate women's section), but there are no stairs leading up
to the balcony anymore.

What is more shocking, finding Wally's old house or discovering his devastated synagogue? Both were invaded and both were
ruined. We all appear to have seen enough. Our children leave us to
return the key to the neighbor next door.

The People in the Village

As we walk down toward the street we meet a few people from the
village: Mrs. Wenz, Adam, and another man who knew Wally's
brother. All are quite friendly. Adam knew Wally's dad because he
had worked for him. Adam tells us that our family made the best len-
til soup. He tells us also that in 1941 after the Roth family had left,
he used to bring fish for the Jewish families who remained in the
village. They came knocking on his window in back of his house so
no one would see them, and they picked up whatever he was able to
garner for them.

Walking along we find the small grocery store that Wally
remembers well. At this corner deli we buy a few things for
memory's sake: *Pflaumenmus* (plum jam), *Gruenkern* (green wheat)
for soup, and a half of a large peasant bread. Back in the car, we
drive by Wally's house again and see the Pfeffers across the street.
They were old-time neighbors and the families knew each other
well. Mr. Pfeffer asks us in. Hesitating, we enter their house. Wally
exchanges recollections with the family. Pfeffer says that the Roths

were a good family, always friendly, "but you could never get too close to them because they never ate at the home of a Gentile."

Pfeffer says, "When you don't eat in your neighbor's house, you can't get close." He offers us sausage and we refuse because we keep kosher just like the Roths in the olden days. "Ach! You are not like your brother," he says to Wally. "Herbert, he loved eating our sausage when he visited us here last year."

I ask the old woman, Pfeffer's mother, to tell us what she remembers about Wally when he was young. She says, *"Der Walter war so jung als seine Mutter starb, und Er war auch sehr traurig. So habe Ich ihn jeden Tag bei mir nach Hause gebracht, und Ich sass mit ihn Stunden lang. Er hat meine Hand gehalten und wollte mich nicht gehen lassen ohne ihn. Ja, Ja, er sass auch Stunden lang auf meinem Schoss."* (Walter was so young when his mother died and he was very sad. Then I would take him to my home every day, and I sat with him for many long hours. He used to hold my hand and would not let me go without him. Yes, yes, he sat for hours on end on my lap.)

After some cold drinks and a couple of beers we take our leave, and slowly walk toward the bridge. There we meet up with other villagers: some are standing around, and some are on their bicycles; it seems they have been waiting for us. Some remember Wally and Irene (Herb and Wally's sister), as well as Herb and Wally's stepmother, Toni; they remember Toni's mother too, who was deported to Riga. Another young woman remembers how, after life had become bad for the Jews, she would bring fruit and milk to Toni's mother and quickly run away for fear of being seen and reported to the Gestapo. We walk down the street and a woman asks me about my German accent. I tell her I was born in Berlin. She says, "Oh, yes, I thought so, what with your *hoch* ('high,' can mean 'snobby') German accent!" The kindest thought I was able to muster was, "Well, this one doesn't tolerate differences very well."

Discussions and Arguments with the
German People of this Village

Some of the men strike up a conversation. We become engaged in two parallel discussions. Our children, Miriam, Gefen, and Ari, have a long conversation with the Pfeffers' son. The general drift of their discussion is, "Should all Germans be held responsible for the deeds the Nazis perpetrated forty years ago?"

Wally and I engage in a discussion with the older men. They talk about their participation in the war and about their losses. Two of the men were on the Russian front in 1942 and participated in the fierce fighting in Russia. Another lost several comrades during the war. "You are lucky, Walter," he says, "that you left when you did. At least you didn't have to go to war."

A man from Niederwalgern asks, "Why did you come back?" Another man, slim in stature with grayish/blond hair, whose name is also Walter, chides the first man: "*Ach du lieber! Er ist hier gekommen um seine Heimat zu sehen!*" (Oh! My dear, he came here to see his homeland!)

That Walter had served in North Africa in 1940, and was captured in 1941. Then, he was sent to Michigan as a prisoner of war. Pfeffer was wounded at the Russian front in 1941 and was sent home. He was eighteen at the time and Walter was seventeen. Now the two men are in-laws.

Pfeffer repeats to Wally, "You are lucky you left, Walter, that way you escaped the whole thing!"

Wally is shocked. "Lucky?" Indeed. But, turning the tables on Pfeffer, he has a comeback. Wally asks, "And how was it here for you when the Nazis took over?"

Pfeffer got his drift immediately, replying, "Things developed so quickly so that those who wanted to resist couldn't, or if they did they were made to stand against the wall and were shot. And Hitler said he wanted to persecute the Jews, but not everyone else, but that clearly wasn't the truth."

Wally: What about the invasions of Russia, France, Holland?

Pfeffer: Let's say this: things have changed now. The Jews are a people, they have their own land, and they are not persecuted anymore.

Wally: Yes, but the only people who wanted to exterminate the Jews and had a plan for total annihilation were the Nazis.

Miriam, who had joined us to tape our conversations with the older people, gives me a broad smile.

We arrive at the bridge and take our leave. Walking a few steps behind us Gefen and Ari are conversing in Hebrew.

Gefen: What are your reactions to the villagers of Roth?

Ari: What I am feeling now is anger, but also some hope. Perhaps one day, people will come to understand each other. After all we were able to talk to each other today.

Gefen: How can I understand them? These people are inviting us to eat and drink with them, but these are the same people who didn't do a thing when the Nazis came!

Ari: You are wondering why they didn't rebel? Maybe they couldn't; not everyone can be a John Reed, like Warren Beatty, you know.

Gefen: Yes, but with them it is as if nothing happened here. People must behave like human beings, and most of them didn't.

Ari: And what do you think about the situation in Lebanon today with Israel asking Jewish citizens to kill Arabs?

Gefen: Yes, but there are people in Israel who disagree with the policies of the state, and they have demonstrations and petitions to protest the policies. But what did the people here do under Nazi rule?

Ari: You're right. There are people who don't have a conscience. Before, when I was sitting in the Pfeffers' living room, I had the feeling that, yes, we are all human beings, but we are also different. It's not only that they are blond and we have heads full of brown curls, but that they are living with a different past. There are differences between people.

I ask Wally to tell us about his village, its history, and the Jews.

Wally: Jews have lived in this area since the thirteenth century. In the village itself Jewish existence can be traced from the year 1630. In the nineteenth century, nearly 200 Jews lived in the village. By 1933 only eight Jewish families, or approximately fifty people, remained. By 1939 only five Jewish families or about thirty people were left in the village. Now there are none. The Christian population of the village in the 1930s approximated 600 people. There is much more to say about our family and its history but that's for another time.

We decide to go to Marburg and visit this old university town. Much history lies buried here, and Wally explains: Marburg was the principal residence of the Hessian rulers. This is their castle on top of the mountain. And here is the great Elisabeth Church that became well known during Martin Luther's time. Also the Grimm Brothers of fairytale fame lived in Marburg, and its university has been a center of learning since medieval times. Hermann Cohen, a great Jewish philosopher lived here, and Hannah Arendt, the well-known Jewish philosopher and political scientist of the mid-twentieth century studied here. Also, the Jewish community of Marburg can be traced to the year 1300. Its synagogue was destroyed on *Kristallnacht*.

The architecture in Marburg is Gothic and the views are fairyland-like. We walk past the Judengasse; there is much to remember here but no relics remain.

Then, we are ready to eat; but only a Chinese restaurant will do for now. Nothing local, I'm afraid. We joke a lot to release tension and pronounce the food exceptionally good. We find our way back to the village, and walk down to the river to unwind.

Ari: On the banks of the River Lahn, outside of Roth, we are listening once again to nature's sounds; geese are honking, swans are swimming in the river or sitting lazily by the babbling brook. "Quaack" says the little swan, "quaack" says the daddy swan; "quaack" says the dying goose. The River Lahn, the amazed child gazes with Wordsworthian wonder. This is the idea of a Roth hike.

We return to the Bellevue for our last night here and have another family pow-wow: where do we go tomorrow? To Munich or Dachau, the concentration camp? And if we go to Dachau why are we going there?

Discussion at the Hotel

Chaya: Why go to Dachau now? Why not Munich?

Miriam: We want to keep everything in its proper perspective. We came to Germany and found things quite pleasant, like this beautiful landscape, for example. But at the same time, I need my angry feelings about Germany to be validated.

Ari: We were saying before that we want to see the Germany of today. We don't want to have only old memories. What exists today is also what existed before World War II. But what we saw today was very sad knowing how much was altered and taken away. Still, we also saw beautiful things. And Munich represents a Germany that has been rebuilt. I guess I'm kind of mixed about where I want to go tomorrow. But we also want to see the tangible evidence of all the terrible things that Germany committed.

Chaya: Here we are talking about how peaceful and beautiful the German countryside is; still I must tell you, the sick feeling I had entering Germany has not gone away. I can't believe that we have been driving here without constraints or borders. No papers, no police, as if nothing ever happened here. Then, coming into this hotel was equally intolerable. We walk in and see German citizens sitting around tables, reading poetry, discussing literature, eating, and reading. Such a cultured people they are. Then, coming into Daddy's village evoked something totally unexpected. It was peaceful and extremely moving.

Ari: I can't separate the village from Daddy. But I agree with you, driving into Germany was strange. Then getting out of the car and going to the cemetery and the forest felt like Daddy fit in.

Gefen: I was shocked at this place, your hometown; I felt estranged. This is not a Jewish place. I can't reconcile this place with you, Daddy.

Miriam: This reminds me of my first trip to Israel. When I came to Israel I expected some divine revelation. But that didn't happen. And coming into Germany I expected absolute hatred and disgust, and that too didn't quite happen.

Monday August 2, 1982

After last night's discussion we agree to go to Dachau and Augsburg. We decide to skip Munich. Leaving Wolfshausen at 9:00 am we arrive in Dachau at 4:15 pm. We are very late; it is almost closing time. Wally and I tell the children what we know about Dachau based on our readings: Dachau was one of the first concentration camps, located in the outskirts of a small town called Dachau, about ten miles from Munich. Himmler announced the opening of the camp in 1933, and the first prisoners there were political enemies of the Nazi regime; they were mostly communists and social democrats. National Socialism terrorized all resistors and tortured political opponents to a bloody pulp; many were imprisoned in the Dachau camp. After *Kristallnacht*, November 9–10, 1938, ten thousand Jews from all over Germany were interned here. Then when the war was all but over, thousands of inmates were forced on a death march in the last three days of the war. They were ill and reduced to mere skeletons and succumbed to a typhus epidemic that was raging in most camps, including Dachau.

The sign over the gate of the camp still reads, *Arbeit Macht Frei* (Work will set you free). We see the watchtower and the old crematoria. The barracks, the toilets, and the prison building all spoke to what happened here. We walk up to the memorial monument and the museum. It is getting late and the museum is closing and soon the camp proper will close as well. Lingering on after the guard closes the museum, we look at the barracks again, the tower, the fence, and the moat. We will not forget, but for now we are quiet. No questions, no comments. As secondhand witnesses we feel that recording what goes on with us is a must. But still, no one speaks. We enter the car and drive off to Augsburg.

The Drive to Augsburg

Wally talks about European history. He thinks that a historical perspective will help integrate our emotional reactions to Dachau. We talk about Germany, its relations to the Jews, and our relations to the Germans now and in the past. Wally explains the Yalta/Potsdam conferences before the end of World War II.[8]

We are entering Augsburg. Here we find a Holiday Inn, the good old United States in the heart of Germany. We watch TV and accidentally come on a channel showing *Holocaust,* the made-for-TV movie, in German. And, of course, we watch it. Then, we go for a swim in the pool. To experience a touch of the United States attended by a German lifeguard is the epitome of culture shock. Orderliness, thoughtlessness, and rigidity prevail. Do you want an extra towel? No, that will not be possible. Can we bring our towels down from our rooms? No, that is strictly forbidden! And sitting on the towels in the sauna is absolutely not allowed; that is the rule. This last rule breaks the camel's back. I walk up to the attendant and he becomes the target of my rage. I shout at him, "What is the matter with you? What are all these nonsense rules? Will you Germans never learn that your inconsiderate and arbitrary rules have been your downfall?" Poor kid, he never knew what hit him and neither did I.

Tuesday, August 3, 1982

We're on our way to Verdun. Driving out of Germany is a relief. Beautiful countryside or not, the German language and behavior have done the job. As we drive, Wally tells us about World War I. It was in Verdun, in 1916, that the fiercest battle of the war occurred. It resulted in enormous and gruesome losses. Germany experienced such bitterness and humiliation for having lost the war, which was followed by an economic debacle, and social and political unrest that led to the rise of Hitler.

We visit the tunnels the French had dug in preparation for World War I; these huge underground tunnels were used to safeguard their troops and as foxholes for attacking the enemy. The tunnels are still intact. We observe where the men slept, their rooms, and the common areas. The fortifications are like underground citadels, meant to be impenetrable forever. But we know that it was not so. During World War II the Nazis invaded France easily by going around many of the fortifications that had been put up.

We visit the battlefields and see a vast expanse of grass and crosses. Three-quarters of a million men died here in World War I. We meet people along the way who guide us to a screening place where a twenty-five-minute film about the battle of Verdun is shown. Verdun was a citadel, a bastion of resistance and attack in World War I. The fortress of Verdun was one of the main barriers on the road to Paris. It was the primary objective in the German campaign in 1916, and the failure to secure it was fatal for Germany.

There is much information to take in. I wonder how our young people are absorbing this history. And there is so much more to come. We are not even one week into our trip! A walk along the canal caps off the day and we stay overnight in a small *auberge* (hotel) located near the road that will lead us into Paris the next day.

Wednesday, August 4, 1982
from Verdun to Paris

Through countryside roads and highway we ultimately drive into Paris. Pleased at our ability to maneuver the car around the highly trafficked plazas, we find our hotel Vendome. The hotel manager offers us three fine rooms and we are amazed at the extravagant furnishings and comfortable accommodations. The kids are no less astonished. "It is like the Plaza in New York City," says Gefen, and we agree. Ari's room is a Parisian garret; under a slanted ceiling and a window overlooking the rooftops, he has the urge to exercise his poetic inspiration. When he joins us at breakfast the following morning, he generously offers us last night's epiphany.

Ari's poem: Song based on "Gee, Officer Krupke" from *West Side Story:*

1.

Dear Travel Information Bureau
Here is my complaint
You promised me a rustic room
Roughing it I ain't.
I'm pent up in the penthouse
Where the maid presses my pants
Why did my parents drag me here to France?

2.

I'd visions of a sleeping bag
And singing 'long the Seine
Eating only cheese and bread
Living by the pen.
A Hemingway with Mom and Dad
I'll never have a chance
Why did I have to go with them to France?

3.

Most young men in my place would live it up, my mom tells me
I tell her "Thanks a lot, but most young men, I'll never be."
"Then, do it for the family, enjoy yourself for us."

They give me my own room and I don't fuss.
Dear Travel Information Bureau
Whatever shall I do?

With this document in hand, Ari's humor finds a way to sidestep some of the upheaval that is beginning to emerge.

Thursday August 5, 1982

We spend the morning at the Louvre. The galleries are mobbed. We see the Mona Lisa, Franz Hals, Diego Rivera, Venus de Milo and the Winged Victory of Samothrace still perched at the top of the stairs. I am reminded of my daily visits to the Louvre when I was sixteen, which leads me to think that I was about the same age as our Miriam is now. Would I have taken a trip with my parents to Europe during summer vacation to revisit my parents' past? I don't know, but I doubt it. Then, why are we foisting this journey on our children?

Our next stop is the Cathedral of Notre Dame. The tour of Notre Dame is intense; the gothic architecture and gargoyles stir up awe and fear. Especially when leaving the cathedral, we are directed to the commemorative dedication to the Jews deported in 1942. I want to tell them about the roundups in Paris at the Vélodrome d'Hiver[9] in July 1942, but I cannot do it today.

At this point, we feel a strong need to be with Jews. We walk over to the Jewish Quarter on the rue des Rosiers. It is a tight area with narrow streets, three- and four-storied, narrow apartment houses with very little light coming down from above, even during daytime. Interestingly, we see few Jews on the street. Looking around, we find a place for supper and then we head back to our hotel where we unwind and speak about the events of the day.

Friday, August 6, 1982
Paris

Yesterday's visits left a painful mark. It is difficult to wrap our thinking around the conflicting aspects of French attitudes toward the Jews. I was greatly affected when I first learned about the French Revolution and later about Napoleon. We look to the French Revolution, with its motto of *Liberté, Egalité, Fraternité* (Liberty, Equality, Brotherhood) to gather the meaning of France's ideals. It is difficult to think of the French as other than our allies in philosophy and world outlook. Historians credit Napoleon's Civil Code, which guaranteed freedom of religion and equality under the law, as his most significant and long-lasting contribution. I found it impossible to make sense of the contrasting attitudes of the French toward the Jews over the course of a 100-year period, during which time there were numerous changes in forms of government. Rights of Jews were abolished, restored, and then abolished again. And the Jews were persecuted again when fascism took root in the prewar 1930s. How could the French have influenced Western thinking at one time, and allied themselves with Vichy's racial laws, abetting the Nazi's killing program at another time?[10]

Back home at the Vendome, we unwind. Today, Wally and the kids set off for the Eiffel Tower. I stay behind. A bit of rest is what I need. We regroup at the Pompidou. Pipes and tubes in primary colors are the exterior of this museum of modern art; Magritte and Dali are the inside. This is a place that does not want to be ignored and we do our best to satisfy its agenda.

Saturday, August 7, 1982
Paris

It is the day before our departure from Paris. We have saved our visit to the house of Rodin till last because we want to savor his works. The kids have learnt about Rodin's works in school and are eager to see some of his works in life. We observe how he brings to life the objects that emerge from the hard stone and the manner in which he chisels his figures to depict society, the essentials of human character, passion, love, and beauty as we idealize them, and God. Leaving

Rodin, our hearts are full.

Sunday, August 8, 1982
Paris-Lyon-Vienne-Orange

The weather is cloudy and cool as we drive out of Paris; it matches our mood. We pass Lyon, the city where in 1942, Mother, Gitta, Luzer, and I briefly stopped to attempt to find an escape route to Switzerland. The rumor that families with young children would be accepted in Switzerland was what made us stop in Lyon. But those families with young children were limited to those who had children below age two. Therefore, our stay in Lyon in 1942 was brief and frightening. We felt threatened there, targeted for roundups and we knew no one to advise us.

Today, we do not linger in Lyon; we move on. But on the radio we hear ominous news from Paris: An explosion outside a Jewish owned store caused damage to the store and the homes nearby. No group or person claims responsibility for this act of terror. Later, we hear that the damage occurred in the restaurant where we had supper on rue des Rosiers. This news is shocking, and we each respond with our personal dread at having escaped what could have been a tragedy.

In this mood we move on to Orange, a town north of Avignon, famous for its Roman history, ruins, and center of learning. The town saw the defeat of a Roman army and later became an important Roman colony. Walking through the town we see a Roman viaduct, more ruins...and a history that on the surface is not related to Jewish history or the *Shoah*.

For the moment our sightseeing in Orange seems to be going well enough. The day is almost over and, though we had no reservations for the night, we did not anticipate that it would be difficult to find lodging in this small town. But, in fact, there were not many hotels in Orange, and the ones we saw were unsuitable, at least to me. Still, it was getting late and Wally worried that with dusk setting in and poorly lit streets, finding lodging would become more difficult.

My family is impatient with me because none of the hotels are to my liking. Finally, we agree on a room in the least objectionable hotel. A suspicious manager takes our passports and we register. Our room is dusty, and in truth, the velvet furniture seems not to have been cleaned since Roman times. I suggest we try to find something better. But it is dark by now, so we decide to stay and deposit our luggage. Eventually, we find a restaurant. It is an ornate dining room with red velvet drapes hanging from the windows and red tapestry covering the chairs. A thin carpet lies rumpled on the floor—it has the appearance of an old oriental rug, I believe. "This place is totally fancy and probably hugely overpriced," I say. No, it isn't. We manage to order from the menu and wait for the food to arrive.

While waiting and chatting, I begin to feel a prickle on my arm, then on my neck, then on my chest and legs. Tiny bugs seem to leap all over me. Within minutes, I itch all over. I imagine there are fleas here jumping from the velvet drapes onto my skin. Wally sits across from me and senses that I am not quite myself. I try to explain, but can't. Whatever it is, I am deeply distressed. I am not prepared for this. In coming back to Europe I expected a rational, even if emotional, experience, but not an actual "reliving" of the past. And wherever we go, the past seems to be raising specters of danger and flight. And this began with our descent to the south of France. I am caught up in something; still, I don't believe that this itching is just "in my head". Perhaps there are live fleas here! Later, I will explain to my family what was going on with me.

After dinner, we settle the bill and head back to the hotel; we are ready to turn in for the night. But our adventure in Orange is only half over. On entering the building, we see that the hotel manager is busy locking the doors to each floor. He does this every night, he says. "*Mais pourquoi?*" (But why?) I ask. Shrugging his shoulders, he does not answer. "Maybe he intends to stop the guests from stealing some of the objects that adorn the rooms, or from leaving the hotel before their bill is fully paid?" Gefen suggests. The locked floors add to our discomfort: Miriam, Gefen, and Ari are visibly taken aback. Wally too is uncomfortable; it shows in his quiet demeanor. He tries to make conversation but we are tired now. Let's just go to sleep. We sleep through the night despite being locked up in Mr. D'Avignon's hotel. Realizing that we are alive and breathing in the morning, we don't wait for any more surprises. We take off in our car and pick up breakfast on the road.

Monday, August 9, 1982
En route to Nice and St. Paul de Vence

Today, we drive to Nice. I am at the wheel and the kids are eager to ask questions they wanted answered earlier. They ask me, "Who was Luzer? When did he meet your mother? When did they get married? Why did your mother not want to talk about this part of her life? And what was the secret?" The questions come, and though I cannot answer in detail, I am relieved to speak. Miriam is taping.

In Vence, when I was almost eight years old, I was picked up, together with Luzer, in a roundup set by the Vichy authorities at the insistence of the Nazis.[11] The date of Luzer's and my arrest was on August 26, 1942, I later learned. I did not understand the reason for our arrest then. But I did know that when we came to Nice in March–April, 1942, we lived on forged papers; therefore, I was not fearful of roundups here. Nice was part of unoccupied France, governed by the Vichy authorities. As a Christian child with the name of Helene Daveau, and a pupil in our boarding school at the Institut Massena that clearly honored Marshal Pétain, the head of the Vichy government, I felt safe. Pétain, whose benign face was framed in a picture that hung in our classroom, was honored and idealized here, and all that gave me a safe feeling.

Before leaving Nice for summer vacation in the month of August, I was told that we were going to Vence, a town located about 21 kilometers above Nice, near the mountains, to get away from the summer's sweltering heat. I remember very little about our stay in Vence or about its surroundings, except this: One day, I was playing alone on the street, hopscotch perhaps. My mother and sister had left in the morning for Nice on some errands. Luzer was indoors at our hotel. I later learned the name of our hotel; it was Hotel de Vence and I believe it was located in the old city. With our false papers we were not in *residence forcée* (enforced residence, in which Jews were supposed to register and daily report to the police). While I was playing by myself on the sidewalk, a French *gendarme* just happened to walk by, or so it seemed to me. "What are you doing here, little girl?" he asked. "Just playing," I said. "Are you all alone here?" he asked. "Yes," I said. "And where are your parents?" he says. "My mother and sister went to market," I said "What is your name?" he asked. "My name is Helene." "Show me where you live, Helene," he said. And, as if it were the most natural thing to do, I pointed to our small hotel right by the sidewalk. He asked me to show him to the entrance, and the manager behind the desk, seeing I was with a *gendarme*, told him our room number. As a result, I brought him straight into our room and delivered Luzer and me to the Vichy police! Whatever was I thinking? Why did I show him our hotel? Why didn't I tell him the same story I had learned to repeat by heart over and over? "I am Helene Daveau and my parents are not here." But instead I led him into our hotel. What was I thinking? There were no Nazis here in Vence, only French *gendarmes*. And I was on familiar terms with Marshal Pétain, the valiant military hero of the First World War and now a kindly head of the Vichy government. I was not afraid of Vichy *gendarmes*, or so I thought. As a result I was totally stunned when we were picked up in one of the memorable roundups in August 26, 1942.

It was the day of the *grande rafle,* when thousands of Jews were rounded up and put into convoys in the Free Zone; Luzer and I were picked up, taken in a van with a blue light circling overhead to the sound of the familiar siren, and driven to Nice to a huge police barracks. At the barracks, adult men and women were shouting and crying. They showed their papers and went into cubicles where French police were processing identity cards. I was shocked—I totally did not understand what was happening. I knew that in the family we had talked about not getting caught or being deported, but I had not yet seen a Nazi in Nice. When the reality hit me that the Vichy French were doing the roundups, I had no grasp of what was happening. I only knew the unthinkable: I was here without my mother and sister. My mind went blank. And when it appeared that Luzer and I were going to be separated too, I panicked. I screamed until my breath gave out. I sobbed, and coughed, and cried. I do not remember what happened after that. I was told that I stayed overnight in the barracks but I do not remember that. All I knew was that we were in a huge barracks with long gray walls on one side, and wired windows high above the walls on the other. To my right were offices: *gendarmes* in each office were examining mounds of papers, and people being were interrogated. We were all Jews and naturally all wanted to be released. Many said they were French Jews, or related to French Jews, meaning that they did not belong here, because at this time the Vichy police were not picking up French Jews.

Was it my idea to go screaming up and down the hallways? Did Luzer coach me about what I should say? Did he tell me to walk away from him? Or did I just walk away from him on my own? Or were we separated, the men from the women, the children from their parents before I understood what was going on? I don't know. I don't remember. I do know that I walked up and down the hallway screaming through my tears, "This is a big mistake—I don't belong here! I am not Jewish! My name is Helene Daveau. My mother will be very angry when she finds out that you brought me here. And she will worry that I am alone; and how will I get home then? You are making a big mistake!"

A serious looking, tall *gendarme* walked up to me and whispered that if I promised to quiet down, he would take me home at the end of the day when his work was done. I quieted down some, but I did not trust him to remember me, so I walked past his office as frequently as I could, looking in on him every time I passed by. When evening came, my *gendarme* stepped into the corridor; he did not have to go looking far, because I stood right there, close to his door. He took my hand, bent down to talk to me at eye level and said, "Now I will take you home, Helene. Then your *maman* will not worry about you anymore." He was a good man, this *gendarme*, and my heart was grateful. But I did not dare show my gratitude to this man, who was, after all, saving me, a Jewish child. I had to be Helene Daveau, the little Christian girl who had been picked up by mistake in the big roundup, mistaken for a Jewish child.

So, I left Luzer—walked away or was taken away from him, never to see him again. Some time later, after I was reunited with my mother, she heard that Luzer had arrived in Drancy; a postcard was the evidence. Later he was transported on convoy #29 headed to Auschwitz; but apparently the train stopped at Schoppinitz, a forced labor camp, and there he died of typhoid fever.

The serious *gendarme* walked me out of the barracks, and he took me to his black Citroën where I sat in the front seat next to him. He asked me where I lived. I expected this question, but I didn't know what to say. What should I tell him? I didn't know where he should drop me off...think! Then, I thought about Luzer's Jewish-French cousin whose little girl had been my playmate ever since I arrived in Nice. So, I said in a natural voice, "Please take me to rue X, this is where we live." When we came to the place, my *gendarme* stopped the car; the French cousin's house was across the street. He offered to walk me over to explain to my mother what had happened to me. I thanked him but declined his offer. "That will not be necessary," I said, "but I thank you very much for bringing me home." I wanted to hug him to show my gratitude, but that did not seem the right thing to do. Instead I just walked away, crossing the street and turning around to wave good-bye.

Yes, I think he knew who I was, but he let me go because he felt sympathy for me. He was just like the customs officer in Périgueux who took us off the train and interrogated us when we tried to cross the border in March 1942 to escape from the German-ruled Occupied Zone of France to the Vichy-ruled Free Zone as we were heading to Nice.

Back to My Release from the Barracks

After leaving the man who saved me from the barracks, I walked up to the second floor of our cousin's building and moved toward the door. It was sealed! I could not ring a bell or knock on the door. Not knowing what to do, I waited long enough until I figured that the *gendarme* had probably left. Then, I resolved to go back down to the street. When I reached the sidewalk, taking a few hesitating steps, I practically bumped into my sister; Gitta just appeared around the street corner I was on. I could not believe my eyes. We fell into each other's arms and cried. Gitta had been frantically looking for me. I had been missing for two days and a night, and everyone in the family thought that the worst had happened to us, because they knew about the roundups now. But Gitta, who knew these streets well, because of all the shopping she was responsible for, had an intuition: if I were let go, or if I had run away and did not know where to find them, I probably would go to Luzer's cousin's house. Laughing, sobbing, embracing each other, she became very serious and said, "Now there is no time to lose, we must hurry home!"

Gitta explained about our new home: it was our hiding place. We were living together with three other families, twelve people in all. And we were living in hiding. The shutters were always closed, and we were not allowed to walk with shoes, only in socks. We were not to flush the toilet during the day and we were not allowed to turn on lights, not by day nor at night; we were not permitted to laugh, or talk out loud, and definitely no one was allowed to scream!

So home, for now, was our apartment on rue Trachel 42 bis, third floor. Across the street was a French police station. Standing behind the shuttered windows, I saw a small group of Jews entering the place. A few people, rounded up, were taken into the station. Given my recent experience with a roundup, I became agitated. What if one of the *gendarmes* inadvertently looked up toward our house and saw some shadow behind the shutters? Mother stayed calm and reasoned otherwise, just as she had in Brussels. "Who would suspect that Jewish people would be hiding in an apartment across the street from a police station? No one, I think," she said. It was a long time before I stood behind those shutters again.

We hid at rue Trachel from August 1942, until November 1942. Life at number 42 bis became boring because there was nothing to do all day; no games to play or books to read; the adults played cards: sixty-six, gin rummy, solitaire, and I got to kibitz and play when they let me. Gitta and Freddy went out shopping for food and stood in line for hours. I was reprimanded often for laughing, talking too much and too loud, and worst of all for experimenting with large scissors. Those scissors lay on the couch one day; I had left them there. When I inadvertently stretched out, the tip of the scissors entered the bottom of my foot; blood came gushing out. Hadn't Mother asked me to remove those scissors earlier? But I was either obstinate or lazy, and didn't budge. Those scissors pierced into the heel of my foot and it hurt badly. But my first reaction was not pain; it was fear. What will happen now? I'll have to leave the house, find a doctor and maybe even go to the hospital. I shrieked; Mother ran and put her hand over my mouth; someone handed her a towel and she stopped the bleeding by applying pressure to the heel of the foot. Then she cleaned the cut with alcohol—that stung! Finally, a strip of cloth finished the job. Now I was an invalid. I overheard the adults bickering about the problems young children pose in a place such as ours. I hated when adults fought, especially when it concerned me who created the problem in the first place. But when they argued about money, who owed what, who paid too little, or who paid more than their share, then I was ashamed because all too often, Mother was accused of buying too much food on the black market, and then the rest had to share in her unnecessary "luxuries." Also, I knew that they were running short of money. Regina, who lived with us and whose husband Willy was a member of the Central Committee of the Jewish Community, apparently overcharged us for bread. But as she and Willy had found the contact person for our source of bread, we were not free to complain. So, for now, the others decided to put up with Regina's exploitation.

But that did not resolve the problem that children pose in hiding. Children are so unpredictable, they said. Are they more unpredictable than adults, or possibly, more vulnerable? I developed a rash. The same rash I told you about when we were in Orange. They said it was because I didn't eat well; I lacked vitamins or perhaps suffered from some other medical condition. I had never seen such a rash, not then, nor later in my adult life. Well, there is no use repeating the entire ordeal. Except that my poor mother blew on the little sores, cooled them with a calamine-type of lotion, and stayed up for hours, gently stroking my arms, legs, back, until I finally was able to sleep.

On November 11, 1942, the Italians occupied Nice, the Alpes-Maritimes, and seven other departments east of the Rhone.[12] The French were fuming and felt dishonored for having their authority displaced by the Italians whom they considered, in any event, inferior to them.

The Jewish population, however, experienced a brief respite during the Italian occupation. Two men were responsible for this safe haven. The first was Guido Lospinoso, governor of the Italian territory, who in sympathy with the Jews played "cat and mouse" with the Germans, who were insisting on receiving names of Jews and lists for future deportations. To their claims and demands, Lospinoso responded that no such lists could be found and therefore, they probably did not exist. The second benefactor was Angelo Donati, the Jewish Italian banker who did all he could to support Lospinoso and worked toward the liberation of the Jewish population in southern France. He planned to lead them toward safe shores, namely toward the coast of North Africa, now occupied by the British. (Zuccotti;[13] See also Poliakov and Sabille[14] and Cavaglion.[15])

In the meantime, the Jews on the French Riviera pursued their daily lives in relative freedom. They walked on the boardwalk in Nice, gambled in the casinos, and occupied most of the beach chairs, much to the displeasure and grumbling of the local inhabitants. Mother found work with a *maison de haute couture* (a fashion house) that gave her a commission for every customer she sent their way. She did the same with a Jewish dentist. For any new patient she referred, she received a moderate commission.

Today, as I am telling about these experiences, we are already driving through Nice; and soon, we reach a road that veers toward St. Paul de Vence. We look out the window holding hands. "You were such a little girl," says Gefen. "Yes, you were, Mommy," echo Miriam and Ari.

Our car manages the hilly ascent and brings us directly to the hotel situated by the side of the road. Le Hameau is a rustic villa, built with heavy, unevenly cut stones (like Jerusalem stone); the arches on the windows and doors show a Spanish influence; the red, blue, and orange bougainvilleas cascade in big bunches over the balconies and on the doorsteps providing a sumptuous foreground—this is the Riviera; it is midday and beastly hot. Le Hameau suits us perfectly, from the rustic beams and the heavy wooden furnishings to the starched white linens and the refreshing temperature indoors. We go to a nearby market and buy fresh bread, cheese, and fruit: figs, peaches, and plums. Everything is brilliantly lush—we eat and rejoice! Then, back home at Le Hameau, we go for a siesta: to relax, change clothes and enjoy the view of dry red earth, pine needles, rocks, the smell of trees, the aroma of southern France. Some people say, "It is like Israel, like the Judean hills." Of course it is, some-what. But it isn't Israel.

While the younger generation goes out exploring, Wally and I stretch out on a king-size bed. With the smell of freshly washed linens, my thoughts race back to Nice. So much happened there that I did not understand. The next day we plan to go down to Nice to find the places where we lived during the War. I struggle constantly with dates.

Tuesday, August 10, 1982

The girls and I spend the morning looking for places I want to see: the center for deportations, rue Trachel 42 bis, and Institut Massena, our boarding school, among others. We find avenue des Fleurs, the street our boarding school was on, but we do not find the deportation center, nor do we find our boarding school. In the basement of the train station in Nice, in the restroom area, we make numerous phone calls. We start with the liberal synagogue, receiving names for the Jewish Archives, the mayor's office, the departmental archives, various churches, St. Pierre, St. Etienne, and the Jewish Social Fund. We do not make a single connection in Nice, perhaps because it is the month of August when almost everyone is on vacation, or because the people we contact by phone are unreceptive to our questions and claim ignorance. One woman from the Jewish Archives says she will call back, but she doesn't. I don't want to carry my search to extremes, aware that what is meaningful to me is not necessarily so for the rest. But my daughters at my side help with phone numbers, dialing, writing notes; I feel protected by their presence. But, so far our search is fruitless.

We pick up Wally and Ari at the beach and hear a string of comments about what they had seen: bare-bosomed women stretched out on the beach! Wally and Ari declare they witnessed the glorifica-tion and the fruits of nature. Together, after refreshments, we take the road back to the rue de France and Miriam and I stop at the *rab-*

binat (rabbinate). I ring the bell; there is no response. In the car, listening to the radio, we hear more news about the terrorist attack and the deaths in the Jewish quarter in Paris, on the rue des Rosiers.

Half-forgotten memories return. The terror on the Paris streets, together with the closed doors to our inquiries here in Nice give me a cold feeling of imminent danger. We drive to the liberal *rabbinat*. Someone lets us in through the street door, but we are not allowed to come up the stairs. Perhaps they are afraid. I leave a message. Someone will return my call: call back the next day, they say. We return the call, but no one answers. I call Mlle. Michaud at the Jewish Archives; I knew the phone line was off the hook because the busy signal is interrupted. The Jewish Social Fund phone line is busy as well.

We take the road back to our hotel. Entering the rugged side road we feel at home. Our hotel manager greets us warmly: the entrance is cool and colorful and we are treated to ice-cold drinks. I raise my concerns: What is happening here? Why are we coming up against an impassable wall? These are Jews like we are—why don't they trust us? Then I think of the terrorist bomb at the rue des Rosiers. Sadly, the answer is too simple: people are fearful because life is becoming dangerous again for the Jews in France.

In the late afternoon we drive to Vence. After inquiring with the management of one hotel whether they remember where the Jews lived *pendant la guerre* (during the war), we are directed to the Villa Beau Sejour. Mr. and Mme. Suivanti, the owners, don't seem to remember much, but after some hesitation, Mr. Suivanti remembers that his father had a registry dating back to 1942. "Many Jews were here," he said. "They all had to be registered officially here and then they had to register daily with the police." He brings us the register and looking through the pages we find long lists of Polish names. Each page has four columns dividing the information of the hotel "guests" by name, date of birth, nationality, and place of origin. Mr. Suivanti's father lost his memory, says the son, and the son was too young perhaps to remember. But perhaps because of the fresh young faces who are with us, the manager seems to remember one more thing; "My father told me that a long time ago, during the war, he had saved a Jew who hid in the back of the house when the Vichy police came on a raid. And my father, knowing where the man was hiding, did not report him to the police." "He saved a human being," I say. I ask him whether he remembers other stories of people hiding in his father's hotel. Does he know of other hotels where Jews were registered? I tell him that I too had lived in a hotel with my parents, but we were not officially registered, and I do not remember the name of that hotel. Mr. Suivanti is not interested apparently; he shrugs his shoulders and walks away, mumbling something under his breath. After we leave them, I feel a sense of emptiness. He tried to communicate with us, but something fell flat.

This was our first encounter with a registry of this sort. And I believe we were shocked by the Suivantis' seeming indifference to the people who had lived under their roof in fear of being arrested. We take a long stroll and the kids ask about the purpose of *residences forcées.* I explain that certain hotels and resorts were designated by the Vichy regime as places where Jews were asked to register and were expected to live during their "limited" stay so that the authorities could tally their whereabouts. The Jews had to report daily to the police and they had to abide by a curfew so that, when the time came, the authorities would know where to find them. It was in the Vichy government's self-interest to institute this policy because they, like the Germans, wanted to track the Jews, possibly to round them up in internment camps and possibly to "nationalize" their property. At the same time, the Germans were expecting long lists of Jewish names from the Vichy authorities for future roundups, and convoys that would head to extermination camps in the East. Predictably, our mother did not register officially in any place where Jews were assigned to reside and register their proper Jewish names. She did not understand why people would put themselves into such dangerous situations.

Coming face to face with the reality of the Suivantis' register was tough. We decide to take a short walk to visit the Chapel Matisse. In this simple white structure, with its tall narrow windows and clean lines, we recognize the Matisse style, his primary colors, and minimalist designs stripped of excess. Here we are breathing deeply and are able to cool off.

Later, we drive to our place in St. Paul de Vence; these two towns, St. Paul de Vence and Vence, are located in the hills some 25 to 30 kilometers northeast of Nice, where the temperatures are cooler than in Nice; they are called twin cities because of their proximity to each other and because in design, dating back to Roman times and the Middle Ages, they have similar layouts. They are built of heavy stone which keeps the interior of the houses cool. Both towns attracted many artists in the 1920s and 30s with whose works we are familiar, such as Matisse, Dufy, Soutine, Chagall, Dubuffet, among many others. And so, we visit the Maeght art museum and rejoice as much in the town's exhibits as we do in its beautiful landscape. I did not visit St. Paul de Vence during the war; therefore my memories cannot cloud today's experience. But Vence itself, I cannot forget.

Wednesday, August 11, 1982
Saint-Martin-Vésubie, la Madonna, and Colle delle Finestre

We leave Le Hameau, our friendly retreat in St. Paul de Vence and are now ready to trace our escape across the mountains from France into Italy on September 8, 1943. The drive up to Saint-Martin-Vésubie is mountainous and the air is cool. At the entrance to the town we see a number of old villas, gardens, and big old trees. I am on the lookout for the one our mother had rented with her Belgian cousin Hindze. But I have no clue what our villa was like. Any one of these could have been the one we had rented. I don't know in which direction to turn, though Gitta told me the villa we rented was close to the entrance of the town. Why did we go to Saint-Martin-

Vésubie from Nice in mid-August, in 1943? It was not because Mother was looking for a safer place to stay, because life was safe enough in Nice under the Italian occupation. It seemed to my sister and me that we went there because Mother's cousin Hindze had rented a place there and she was interested in sharing the place and its rental with our mother, as well as to get away from Nice and the summer's heat. But we did not go for the entire summer. We had our apartment on rue Trachel and I believe Mother felt that renting a villa in Saint-Martin-Vésubie would be too expensive. Moreover, she had her business in Nice that required attention, both at the boutique as well as at the dentist's in order to collect what was due to her. She must have heard about people's experiences in Saint-Martin-Vésubie; the daily registrations with the Italian authorities could not have gone unnoticed. But neither my sister nor I have any memory of such registrations. I do believe that we did not mingle with the Jewish community. And while Gitta and I heard of the organization of school activities, youth movements, and other goings on, I did not participate in any, and neither did Mother or Hindze. I believe that my sister did meet up with a few friends while we were there.

Now, we are walking on cobblestone streets and look around to find our bearings. At the corner, where two streets intersect, we see a bar. I suggest we enter and ask there if the owner could provide some information about the time in 1943 when the Jews who lived here took flight across the mountains. We pick a roomy table against the wall and order cold drinks; opening our map of southern France we try to locate ourselves. I notice some men standing at the bar, talking boisterously. I decide to walk up to them and ask in French whether someone remembers the war years of the 1940s when the Jews lived here in Saint-Martin-Vésubie. There is no immediate response. Then, a man, perhaps the owner, tells me he knows the man I am looking for. "He is sitting right here [on a barstool]." He calls the man over, "Heh, Cergier, come on over here a minute, these people are looking for information about 1943 when the Jews lived here."

Cergier, a man in his late fifties or early sixties, must have been a youth back then. In spite of his age, he was a handsome man, with a good face, strong and stocky build, gray-haired and balding at the crown. He tells me he remembers what happened here. Invited to join us at our table, he greets my family and they him. He bends over the map spread before us and tells us the following: Yes, he did participate in the Jewish escape from Saint-Martin-Vésubie. Approximately 800 Jews fled Saint-Martin-Vésubie on September 8–9, 1943, that was after the Italians capitulated to the Allies on September 8, 1943. He remembers that Jewish people were coming out of their houses at the crack of dawn the very next day, maybe before 5 am, and heading toward the mountains. Cergier brought the firewood they would need for the road. Why firewood for the road? I wondered, but I didn't ask; I assumed it was to make a fire during the night, for warmth, and possibly for heating up some hot water. He, along with a couple of other young men, served as volunteers in this getaway. It was a massive exodus.

It would be a treacherous road across high mountains, with narrow paths, dangerous ridges, and steep cliffs. It would take two or three nights to get to the border and not everyone would make it. According to Zuccotti and Cavaglion, some of the people who started up on the climb turned back. One little girl remained in town. The villagers brought her to Nice. The man who directed the passing no longer lives here, says Cergier. But it is true that 800–900 people left toward one of two summits, the Colle delle Finestre (the summit of the windows) and the Colle delle Ciriegia (the summit of the cherries) to cross into Italy.

Now Cergier gets up from his chair and moves away from us. It seems he has exhausted the fund of what he wants to say. I want to ask him to tell me more about the passing and what it was like, and what he remembers. But once again I see that hint of "let's not get into this too deeply." Before leaving our table, however, he offers the following unsolicited remark: "Many Frenchmen betrayed Jews to the Gestapo and many Jews who did not leave Saint-Martin-Vésubie in 1943 were caught by the *boches* (Germans)." I wish I had asked him to stay, or at least asked to meet him for a drink later with my husband. Because his remark seemed so full of undertones and bad feelings about his compatriots, I thought that he wanted to tell someone what was weighing on him.

Was he telling us that here too the Jews encountered anti-Semitism with local residents who would have preferred seeing them leave, or possibly would have wanted to turn Jews over to the Nazis—possibly for some recompense? I translate Cergier's words to my family; we look at each other and seem to be getting the same message from Cergier.

Zuccotti clarifies the nature of the disarray on September 8, 1943: "The armistice, signed by Badoglio, was not scheduled to be made public till the end of the month ...the premature announcement ...on September 8, 1943 [by General Eisenhower] caught everyone but the Germans unprepared .... The [Italian] army immediately disintegrated and ... [the] soldiers scrambled across their frontier."[16]

We drive up to the church of the Madonna. This road is steeper than the one we drove on earlier. We arrive at the foothills of the Alps. To our right is the church of the Madonna. It is a small church; the outside walls are grayish white and in disrepair; it stands at the far end of an unpaved, pebble-strewn, open walkway. We are facing the Alps; they rise before us like stark slabs of gray slate. The valley of the Vésubie is below us, an uninviting, forbidding place. We walk to the church. Here is the place where many of us slept on that first night before the crossing. Gitta told me that she slept in the church, but I thought I slept outside to the left of the Madonna, in a large open space together with many other people. I may be wrong. Perhaps that night I slept with her, next to my mother and Uncle Herman, and only the next night did we all sleep under the stars on a huge grassy plateau. Gitta did not remember the plateau. She remembered singing by the fireside with many young people and Italian soldiers, drinking hot coffee or tea. I remembered lying on my back, looking up toward a star-speckled sky, hearing the voice of a little boy rising in our midst. He began with the well-known Yiddish song, "Oyf'n Pripitchik." It was the sweetest voice I ever heard. After a while, many of us lying on the grass joined him in song. It was a night I would not forget.

When I finish my story Ari sings "Oyf'n Pripitchik". A shudder runs through us: Here in 1982, we feel like 1942 could have been yesterday. What matters is that we are here now and the war is decades behind us. We climb toward the Colle delle Finestre; I tell them that the Colle was known for being one of the steepest summits in the Alps, used by professional skiers who sought to be challenged. We drink icy water from the river and skip over the rocks. I am wearing sandals now, just as I did when we escaped from Saint-Martin-Vésubie.

I feel exhilarated and continue climbing; Wally is tired and sits back against a large rock. Ari and Miriam join me on the climb, but Gefen stays behind to be with Wally. No one should stay alone on an outing such as this. I tell the kids about the huge rocks we climbed just before reaching the Italian border, about a pregnant woman who fell behind me in 1943. My mother said, "Don't look back; a woman just fell but she will be OK." Very carefully I looked ahead at my feet, so as not to accidentally misplace a rock, which could cause an avalanche of rocks to roll down behind me.

Now I tell the children about the Italian soldier who stood guard at the Italian border: "My mother was afraid he would ask us for papers but he turned his back on us, and looking toward the mountains, he just waved us through."

Then, Ari and Miriam turn toward me. "We have climbed far enough. It is time to go back," they say. I could have gone on. Something inside me takes over and I become totally energized when I am in these mountains, but I listen to my wise kids and we stop. After all, I am no longer eight years and eleven months old.

On our way back we pick flowers, blue and yellow mountain flowers, and a piece of wood. The flowers are still here in our Chicago home; twenty years later I find them accidentally among the pages of my diary. The long, flat, gray piece of wood is hanging on our mantle in our Michigan home. We all remember its origin and we can't miss looking at it when we are there.

Coming down the mountain Miriam's foot accidentally kicks a stone and causes it to tumble. It bounces toward me and hits Ari, who stands below me. Unintentionally, it seems we have recreated the "rocky" climb of thirty-nine years ago. A reenactment is a very powerful thing: it is like a strange current that grips one person, then another and then a third. You can't explain exactly what you're doing or why, but it feels as though you have been there before. We pick up Gefen and Wally and return to the Madonna. How good it is.

In the evening we drive into Nice and dine at Chez Charly, a great noisy, simple and happy place. Wally is tired, Ari is into himself, and Miriam and Gefen move closer to each other. Miriam said that these past couple of hours had been very difficult for her. Gefen agrees. I wonder how I would have felt were I in their shoes, participating in retracing my mother's past.

Friday, August 13, 1982
Valdieri, Borgo San Dalmazzo, Cuneo (Lugere)

We drive across the mountains—the roads, though narrow, are passable. Winding our way down, we arrive in Valdieri energized and ready to go. Our mission today is to find Andreina; but I have no other name for her except her proper name. We had not kept in touch with her since we escaped here in 1944. There were reasons for our silence but I didn't know what they were, except that survivors needed to move on with life and wanted to forget. They had to build new lives, new families, and new professions. So they did not return to the places where they were during the war and they did not search for their helpers and saviors.

But now in August 1982 we want to find her. The kids too are into it totally, having heard about Andreina for many years. As we don't know a soul in Valdieri, we enter the town and look for the piazza. Three elderly men are sitting on a stone bench under arched columns. This looks like Valdieri's City Hall. The men are talking, and as they see me approaching, their conversation stops. Their looks are sullen and suspicious. I approach them and in my rusty Italian tell them that I was here during the war *("nella guerra di 1943–1944")* with my sister and mother, and we were hiding in a *cava* that belonged to Andreina. They want to know which Andreina. And for me there is only one Andreina but I don't know her family name. One of the men confirms that there are several Andreinas in the area. The men are jovial now and the one who spoke to me first says that his companion, sitting between them, had been a collaborator during the war! I don't see the joke. But I do see that they are suspicious of my family and me. The man who spoke first may have felt that his comment was out of place because he gets hold of himself and, speaking in a kinder tone, tells me to go across the piazza to the grocery store. There, the owner will probably be able to help in our search.

Miriam, Gefen and I enter the store. The owner is a woman in her forties. No sooner does she hear that I was here during the war of 1943 then she brings her hands to her face and tears come streaming down her cheeks; she shakes her head: *"Oh! Che brutta guerra!"* (Oh! What a terrible war! How difficult it was for you!) In response to her genuine compassion, tears start rolling down my cheeks. I embrace her. We both cry. She tells me about her father, who did not come back from the war. She helps me sort out which of the Andreinas is ours. The one I am looking for lives in Borgo San Dalmazzo, she says. But in order to get better information, she sends us to a small hotel on the far end of the piazza. I translate for Gefen, Miriam, Ari and Wally. The five of us re-group and make our way across the piazza where we meet an older woman named Margarita. She too, hearing my story, responds immediately with great excitement. Of course, she knows Andreina Blua! She also knew "Gisele", my sister, and "Elena", me. *"La povera Elena, quanto ha parlato di lei! E della sua mama e delle bambine!"* (Poor Elena, she spoke so often of you, your mama and her two children!) Margarita cries as she cups her face in her hands; I cry too at her compassion and at the thought that she remembers us after so many decades. I am deeply moved, as are the children and Wally. What is happening here is so real, as if it all happened yesterday; but thank God, it is not happening now. Margarita shows us the way to the *cava* and then tells us how to get to Borgo to find Anna Marabotto, Andreina's daughter.

We drive up the road away from the piazza and reach a stone quarry. A church stands at the corner between the main road and the side road going up. We see two women walking up the road; I stop the car and ask them about Andreina's *cava* in the mountains. No sooner do I mention who we are than they begin to talk about the two little girls. They send us up to the *cava*. I remember it being to the left and the quarry the right side of the road. We go further up and then we see an igloo-like stone structure that has no window, just a wooden door. The place looks as if it could have been our *cava*; we see the small entrance, the area in the back that was black from making fires without a flue, and we see the blackened ceiling. That would have been the place where we cooked and ate. Next-door stands a longer, wooden structure. A ladder stands against the wall. I climb up the ladder and see what used to be a barn, but I don't recognize the place. I am not sure any more. Ari, Gefen and Miriam take turns climbing up. They want to know for sure. "Are you sure this was the *cava*, and this was the barn?" "No, I am not sure. It could be, but I cannot say for sure." I cannot say, because I do not fully recognize the place. But it could have been. We drive on.

Along the way we meet Giovanni, a small, bony man; he looks as if he were in his seventies: several teeth are missing and he is stooped over. Yes, he remembers Andreina. He shows us her house. It is a real house, not a *cava* like we just saw. He picks up bits and pieces of marble for us. We meet the family that lives next door. Andreina had a *cava* but it was too close to Valdieri and she feared not only the Germans but also her neighbors who could not be trusted to keep silent about the "foreign visitors" occupying her *cava*. A Jewish family with a tiny baby lived there, he said, they had a little girl. One day, they went away and didn't return.

We stop to pick up more marble stones for Gitta and take leave of Giovanni. He tells me to mention his name to Andreina. Then we drive down to Borgo San Dalmazzo to the store that belongs to Anna and her husband.

A man on a bicycle shows us the way and we meet Anna. And again the recognition comes with an exclamation: *"Ah!! Mama ha tanto parlato di lei. E quanto aveva paura dei tedeschi."* (Ah! My mama spoke so much about you and how she feared the Germans.) Tears, laughter, arms wide open, we hug and kiss. They admire the beautiful children Gefen, Miriam and Ari. Happy, yes, but already I sensed remorse in her tone. Had they been afraid for us, but also relieved perhaps after we departed? And then, when the war was over and we did not let them know that we were alive, they must have been worried for us. Anna calls her mother and we speak on the phone; then Anna brings us over to her mother's house. Andreina is brimming with joy. Uncannily, she looks like our mother, Hannah, and, of course, she wants to feed us immediately! *"La cena e poi dormire qui!"* (First you have dinner and then you sleep here!) She has room for three beds; she calls me over and shows me her spacious bedroom. I wish my mother were here with us. Andreina serves wine and cookies; she is stirred up and excited, and we both have tears rolling down our faces. The children too are moved. What a contrast between the human engagement we experience here, and the indifference we encountered among many Germans and Frenchmen we met.

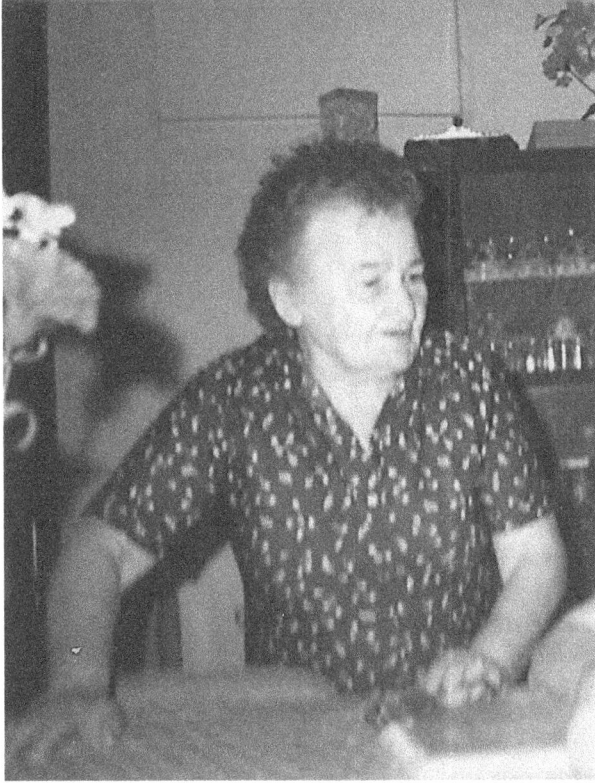

Photo 6.1   Andreina Blua, Borgo San Dalmazzo, 1982. "You can all sleep here!"

I ask Andreina how it had been for her in the war and what she remembers. She remembers how we had to leave. "It was no longer safe up here in the mountains. In March or April 1944, your mother asked me to please accompany you to the train station. She wanted me to sit with you and pretend you were my little girls, then the Nazis would not take you to be Jewish." Andreina recalls saying, "But this is very dangerous—you know what the Germans do to Italians who help Jews? They shoot them!" Then, remorsefully she tells us that she asked our mother for her gold watch; after a brief hesitation, Mother gave it to her. Now Andreina says, "I should not have asked her for the watch. She needed the watch to trade for food and other things—but, the watch was not really all gold. Later, when the

Germans came to take everything we owned, they took my wedding ring and the watch, and I was glad that it was not really gold. Still, I was so upset that I had asked her for it. I went to confession many times to talk about this terrible thing I did." Her humanity was immense. I am thinking today, as I write these words, that Andreina did not deserve this grief. Her life was on the line so many times, every day, during the six months that we stayed in her *cava*. After our visit with Andreina, Anna insists that we go to her for a *festina* (little party) with the family, and then to sleep over. I am inclined to accept the invitation, but I sense that my family is not enthusiastic. Perhaps it is the barrier in language that deters them or perhaps they just need to unwind. I turn to them and Wally for a reaction. Their response is unanimous, they are tired and these visits are draining. It has been a long day and I suspect that I am imposing more than they want to experience. There is, however, another possibility. I am thinking of my discomfort with Andreina, and hers with me. I cannot doubt her warmth, her love, or her sorrow when we left her in March 1944. But what distresses me today, as I am writing these words, is my realization that we hit some sort of moral impasse: here Andreina refuses to grant Mother's request that she accompany us to the Turin train station; she explains to Mother the dire consequences of such an act to her and her family should she be caught: "people have been shot for harboring Jews." Sure, our family was in terrible danger; the Germans, in March 1944, must have known that the Allies would soon conquer Italy but their continuous hunt for Jews was their last stronghold here in these mountains. And so we were in great danger too. Andreina had come to the rescue by sending us to Don Francesco Brondello who provided a new set of false papers, thereby making it possible for us to escape and hopefully make our way to Rome. But when Mother asked her to accompany us to the Turin station, pretending we were her little girls, and Andreina, fearing for herself and her family, hesitated, she asked Mother for her gold watch and Mother settled the arrangement by giving it to her. Did

Mother understand the danger to Andreina? Did she know that her watch was not gold? But whether the watch was gold or not, it did not lessen the danger to Andreina in any way. The terrible dilemma was that Mother, on the one hand, had no choice but to ask Andreina to sit with us at the train station to save us from a possible death, but Andreina's life was on the line as well, and not being able to say no to my mother, she asked her for her gold watch?! To what end?

It is not surprising that I did not insist that we return to Anna's that night. I have regretted not having gone back to the Blua family. I should have spoken with every person in the family and their friends and learned about what they went through during those years and how our presence in their midst was not only a burden but a great danger to them. I should have returned and talked to *la gente,* the people of Valdieri, and Borgo, and asked about Andreina's cousin who brought her to us in early September 1943 when we were fleeing back into the mountains after our arrival in Valdieri. I wanted to know what the Italian people in these surrounds thought about helping us, and there were many here during the war; I should have, but I didn't.

Gefen is listening intently, Ari is taking pictures, Miriam is tape-recording, and Wally is pensive. We spend the night in Cuneo. Early in the morning, as we leave the city, we speak about the people we are leaving behind in Borgo and Valdieri knowing that we are leaving some of the best, most courageous and caring human beings we encountered during the war.

Saturday, August 14, 1982
Venice

This romantic city, known in modern times for its gondolas and lovers who grace the waters with their presence, has a famous history. But we are exhausted from our ride; though it was not a terribly long ride, the weather is steaming, unbearably hot. My impressions are that the city is dirty and in an apparent state of disorganization. Parking, bringing our luggage with us, out of the car, finding *il vaporetto,* the little ferry-boat, combined with the heat is at best, exceedingly tiring. We maneuver to our destination and become adept at map reading. The hotel, La Serenissima, has lovely frescos on the walls. The weather, I seem to come back to it, is hot and sticky; and the city, sad to say, is dirty, crowded, and smelly. But the sights make up for all the inconvenience of getting here. The buildings are majestic, the canals and bridges, the contrast of colors, the entire layout of the city make us forget about the decaying interiors. Venice was once one of the finest of architectural sights in the country; unfortunately, it is sinking, slowly sinking into the sea. In the evening we dine in the courtyard of an intimate restaurant. We take, per force, a gondola ride. Though commercial, we see San Marco and the palace of the Doge. This is real sightseeing!

Sunday August 15, 1982

Today, we visit the Jewish Ghetto in Venice, the old and the new ghettos; we see the commemorative plaque for the 247 Jews who were deported between November 1943 and August 1944. According to Rebecca Weiner,[17] "The Holocaust memorials [were] designed by sculptor Arbit Blatas…. One of the monuments is a bronze panel depicting the Last Train, the other monument has bronze reliefs that show the Nazi brutality against the Jews."

About 1,200 Jews were living in Venice when German troops occupied the city in 1943. Between November 9, 1943 and August 17, 1944, 247 people were deported to extermination camps. At the end of World War II, 1,500 Jews were living in Venice and the number decreased gradually over the years. (Mann[18] cites 205 deported, and Zuccotti[19] cites 212 deported and 15 returned.)

We meet a Jewish glass blower, Giovanni Toso is his name. (I believe his store is located in the New Ghetto.) Giovanni is one of several generations of glassblowers and he produces fine figurines with Jewish themes. He is orthodox, self-righteous, and has an acerbic tongue. He is arrogant, mercenary and tries to appear disinterested in making a sale. He accentuates this disinterest by whistling through the wide spaces between his teeth while we look admiringly at his artistic works. He borders on being brash, maybe even insulting, but I like his cheekiness; he has pride. He is after all, a remnant of a long, honorable line of Jewish artisans. He is stuck here like an immovable relic in this sinking city. We look through his glass blown pieces and decide on a Hasidic rabbi holding a lantern, exquisitely designed. When we come to pay, he charges us seventy dollars. We buy it, in spite of Ari, Gefen and Miriam's opinion that "this is highway robbery!" Maybe so, but he is an artist after all.

August 16, 17, and 18, 1982
On the Way to Florence

The drive to Florence from Venice is long but not strenuous. The landscape is breathtaking and driving into Florence we see elegant and beautiful exteriors: churches, mosaics, and marble; the interior of the Duomo; the Uffizi galleries; the Palazzo Pitti; the gardens; the David; the Pietà—riches this city possesses. The grand old synagogue is locked; we can only get glimpses through the windows because it is undergoing repairs, we are told.

Our dinners are memorable here. No one will forget the elegant torte decorated with thinly shaved chocolate swirls and chocolate whipped cream at La Zia Rosa restaurant. That night the kids are looking for adventure and improvisation. They want to visit some bars or coffee houses to hear some good music and singing, but Wally thinks we have to retire early. It has been a long day. The conflict here is mostly between father and son. The way I see it, Ari is saying it's time for some excitement and independent exploration. Two weeks of non-stop togetherness is more than any young person should be expected to abide by, and that holds probably for Gefen and Miriam as well.

But our villa-hotel in Florence brings smiles to our faces.

The place is a dream: spacious, almost regal, with columns at every entrance, and a balcony, overlooking the gardens and the pool, just hangs there; no stairs that lead up to it, and none that lead down either. It hangs there, apparently "just for fun"; which reminds me of Tevye's song "If I Were a Rich Man" in *Fiddler on the Roof.* We feel enriched indeed. It is beautiful here, the landscape, the vegetation, the surroundings, and all. But I sense a strong undertow steadily moving into me; it is a reminder of our experience in Florence, in March or April of 1944 when we were held up in Florence, Mother, Gitta and I, because the train tracks had been bombarded and we had nowhere to go. The people at Andreina's had been talking about roundups that took place that took place in 1943 when we were in the mountains in Andreina's *cava*. The Germans turned on the Jews in Milan, Turin, Venice, Genoa, Florence and more. And in Rome the roundups were bestial.[20] We did not know what all was happening, but discovered later the tragedies that befell the Jews. Our luck was that we were hidden in Andreina's *cava* and we were spared the multiple disasters that took place, yet, I never cease to ask, "What if?

Thursday, August 19, 1982
From Florence through Siena to Rome

It is unbearably hot as we enter the car but the drive to Siena is hilly and a gentle breeze breaks up the heat. I think we might be tiring of our intense visits. Some of us complain of digestive problems. Wally says it all comes from eating unwashed fruit; and I do believe that he is right. At about 3 pm we enter Rome and find our hotel, La Residenza; we lucked out again: the place is a bit like an apartment hotel with air conditioning, a veranda, and plenty of room. We want to take in the sights before evening and so we walk to the Piazza del Popolo. Rome's buildings are dark, blackened by soot; they look old and dingy. On the walls of many buildings there are enormous graffiti, but the city is less noisy than I expected, and there is less traffic than I thought there would be. Rome is friendlier than Paris, but also dirtier. In Rome you feel that the architectural splendors have been left alone, in benign neglect. In Paris the carelessness feels more like French smugness.

After a long walk, hot and exhausted we return to our hotel, to eat and sleep in our rooms. The air conditioning had broken down.

Friday, August 20, 1982
Rome: The Vatican

We face another very hot day. Breakfasts are great: Gefen found the most delicious fresh fruit, blue and green figs, peaches, and apricots galore. We visit the Vatican, the Pietà, the Sistine Chapel, and the Musei Vaticani. We rest and have lunch in a restaurant close to the Vatican. Then we decide to walk over to the Convent of the Dorothean Sisters and the School of the Dorothei, on Via Sant'Onofrio, 26, where Gitta and I stayed for three months in 1944, until the June 4 liberation.

Walking in, I remember the rotund entry hall and beyond it the garden. I am eager to see the Chapel, the glass case under the altar in which the Beata Dorothea's body was encased in an oxygen-free space. I also think about the confessions booth. The Mother Superior greets us; she is in her late eighties and hails from Naples. She is not the one who knew me back then, thirty-eight years ago. I am told that the other Mother Superior was placed in another convent a few years ago. The new Mother Superior is tiny, thin, short, and kind. She treats me like one of her students. She directs me to turn on the lights on the side of the altar, and I oblige. Wally and the kids are astonished, perhaps shocked, by my familiarity and apparent ease. Am I really at ease here? Or am I comfortable because I feel sheltered by my family? I am sure it is the latter. So, I performed. The old nun shows us around and I help her up the stairs. She is in her eighties after all. She asks if we are Catholic and I say, "No." She says, "I thought you had converted, no?" I reply, "We did not convert. You protected us when we needed you in 1944 and for this

we were grateful; because of you, we were able to remain *Ebrei.*"
Our Mother Superior did not give up easily. "But the Catholic religion sprung forth from the Hebrews," she says, "so, why didn't you
just you go along with the Catholics and continue to develop, and
accept *Gesù?*" I laugh and hug her; I tell her there is room for both
religions in this world. She shakes her head. Now she is critical of
Sharon and Begin and their actions in Lebanon. "And so are we," I
say. Then, she says, "How many million Jews are there in the world?
By my count there must be fifteen million."

I wondered about the flow of her associations. What was she
thinking? If fifteen million Jews converted, there would be that
many more Catholics in the world? Or worse, in spite of their destruction during the war, those Jews are still so stubborn and out-
spoken? Or is she thinking, how long will you *Ebrei* hold out?

The Mother Superior asks, "Do your children speak Italian?"
"No," I say, "They speak Hebrew and some French. But I do hope
that someday they will want to learn Italian; it is a beautiful language." She does not understand. She may be wondering, "How
could this nice little Italian-speaking novice be so different from me?
What went wrong here?" Clearly her questions stir me up and our
young people appear to be uncomfortable as well. They do not understand the language but they understand the melody.

Eventually, we take our leave. In the evening we have supper
with American friends. It is a nice break.

Saturday, August 21, 1982

We visit the Colosseum, the Forum, and the Moses in St. Peter's
Church. A torrential downpour catches up with us in the Forum. We
are soaked by the time we arrive at the Moses.

Sunday, August 22, 1982

We visit the old Jewish synagogue, the museum, and the old Jewish streets behind the synagogue. According to Zuccotti, "at least 1,700 Jews were deported during the brief nine months of occupation."[21] The Jews in Rome seem frightened today. They recall World War II unwillingly; the conversion to Catholicism of Rabbi Israel Zolli, the Chief Rabbi of Rome, in 1945, is never mentioned. We read an inscription from Isaiah on the facade of a nearby church, "You have angered your God, and I carry the anger on my forehead." Is this is the Catholic moral to us Jews?

We visit the market—it is huge but meager. Fruit is plentiful, however, and the kosher meats we bought at the Cafe de Paris suffice for our evening repast. Rome is dead. At 6:30 pm we are driven by private car to the Villa d'Este; it is closed and will reopen at 9:00 am. We walk around and see the park. Ari, Gefen and Miriam keep our spirits up as they cavort around.

The following day we leave Rome. Our trip is over.

PART III

FAMILY DIALOGUES

CHAPTER SEVEN

THE FAMILY INTERVIEWS, 2000[1]

This chapter illustrates how and why the generations in our extended family handed down stories about the war. Not only were memories preserved by way of tape recordings, family discussions, and individual diaries concerning what we experienced during the war, but also by way of asking and listening to the children in order to hear what they had absorbed and integrated, what they rejected, and in what directions their spirits have taken them in light of the baggage that was placed on their shoulders throughout their growing-up years. This chapter follows the course of select memories told by Hannah, Gitta, and Chaya, and what the children and grandchildren made of them. The memories illustrate why they shared what they did, how they sharpened their memories, corrected some, and never recovered others, in spite of the many attempts made at uncovering significant gaps.

Hannah spoke without prompts about the experiences that were central to her; the questions had not been formulated at the time, but in her associations she included her values, ideals, and beliefs as a matter of course.

Gitta and Chaya, who inherited their parents' values, clarified in the interviews their reasons for handing down their experiences.

Their children, now called the second[2] generation, born after the Holocaust, and their children, the third generation, speak clearly, addressing their parents, possibly their grandparents and great-grandparents, and most importantly their own children and those who have not yet been conceived.

The Format

Nine members of Hannah's extended family, representing three generations, explored aspects associated with memory and transmission of the Holocaust, and their values, ideals, and beliefs about the necessity of transmission to the next generation. The information was gathered in open-ended style that included semi-structured questions. A trained interviewer posed similar but not identical questions to members of all generations. (Hannah, however, spoke freely without such guided questions since she was tape-recorded at least fifteen years before the start of this project.) In the course of the interviews, questions varied from person to person, and the content reflects these differences.

In general, questions posed to the three parent generations were: what did you (as parents) want to tell your children about the Holocaust? Do you think you were successful in conveying to them what you wanted them to know? Have your memories of the Holocaust changed over the years? Have you been able to share your values, ideals, and beliefs with others, and were these in any way connected to the Holocaust?

The children, born after the Holocaust, were asked different questions, such as: when did you first hear about the Holocaust? What are some stories you remember being told? Have your parents told you how to live your life, specifically because you are a descendant of survivors? Were your values, ideals, and beliefs tied to being survivors or descendants of survivors? Did you feel you had a special inheritance that set you apart from others? How do you plan to transmit the Holocaust to your children and grandchildren?

The Family Participants

1. **Hannah** (1908–1988), first generation, adult survivor, interviewed during the years 1976–1985, between ages sixty-six and seventy-seven.
2. **Gitta** (1930–), Hannah's daughter, first generation, hidden child survivor, interviewed at age seventy.
3. **Chaya** (1934–), Hannah's daughter, first generation, hidden child survivor, interviewed at age sixty-six.
4. **Dan** (1960–), son of Gitta and Sam, second generation, interviewed at age forty.
5. **Ari** (1961–), son of Chaya and Walter, second generation, interviewed at age forty.
6. **Sasha** (1988–), daughter of Dan and C., grandchild of Sam and Gitta, third generation, interviewed at age twelve.
7. **Isabel** (1989–), daughter of Ari and Kate, grandchild of Chaya and Walter, third generation, interviewed at age eleven.

The Interviews

Hannah (1908–1988)

First Generation, Adult Survivor,
interviewed during the years 1976–1985,
between ages sixty-six and seventy-seven

How Hannah Coped with the Tragedies of the Holocaust

Like my grandfather who handled unbelievable situations in Poland in 1915 with Hindenburg and later in Berlin where he had relationships with men high up in government, I always held my head up high. I was not afraid of anyone. I knew how to handle myself with people, especially in business matters. You know, the factory was in my name and I was the one in charge and told *die Angestellte* (the employees) what to do. And because I had connections, I was able to seize all sorts of opportunities in order to save us—but I could not save Papa.

How Hannah Wanted to Preserve the Children's Identity and the Memory of Their Father

I told you after Papa was killed that you must always remember that you are Jewish, no matter what happens. "Deep down you are Jewish children," I said, "regardless of what names you carry or what religion is written on your papers, you will always be Jewish." And I told you to remember to say the *Shema* (daily prayer "Hear oh Israel") every night, just as you did with Papa when he was alive. If you do that, you will remember Papa and you will always know who you are.

Hannah Instructed the Children on How to Manage Dangerous Situations

I wanted you to know that it is important to be smart, street smart, I mean. You must listen and remember what you hear and see. You must be vigilant and you must not trust anyone, not until the person proves to you that he can be trusted. And most importantly, you must be polite and have good manners; then people will like you and will want to help you. Later, when we were running from place to place, I told you how important it is to keep yourselves clean to prevent sickness. You must always try to wash even if it means washing with snow...but you got lice anyway.

I told you that I will always try to get something for you to eat...even if it is just biscuits. And the proof is that I did; you never went hungry during the war. And Gitta was a big help to me, because she ran the errands for the family; but I gave her the money to do it.

Later, when the war was over, I told you to work hard, so you'll be successful in school. And I made sure you knew the value of money, because without money I could not have saved us.

Memory and Maintaining Good Values and Ideals Was a Daily Affair

After the war, after I brought you back from Israel, I often asked you when you came home from school, "Well, what have you learned today, and what have you done for humanity?" This was not an idle question even if it did sound a bit pretentious. And you knew what I meant. It mattered a lot that you should never forget the persecutions and that you should try to make this a better world because of what we went through.

Gitta

First Generation, Hidden Child Survivor,
Hannah's daughter, interviewed in 2000 at age seventy

What I Told My Children about the Holocaust

In the beginning I did not talk much about the war or the Holocaust. Sam and I were both hidden "children"[3] and we were too close to the war and the pain. When I talked about the war, it was in bits and pieces. But with each child—I had three—as time passed I spoke more freely. I told them incidents that happened. During the war, I was scared all the time. Because I was the big girl, I also had more obligations. And bringing food from the village or the market was one of my obligations. My experience of being lost in the mountains, losing my shoe, and almost freezing to death is a story I told often, and the children and grandchildren want to hear it time and again. The story speaks of the terrible living conditions, the fierce winter, getting lost in the mountains, giving up hope, and almost wanting to give up living at the age of thirteen. But somewhere inside me I managed to give myself one last push and I made it down that mountain. A farmer gave me shelter and brought me to a Jewish woman who was hiding in the village and she helped me to get back on my feet. That is how I made it back up the mountain to find the family and save myself. As a result of these and other experiences I see my-self as someone who can always trust herself to get things done, no matter where I am.

What I Wanted to Pass on to My Children

I tried to hand down my beliefs by setting an example: by observing the holidays, the Shabbat, going to *shul*, giving the children a Jewish education, and sending them to Hebrew school and day school, and sharing with them my love for Israel.

And deep down I think the kids are Jewishly identified; it pains me that in their actions they are not as committed to Jewish causes as I'd like them to be, but each of the children has been to Israel to study and work. Perhaps it is more difficult to commit one-self to causes these days, if only time-wise. I guess they are doing their own thing now.

What I Transmitted to My Grandchildren

I did the same thing with my grandchildren as with my children. I tried to teach them about my beliefs by setting an example. I ob-served the holidays, we baked cookies for the holidays, we observed Friday nights, we went to *shul* together, and I encouraged their par-ents to send them to [Jewish] day school or Hebrew school. My old-est granddaughter went to Israel to study and then to Poland, where she learned about the concentration camps; she also keeps a kosher house and now she studies medicine in Israel.

About the Holocaust

I had a stronger influence on the kids when it came to the Holocaust. The children know more about the Holocaust than about the practice of the Jewish religion. We commemorated *Yom HaShoah* (Holocaust Remembrance Day) and we went as a family to some of the coun-tries where we were during the war. So, yes, I can say I was successful in transmitting the Holocaust to them and also my beliefs.

Chaya

First Generation, Hidden Child Survivor,
Hannah's daughter, interviewed in 2000 at age sixty-six

What I Told My Children about the Holocaust

I had to tell my three children where I came from and about the war as soon as they were old enough to communicate in a conversation. They were very young at the time but I needed them to know me. My memories tumbled out like adventure stories in which my mother, sister, and I were able to extricate ourselves from very dangerous situations. The stories I told were tension-packed but they usually had good endings. Also, I conveyed a kind of excitement and bravery that was part of my experience as a young child. That is why, I think, these stories were so invigorating to them and to me. And the story about the roundup in Nice was one of the stories I told more often than the others: first, because I needed to talk about it and second, because they asked for it very often.

What I Wanted to Transmit to My Children

In telling the children about the Holocaust I wanted them to appreciate what courage it took to run and hide. Later, I realized that it also took courage not to run. Still, what happened to our father was difficult to accept. My mother's anger at him for not wanting to leave Berlin and not seizing the chance to emigrate from Germany to the United States also influenced how I saw my father. I saw him as a frightened man for not wanting to start a new life elsewhere. I did not recognize that staying close to Rav Itsche was also an act of bravery.

When I was seven or eight, I felt that I shouldn't have to run, hide, tell people my false name, and lie about who I am. So, I im-

pressed on my kids the importance of being vigilant about discrimination, just as my mother did. I wanted them to be ready to deal with
bad situations such as when kids in the neighborhood threatened or
harassed them (because we lived in a neighborhood that was changing rapidly). I did not want them to let things slide. "When you see
danger," I said, "you must form a plan about how to act."

Also, I wanted them to know that even one person can make
a difference in another person's life; and that during the war, my
family and I were helped by a number of people: the German officer
in La Panne who allowed our mother to buy gasoline for our trip
back to Antwerp; the Vichy officer in Périgueux, at the border between Occupied France and the Free Zone who let us pass; the Vichy officer who took me out of the barracks in Nice where Jews
were rounded up at the caserne Auvare on August 26, 1942 and then
transported to Drancy and Auschwitz; Andreina, the woman who let
us stay in her *cava* in the Alps; Don Brondello, the young assistant
priest in the parish of Valdieri, who brought us the much needed
forged papers that allowed us to leave the mountains and head to
Rome; the farmer who let Gitta sleep in his barn; the Jewish woman
who took care of Gitta's frostbitten hands and feet and fixed her
shoe; the nuns in Rome who kept us in the convent knowing or not
knowing whether we were Jews; and the German driver heading the
convoy, carrying explosives, who brought us to the outskirts of
Rome—all these individuals helped us, one way or another, and
made it possible for us to survive.

Was I Successful in Transmitting My Values?

I think the children heard me. I did not preach to them about religion, but we kept a kosher home and celebrated the holidays and the
Shabbat. We sang a lot, and there was much laughter in our house.
But I did not speak much about God. When my first-born son Ari
asked me, at age five "Mom, do you believe in God?" I told him, "I
don't know much about God, but your father will be able to tell you

better than I can because he thinks more about God than I do."

I do not pray when I go to *shul*; I go to be with my family and to feel part of the community. My husband Wally was more committed to going to *shul* than I, so the children went to synagogue with him. Often they walked to *shul* and spoke together while walking, and these were memorable walks for them. I usually joined the family midway or toward the end of services.

Although I did not preach about religion, I did pontificate about values and ideals: first, I wanted them to know that values begin at home; you apply them next to the outside world. I told them never to gang up on each other or on anyone else. And the same would have to apply for their behavior in school or in their youth organizations. I think if I transmitted anything it probably was that conflict is a normal state of affairs, and tackling conflict builds character and makes you a deeper person. When I say I preached, I mean that I was always on some bandwagon or other about values; nor did I speak softly; I tended to yell a lot at them and I also hit my children when they were small. This was not only painful for me but also humiliating for them. However, my adherence to Zionism and commitment to Israel was not a yelling matter; these were and continue to be my most positive ideals. Throughout the children's growing-up years, I was involved in working with Israel by helping with the volunteers who went over after the 1967 War; I volunteered as a psychologist in a mental hospital in Jerusalem; I taught seminars on parent-child treatment at Hebrew University and the University of Haifa; and I continue to be associated with colleagues in my field in Israel.

As for our children, they studied one year each at Hebrew University; the girls, Gefen and Miri, went there as volunteers; Gefen worked with underprivileged Jewish children, and Miri with Arab children in Nazareth. Gefen in her adult years continues to be associated with Israel projects concerning the effects of trauma during the *Intifada* (Palestinian uprising). She and her husband also visited

Israel with their young children; Miri and her husband helped found a new kibbutz in northern Israel and worked there for two years. Later, they spent a summer sabbatical in Israel, and visited the country with their young children. Ari and his wife Kate went to Tel Aviv University for one full year, where Kate was an invited scholar. Ari taught playwriting workshops in his adult years and went to Egypt to collaborate with an Egyptian playwright on Arab-Israeli relations and conflict. He now directs a Jewish theater in Washington, DC, where the works he produces draw on universal, social, and family themes, as well as Jewish- and Israel-oriented social and political conflicts. Thus, the family's involvement with Israel continues to be an active concern and has taken on new directions. Wally and I are no longer in the lead—sometimes we participate in their projects and other times we don't.

What I Told My Grandchildren

I have thought a lot about how to talk about the Holocaust to our grandchildren. The bottom line is that I didn't think that subjects of the Holocaust, religious beliefs, or Jewish values were my prerogatives to instill in them. I also worried that my own children would disapprove of my meddling. If the grandchildren wanted to know something about the Holocaust, I told them to first ask their parents. Then, when their parents wanted Wally and me to participate in sharing stories or experiences, they would turn to us and ask us to tell the children about the Holocaust, or about any topic of a historical moment.

Also, I have taken a back seat in the telling about our family's experiences during the war because I generally hold strong opinions, as do my children. And they believe that since they are the children's parents, they should be first to convey the Holocaust, their beliefs, and their values to their children. I must say that I wholeheartedly agree with them. Sure, I tell the grandkids about what happened to me during the war and I respond to their questions, but I do it carefully, because I am not sure what my children want them to know, and when. It is their parents' turn to pass on what they think the children should know and remember. And in truth, I felt some guilt about having burdened my own children with the Holocaust, especially our family's experiences, too early in their lives with insufficient consideration for their other needs. All these thoughts are hindsight. I don't think I could have done anything but what I did.

Dan

Second generation, Child of Survivors,
Gitta and Sam's son, interviewed in 2000 at age forty

When I First Heard about the Holocaust

I first heard about the Holocaust in my preschool years. The story I remember best is about my mother getting stuck in the mountains without her boot. I heard about my grandmother, Hannah too, who was the leader and saved them all in escaping the Nazis.

My mother was fairly talkative with me, more than with my older brother and sister. She told me things in the car because I was the youngest; when she drove me to school we usually were alone in the car. When I was about eight or nine years old, she told me about her father being beaten to death in a concentration camp. Then, she told me how her mother paid a smuggler to take her and her sister across the borders to Belgium; she had to take care of her little sister even though she herself was only nine years old.

My grandmother told many stories when she came to visit us from Belgium, but my father did not speak much, not about the war and not about most things; he was quite reticent in general. His family suffered a great deal toward the end of the war. He and his brother were caught trying to escape in the last roundup in Belgium. His father, mother, and sister were caught too. My father was brutally beaten when he was interrogated; as a result he lost his hearing in one ear. His father was also beaten so that he had to be hospitalized when Belgium was liberated. His mother's face and eye were bashed in. His brother was interrogated, tortured, and beaten to death. His sister was totally traumatized, and we don't know to this day what happened to her. She is a total recluse now; even though she is still highly intelligent, she has been a recluse for most of her life since the war ended.

They were all going to be put on the next train to Auschwitz, but the day after they were caught the war came to an end. So, part of my growing up was to face up to my father and discover who he was and what the cause of his enormous pain was.

My mother's purpose in telling us about the war was to educate us, to share with us her experiences, and to make sure we follow a certain path; that is, she was totally wrapped around being observant of the Sabbath, the holidays, praying, and remembering those who died.

Another source of education was our Jewish day school toward which I had very angry feelings. Growing up, I felt isolated from my classmates. In those days no one seemed to be interested in hearing that I was the son of two survivors. Not even the teachers. And when I told them that I am the child of survivors, they said, "Oh yeah?" I blame the teachers for not helping me then to bring this out. I felt isolated from the kids and vulnerable, and I was a pretty shy kid. I also had a fear that anti-Semitism could crop up here too. But at the same time, I was amazed that I'm able to breathe in this world considering the infinitesimal odds against which my parents made it. Then, when I entered high school, I asked my mother to tell me again some of the stories she had told me before because I wanted to put them in a broader context. And she did.

Did My Parents Talk to Me about Jewish Values, Religion?

Yes, all the time. My mother was big on Jewish values, observing the laws, such as the laws of *kashrut* (the dietary laws), but not so much on God. I had to discover for myself about the war, so I went back to Europe, to Dachau, and to Israel and Ben Shemen where my mother and my aunt were after the war. I learned about the Holocaust, the statistics, how many Jews died where; I read Elie Wiesel's books and others. I did not pursue further Jewish studies but I took a course on the Holocaust with Wiesel at Boston University.

Did the Holocaust Experience Help Me Identify as a Jew?

I'd say quite a bit. No one came to our help from the secular world or the Gentile world, no one really tried to understand what it was like, to be born here, but to feel like an outsider. Now, as a lawyer, I think our system of government works: the Constitution, the justice system, free speech amendment, they all work. But there is racism, anti-Semitism, hatred, and bigotry here. And yes, I feel vulnerable. There is an element of danger in our society these days and it upsets me.

I was happy when my kids took up karate. But when they started sparring, I didn't want them to continue, so I asked myself do I have to train my children to become warriors? Having said that, my best experience about being Jewish, Israel-oriented, Holocaust-oriented and civil liberties-oriented came from being at camp. It was a joyous experience to learn and be with people who enjoy life, who are energetic and idealists, and I felt that I was one of them.

What I Want to Pass on to My Children

I want them to learn history and I want to pass on my mother's and father's stories during the war, because their stories are not at all similar. I read stories to the children about other people during the Holocaust. I also want them to learn Hebrew and to have their Bar and Bat Mitzvahs for which they have tutors, but no Jewish day school for them!

Did I Ever Want to Turn Away from the Burden of Remembering?

Yes, I did. I don't want to deny the past, but I don't want to be burdened by it always or to foist it on my children. I also married a woman who is idealistic. She loves life, children, sports, and she simplifies living. No guilt hovering over us there; and she is a wonderful mother and mate. She is really American-born and her parents are of English descent. She came into my life like a breath of fresh air. For her, family is a place where you can let your hair down and be accepted one hundred percent, unconditionally; that certainly was not true in my family.

Ari

Second Generation, Child of Survivors,
Chaya and Wally's son, interviewed in 2000 at age forty

When I First Heard about the Holocaust

I first heard about the Holocaust when I was playing in the bathtub and my mother told me stories about the war. We also heard stories around the dinner table or in the car. I heard about Germany, Belgium, Dunkirk, France, Italy, and Palestine. I remember stories of my mom as a young girl doing something heroic, defying a police officer, being held in police barracks and crying, screaming until she was finally let go. I remember hearing of my grandmother finding a can of peaches in Dunkirk during a bombing and giving it to my mother and aunt.

But these are so many half stories, bits and pieces. Then, my mother would stop and say, "OK, time to get out of the bath now," or "Tomorrow is another day." Or, when we'd arrive at school, she'd say, "Time to go to class now, we'll continue later." And later might be tomorrow or another day. These were half stories delivered to children: stories about the Vatican, the convent, the Alps, Nice; but not whole stories, just episodes. Also, there were stories about her father who was killed in a concentration camp with different versions about how he died.

Later, when we were in college and my youngest sister was finishing high school, our family went back to Europe, in 1982; our parents wanted to show us where they came from, and my dad and mom filled in the gaps with history of the war. I too filled the gaps by writing a number of fictionalized pieces about my mom and her family's experiences; and sometimes, what I wrote and what she told me merged in my mind. But it allowed me to give a structure to the stories she told and to put them in a larger context.

Did my parents tell us about the Holocaust?
Did they share their values, ideals, and religion with us?

Of course they did. Inculcating us with the Holocaust, with who we are, were ongoing efforts on my mother's part. You wear a part of an army uniform, just the pants, mind you, and she'd say: "No son of mine is going to wear army pants in school!" Her mantra was, "You are children of refugees and you are not free to behave any which way." My mother never used the word survivors, only refugees. When I was younger, I felt different from everyone else in my school. I felt like I was cut off from the others, so I struggled to break out from that view of myself with the help of my teachers and friends. Later, I rebelled, and it came down to my having to assert myself and spell out to my mother that there are radical differences between us. She was the different one, she was the survivor refugee; but we were Jewish-American kids and she'd have to live with that difference.

But in truth, we were not only different from other Jews; we were different from other survivors. Both our mother and father were orphaned, having only one living parent from the time they were both five. So whereas other survivors were really wounded orphans, our parents were only "wounded refugees." And we were the children of refugees. That meant we had to have the tenacity to survive because they had, but we weren't really the children of survivors, only of refugees. Still their pain was that of people who survived the Holocaust.

My mother made it to Palestine with her sister after the war, and then she immigrated to the United States in 1953. So we went to Israel many times, to visit, study, and work, first as a family, and then on our own.

She went to school here, got a PhD (wrote the shortest dissertation ever at the university), and became a psychologist. And my dad, who had immigrated with his family to the States in 1938, went to law school, graduated second or third in his class, and became an attorney. So, there was much to live up to. Sure, we thought our family was special, but that specialness also set us apart. And by the way, we weren't always treated by the outside world as though we were special. So that's where the discrepancy came in: when you are the inheritor of this history you can feel like the owner of something that is terribly profound and you have a job to do, a mission. But that's a difficult road to embark on and find happiness in.

You know, for my mother, family is the most important thing in her life. There is nothing more important. And her children are an important source of company and companionship. She didn't want to raise strangers; she wanted to raise people who are familiar to her. Early on, during our childhood, her stories were exhilarating, tragic, triumphant, and exciting. But stories evolve in time, so, as we grew older, my mother grew older, and we got to know our mother and her pains in a deeper way. And when we realized that we had created myths based on her earliest experiences, we became free.

Still, there was much joy in our life; we observed the holidays, we sang, we went to *shul* with my father—Mom usually came late. We played hard, and my mother was my first guitar teacher. My sisters and I went to a good camp; I was very much out there and had good friends. And our day school experience was a good one too. My father was the chairman of the school board, and I was one of the first kids who attended that school from kindergarten on. In short, I felt that I belonged and I felt good about our life.

Did My Family's Holocaust Experience
Help Me to Identify as a Jew?

For me, the Holocaust as I experienced it through my mother and father, and our day school, and Israel, and Jewish history, and Jewish religion are all part of my Jewish identity. My father, we had to draw out, but eventually he did tell us about his life in his village in Germany and the people he lost. My mother, she just told us, "This, I want you to know" and then she'd tell us one story or another. And then, there was this whole Israel bit, she wanted to go on *aliyah* (immigration to Israel), and we all went to Israel many times. Finally I said, "OK, enough now; my life must go forward."

Then I met a wonderful woman who spoke many languages (Slavic languages), had lived in Japan when she was seven, and her father was a journalist, her mother too; they were anticonventional; and they did not need their children to do or be anything in particular; and so, my wife Kate is the most supportive person for me and my career. I don't have to be anyone special for her; she is very accomplished herself, but life is not as heavy for her as it was for me. And I cherish her for all that she is. She is not the Jewish guilt type, she has fewer inhibitions; she does what feels good. I deliberate: I want this, but I hold on to the past; I obsess and feel guilty, but still I want to be free. And Kate says: "Let's do this! Let's celebrate! Let's not wait. I want it now!!" She was the right choice for me. I needed her; but I didn't need her temper; hers is just like my mother's!

What I Want to Transmit to My Children

Of course I told my girls about the Holocaust! I was raised on my mother's stories. But do I speak about the Holocaust at the breakfast table, in the car, or at dinner like my mother did? Of course not! There is homework to be discussed, after-school lessons, my own work, and my wife's work to attend to; plus the fact that my wife does not want to place that much emphasis on the Holocaust in our lives.

Well, they have gotten the comprehensive treatment: my mother's stories and my father's, the history of the Holocaust, the war, but not enough. I have not taken them to the Holocaust Museum yet; I believe there is still time for that. They'll get it; it's in the air. They know it's coming, but you'll never hear me say to my children, "You are the grandchild of a child survivor!" In conversations with my cousin, he and I agreed on this: we were all wounded by our parents' inability to give us their unconditional love and to express it fully. As parents, they were not as good as we are because they were so hurt—and we were the lucky ones.

Sasha

Third Generation, Grandchild of Survivors,
Dan and C.'s daughter, interviewed in 2000 at age twelve

What I Know about the Holocaust

We haven't talked about the Holocaust that much but my grandmother would tell me about how her father had gotten killed or how Grandpa Sam's brother got killed, but I don't remember talking about it until a few years ago. I just don't know. I guess I was about seven when I first heard.

Specifically I didn't hear much, just that my great-grandfather was taken away and was killed.

My grandma talked a little about what happened to her, such as when she was nine and her sister was five she was almost like a mother to Chaya because there was no one else. And our great-grandmother did not want to wear the yellow star that they were ordered to wear. And for a while she was separated from her mom, only she and her sister left Germany, without their mother, with a smuggler. I think I was about five when she told me that. And it felt kind of strange hearing the stories from my grandmother, because until then I only heard about the Holocaust in books that my dad read to me, and I never thought about those stories as real. But my grandma never told me about her father. Actually, it was probably my mom or dad who told me that Grandma's father was killed, and things like that. You know, I was about seven when my parents talked about things like that.

But I know nothing about concentration camps. Well, I know that the Nazis came and they took many Jews to the concentration camps. I don't know much about that except that many people were killed there. It seems like such a long time ago. But my dad did read to me *The Upstairs Room* by Johanna Reiss at bedtime; actually he just stopped reading to me last year. He read me these stories about people hiding in attics or basements so no one could find them. And then in most of the stories the people stayed alive, except in this one their entire families were killed, and their parents too, because they did not go into hiding.

My dad read to me and I liked that, but he did not read that many Holocaust stories. Those stories were interesting because they were just fiction. But then I found out that such things actually did happen to people. I read a little of Anne Frank but I didn't finish it— it was so sad. My grandma told me things when the other children were out of the room, how she had to take care of her sister, about the people in concentration camps who were suffering, and how badly they were treated. I never saw movies about the Holocaust. And my Hebrew tutor never brought up the Holocaust. I was just learning Hebrew. So most of what I learned about the Holocaust was in our family.

What I Will Tell My Children about the Holocaust

When I marry and have kids, I want to raise them to observe the holidays, maybe not like my grandma so much, but close. And I will teach my children about the Holocaust. I will tell them about my grandma and Aunt Chaya, and I'll read books to them too like my dad did to me because I would want them to know what our family went through and what it was like.

And I would tell them about my father too. How he was raised very religious just the same as my grandmother, but then he met the woman he loved, my mom, and she was not religious, so they had to do a lot of compromising. So sometimes he and my grandma would argue that he is not religious enough and not teaching us enough.

Do I Talk with My Friends about the Holocaust?

You know, I never talk to my friends about people who were in the Holocaust. And I don't think it is important to do so.

Do I Feel more Jewish Because of
What I Know about Our Family?

Well, I'm not really sure. But I know that my grandma is really into being religious and having a Jewish family. Because she lost people in her family it is real important to her that we are Jewish and celebrate the Jewish holidays, and that we remember the people who died. I never thought about it that much, but my mom explained to me why Grandma is so into religion. We never talked about this so much until my mom told me about this interview.

So we go to her house for Shabbat and she takes us to synagogue every Saturday. I know that she really cares about that. She wants to fill us with Jewishness because our family is really not as religious as all that. But I think that it's nice that she is, because we learn a lot of things about the holidays and why they are important.

Sometimes I feel sad for my grandma because her dad died. If my dad died it would be terrible to grow up for the rest of your life without a dad. And then sometimes she wouldn't get to see her mom because she had to hide. That must have been pretty hard.

I also remember my great-grandmother. I don't know what she was really like because I was just born, and then a year later she died, but she was very protective of her children; she did not let them wear the Jewish star; she did not want them to act like they were Jewish; well, she did not want them to be caught by the Nazis for wearing a Jewish star. I heard stories from Chaya; when she was little and how they captured her, and she screamed she was not Jewish, and finally, because they couldn't control her they let her go. My grandmother told me that story. Then, a few months ago, maybe in preparation for this interview, my grandmother told me how her father died in a concentration camp. I didn't know that until a few months ago.

And from all that I learned how not to treat other people badly just because of their race or religion. My mom taught me that, and I feel that I am a little more open-minded because of what I learned about the Holocaust.

Would I Like to Learn More about the Holocaust?

Yes, I would. I'd like to read more books, but I've never really looked at anything and I'd like to know a little bit more.

Isabel

Third Generation, Grandchild of Survivors,
Ari and Kate's daughter, interviewed in 2000 at age eleven

What Do I Know about the Holocaust?

I first heard about the Holocaust when I was in my old day school in Michigan, and I was six years old in first grade. I didn't know much except for lighting six candles for six million Jews. By third grade I heard about Hitler and that kind of stuff. But when I think of it, I really started to hear about the Holocaust when I was with my grandma Chaya when I was five or six. I'm a big eavesdropper and so I listen to adult conversations and heard when she would be talking to Mom or Dad, or my other grandparents.

A book I read recently that made a very big impression is *The Devil's Arithmetic* by Jane Yolen, and I really understood the girl and what she went through; and I learned about the camps, even though nobody believed her, and the "showers" meaning the gas, and the numbers, the tattooed numbers. And the girl did not understand, she thought it was crazy. And I was experiencing the book and her very much.

Did My Parents Talk to Me about the Holocaust?

They did not talk to me about the Holocaust until I was in third grade, and never in a discussion like this. My parents talked to me about the Holocaust as history of our people. And I overheard one of the stories about my grandma who was caught and screamed and yelled until they let her go. And this guy slapped her and pushed her and said go in this line, and I believe it was the hand of God. I don't know very much more; but I know that they hid in the Alps and my grandma's mother Hannah was like their savior, always knowing when to run away. I'd like to ask more, but I'm afraid to because when we see each other it's always when we visit them or they visit us and why talk about scary stuff then?

I know about my grandfather's stepmother, my great-grandma, and there is a picture where she walks with a cane and I hold her hand; I was about three then and I couldn't believe that it was me with her. And when she died we heard stories about her in Germany.

About my great-grandfather, all I know is that he was a tailor, or was it my mother's father? It gets confusing. But he died, I think in a camp. I do remember that my grandma Chaya was caught in France with her second father and they both went to a place from where he was put on a train to Auschwitz, and she was very lucky; she was freed by a police captain, and then she went into hiding and everyone was very lucky to have survived in hiding.

About Me and the Holocaust

I feel kind of special that my family survived; many of my friends also have grandparents who survived, but a lot of people didn't. Sometimes I think that if my family hadn't survived I wouldn't be here but more often I think, "Whoa, I'm a person and I'm Isabel, I don't have to worry about every little thing, if my homework isn't done yet, if my girlfriend has a birthday and I didn't make a birthday sign yet; I can still go to school." I mean sometimes I just say, "I exist and that's pretty amazing, and I was formed inside someone's body!"

I have a pile of books on the Holocaust, but I don't think I read many so far. And I have some friends whose grandparents were in concentration camps, but none died. My grandma Toni (Wally's mother) lost everyone in the Holocaust, and my grandmother (Chaya) and her sister lost their father and their stepfather. And Hitler committing suicide, I think he committed suicide out of guilt that he killed so many millions. It's too much guilt I think for such a man, so he had to kill himself.

Also, I saw pictures of the Holocaust and the camps. People in the camps were like dead looking, but I have not been to any museums; my parents say, "Next year." But I've heard a lot about the Holocaust Museum and the shoe room; that is so sad. And I know about the passports you share with a person who was killed. I also saw *The Sound of Music* a zillion times.

And it's interesting as a Jew: I'm going to Jewish school, and all I hear about is the millions of Jews who were killed. But then I learned it was much more than the Jews who were killed; the war was a terrible thing for everybody. I think the war went on from 1936–1937 to 1945, I think. And then came the State of Israel, I think in 1948; but the fight for a Jewish State, it really started much earlier, like in the 1920s or 1930s.

What do I remember about Israel? I was about two or three when we lived there for a year. And I went to nursery school and I hated my teacher; she was really mean. But I remember candy tooth-brushes, Bamba, and Bisli, like curly noodles?

But I don't think about the Holocaust so much; I think about how people—survivors—manage to live now, and life is a little eas-ier for them now. I don't know if that relates directly to the Holo-caust but maybe indirectly, yes.

Will I Teach My Children about the Holocaust Someday?

Well yes, but I'd like them to read a book first, or something like that. I'd introduce them to a novel or something that would have to do with the Holocaust or the whole World War story. Have them get curious first, and then tell them. Not out of the blue, Ah well you know the war? And blah blah blah blah happened. And then, I think they would ask me questions; only then would I talk about the Holo-caust in our family. I think, I'm saying that the Holocaust you must want to learn about it, and then I will tell them. I think it would be weird if they didn't ask. But if they don't ask and they're old enough, then, I think I would tell them. But I would want to intrigue them before I tell them; I wouldn't force it on them.

Did I Ever Feel That the Holocaust Was Forced on Me?

No, not really. It all depends on your maturity. Are you ready for this? It's like going to the Holocaust Museum, am I ready for this?

What Part I'd Tell the Children

I'd tell them the larger history of the Holocaust first. And then I would tell them about my family because otherwise the children wouldn't understand why people in our family were picked up, why they had to hide, why some were killed in concentration camps. And they wouldn't understand that the same thing happened to other Jewish people too. I'd want them to see the bigger picture first, and then tell them about our family, so they won't be shocked. And I'd tell them this when they are about in third grade, like I was, or maybe in second grade, I'm not sure about that.

The truth is I feel kind of special that my family survived but I have to remember that many of my friends also have grandparents who survived; and then, many millions didn't.

♦♦♦ Discussion ♦♦♦

Memory, Legacy, Psychological Trauma, and Existential Vitality

Primo Levi[4] sees memory as a gift. It is our duty to cultivate our memories and not to let them fade away or go to ruin, he says. And he urges us not to lose the ability to store new memories. By storing new memories he means that life must go on. I believe that Levi means that the aim of preserving the memories of the Holocaust is for survivors and their descendants to integrate the past with the present so as to create new experiences that can be remembered. J. K. Roth[5] speaks of the preservation and nurturing of memories. He writes that while "memories can blur and decay...become selective, stylized, embellished and influenced by later experiences...repressed, denied and falsified, they can [also] be sharpened, recorded, intensified, documented and even corrected."

What then Is the Legacy of the Holocaust?

One way of viewing the legacy of the Holocaust is that it is an evolving, nonlinear, and multifaceted process, meaning that what is transmitted is done indirectly and what the listeners hear and absorb is unpredictable. A linear view on transmission is similar to the ways a museum, an archive, or a reference book transmits information about past events: namely, with visible objects, accurate descriptions, scores of documents, and immutable timetables. To the extent that anything is only more or less predictable, this linear manner of absorbing information is partially predictable. Human thinking and actions, however, tend to be affected by multiple processes, both linear and continuously evolving transformations. What descendants of survivors and child survivors have absorbed from their elders and then have handed down to their children cannot even be guessed at. In order to know the nature of such transmission there is only one thing to do: it is to listen to the remaining survivors, to hear what they think they told their children; and to listen to the children and hear what they say they were told, what they are transmitting to their children, and what these children in turn plan to tell their children in the future. Then, having heard and listened, we still cannot be sure about the underlying content of what has been transmitted. In general, we tend to speak of handing down memories of the Holocaust and sharing our experiences in a straightforward manner; we expect that our offspring will have heard what we have conveyed; that they will remember and will then continue to transmit the legacy they have received together with what they experienced as children of survivors. What the unconscious processes do with our memories is another matter altogether, and one that, as a mother of children speaking in these interviews, I cannot address.

I began telling the children what happened to my family during the war when they were quite young (each between the ages of four to six). My purpose was to help the children to get to know me just as I was getting to know them. I told them where I was born, what the meaning of my name was, and how I came to the United States. I told them various stories that spoke about the war when I was a year or two older than they were at the time. These stories were substitutes for the fairytales they later would hear.

Looking back, at first I thought of our Holocaust legacy as a bequest of significant memories (rescued objects, letters, poems, and photographs), and most importantly, of values and ideals that we and other parents who survived want to hand down to their children. I thought that in imparting our values and ideals, our memories and experiences with fervor and truth, the memory of our experiences would be available for retrieval to our children and to the children's children forever.

But as the years went by, I learned that memory of the Holocaust is not a static phenomenon. The stories that parents and grandparents tell their offspring are not necessarily accepted as givens. Rather, our children hear our stories through their respective and unique modes of perception. While they appear to take in what they are told, in the process of becoming youths, young adults, and parents themselves, they bring their specific styles of thinking to remembering and telling about the Holocaust that are consistent with the inner workings of their minds. These are not mere repetitions of what they heard, but rather of what they thought they understood.

I learned to appreciate that our children complemented the knowledge they gathered from us with information from other sources, such as friends, teachers, rabbis, schools, colleges, universities, synagogues, and communities, as well as through books, museums, archives, artistic presentations, plays, movies, classes, workshops, videotaped interviews with survivors and their children, conferences, and the like.

Thus, Holocaust legacy, linear or developmentally ongoing, shows infinite evolution with unpredictable and random input from outside sources. Reciprocal feedback between the survivors and their children also contributes to the amalgam of influences that give meaning to the concept of Holocaust legacy. But there is more.

According to systems theory,[6] communication is governed by two principles: transactionalism and feedback. The moment a narrative is offered by a teller to a listener's ear, not only is the teller transformed by the act of the telling but also the narrative itself is transformed through that same act of the telling. As such, the principle of transactionalism is applicable to understanding how the legacy of the Holocaust is transmitted and that is what makes Holocaust legacy unpredictable and random.

In our families, Gitta's and mine, we shared our memories with our children. Told by two forceful women, our sons understood the moral of our stories as directives. "This, I want you to know," Ari remembers Chaya (me) saying. The directives were, "You shall not forget!" "It is your duty to remember who you are and what happened to our family." Ari reflects that, "this is a difficult road to embark on and find happiness in."

What our children, and we as parents, had to confront was how to transmit our memories. For Hannah transmission was clear and to the point: in order to survive you must do such and such. There is no evidence of hesitation; these are times of war and there is only one agenda: we must save our lives. For Gitta the dominant purpose was to be a dependable and consistent role model, carrier of the faith, transmitter of the Holocaust, and a committed Zionist. For me, "go tell it to the children" has been an oft-repeated refrain; I meant that the children must know everything that we know, but not all at the same time. Such an agenda is not a simple affair. To know one's family history is the conduit to understanding the history of the war and the Holocaust. Gitta and I, I believe, did mark our sons, Dan and Ari, with our cornerstone value: they must remember the Holocaust and must undertake the mission to transmit it for future generations. Each of our descendants knows some of our stories, including our mother's, if not in fully formed themes, then in part. However, they show clear resistance to forging their individual paths with these memories alone. All expressed hesitancy at going on with this unidimensional transmission of the Holocaust. They all stated, one way or another, that they must enlarge on the Holocaust transmission and broaden the scope of their commitments, values, and ideals, to reach not only the Jewish communities, but also the multi-ethnic communities that suffer under the impact of ethnic discrimination, wars, disease, hunger, and more.

Psychological Trauma and Existential Vitality

Psychological trauma and pain, intentionally inflicted, can cause unexpected, humiliating, shameful and unacceptable gashes to the human spirit. But psychological trauma and pain do not nullify existential vitality. Scholars of the Holocaust elaborate on these experiences. (See Sigal;[7] Ornstein;[8] Bar-On;[9] T. Des Pres;[10] Fogelman.[11]) Danieli[12] summarizes the issues succinctly, maintaining that in the course of the most abysmal living conditions human beings manifest an ongoing and unpredictable inner interplay between the pangs of trauma and the uncanny strengths for regeneration of personal inner reserves.

In the beginning, when the children were young, Gitta and I chose to talk about those experiences that showed us grappling courageously and with great cunning with difficult situations. We told our children, like so many survivors have told theirs, that they too should be prepared to face tough moments as they grew up and that being smart and streetwise is an important survival skill. But for good measure, each of us also tried to reassure the children that here in America, they will never face persecution.

Later, our stories changed. We experienced more pain, and I, who was always the more verbal part of our sisterly dyad, became more reticent and despondent too. As a by-product of my psychoanalytic treatment, I became depressed. And while that was painful for me, it was helpful for the children because it enabled them to identify themselves as individuals in their own right, to distinguish themselves from us, and to attend to the many tasks that growing up demanded of them. They were grateful for the distance with which my sadness enveloped me. Consequently, they did not feel incessantly subjected to the intrusiveness of my stories and my demands. Later, when the children became young adults and parents themselves, they became interested in reexploring our early narratives and discarding from my imposed baggage what they thought was ripe for disposal.

Hannah, who survived the war, amply demonstrates that psychic trauma does not vitiate spiritual vitality. Hannah appears to be strong when she is first described. She is learned, has a wealthy background; she knows how to behave in society and is savvy with financial matters. She experiences severe trauma with the murder of her spouse and is temporarily incapacitated (physically blinded due to psychological trauma), requiring a period of intense care and recuperation. She separates from her children, sends them away to temporary safety, and after considerable difficulties, succeeds in reuniting with them. From then on, she is back on her feet and manages the family with uncanny foresight, if not intuition, and with competence. Still the shock and misery of having been truncated from her husband never vanishes. When she remarries and suffers a second tragic loss, she pulls herself together and saves the family by crossing the Alps and finding the means for the next necessary escape.

After the war, however, as we separate from her, attempting to forge our own way in the world, she becomes painfully depressed. The depressions are cyclical and intermittent, and Gitta and I, living in the United States, must fly over to Belgium to attend to her and support her toward a more positive outlook in her daily functioning.

Gitta and I each demonstrate that psychic trauma and existential vitality can be contained in one and the same individual. Two little girls on the run, we had suffered the death of our father and separation from our mother, escaped to new places and new schools, and we showed the effects of psychic trauma. Gitta, lost in the mountains, is ready to give up and almost gives in to the torpor that sets in before her body begins to freeze. Yet she emerges from the episode on the mountain, after a powerfully treacherous struggle with nature and her own feeling of vulnerability, strong, capable, and able to "manage just about anything." For Gitta, being in control of a difficult situation becomes a distinctive aspect of her character.

I come away from the roundup barracks feeling deep guilt and conflict. My mind does not want to remember how my step-father and I were separated and why I ended up alone in a hallway with all the Jewish detainees. I am overcome with panic at being separated from my stepfather; I am terrified that I may never see my mother or sister again. But I also realize that I only succeeded in "saving myself" because a compassionate stranger gave me a help-ing hand. This painful experience together with the gratitude I felt for the Vichy *gendarme* prompted the vow I made shortly after I was reunited with my family in the hiding-apartment in Nice, on rue Tra-chel. When I grow up, I vow, I will help little children and prevent them from being subjected to the type of persecution and pain that I have experienced.

Dan and Ari absorb Gitta's and my anguish and daring, and in the process they inherit both: anguish and daring. In school, they feel like outsiders. They both manifest that they are capable of ener-getic coping, but they also realize that they come by their feelings of "alienation" honestly. Dan struggles because of his double in-heritance: his father's torture and wounds that led to silence and failure to communicate with the family. Ari says that he "stepped out" of his feelings of estrangement by actively striving to be "out there in sports, music, friends, and studies," and by looking up to his father, a refugee, as a role model of leadership. Dan finds joy, ex-citement, and acceptance in a Jewish youth group where he is among friends with whom he shares socialist ideals and Zionism, songs and sports. But he does not feel free to be himself until he discovers the truth about his father's story.

The boys grow up to be men; they are professionally accom-plished and they married women who do not impose agendas on them; they have children, and they are devoted parents, and withal are caring and empathic sons. But Dan and Ari agree, "We are all wounded by our parents' inability to give us their unconditional love and to express it fully." Dan was hurt by his father's silence, Ari by my invasiveness and his father's reticence. "Don't ever forget that you are the son of refugees!" still rings in his ears. Most children of survivors remember their parents' stories only in bits and pieces, says Danieli,[13] and Ari brings this up in his discussion as well.

Sasha and Isabel are awed by the realization that they would never have been born if their grandmothers had not survived. This frightful feeling has stayed with them; it only takes the barest of allusions to the Holocaust for that realization to return. The girls feel for their grandmothers' experiences, but they do not relish lingering on those memories. It is interesting that Sasha recalls the intimacy with her father's reading of Holocaust stories and wants to introduce her future children to the Holocaust with a similar approach. And after that she wants to pass on to her children the Holocaust stories her grandma told her. However, she comments, she does not speak about the Holocaust and her family's participation in it to anyone. It is not important for them to know that, she says.

Isabel sets forth an entire curriculum for introducing the Holocaust to her future children: she wants to expose them to the Holocaust gradually. First, she intends to focus on history of World War II, next on the Holocaust as it happened to others, and only after they know the larger picture, will she tell the children that her family too endured significant losses and dangerous situations during the Holocaust. Finally, she would have her children learn that the war damaged and killed many more millions of non-Jewish people than the six million Jews who perished. She attempts to provide a broader view of the appalling consequences of World War II without minimizing the tragedy of the Holocaust.

Final Remarks

It is true that we, Hannah's daughters, have veered away little from our values and ideals. We tell our stories, study the history of the Holocaust, engage in teaching the history of the Holocaust to current generations of children, and record survivors' memories. Our family has honored an Italian priest who helped saved our lives and we participated in the process that would enable Yad Vashem to recognize this gentle priest as one of the Righteous Among the Nations. All twenty-five children and grandchildren, from age fifty-three down to age four, participated in the ceremony in Cuneo, Italy and spoke of it as a culminating and unforgettable experience.

Our children are in the helping, teaching, legal, medical, and playwriting professions. They have expanded, however, on Gitta's and my ideals: they are politically, psychologically, and educationally more active than either of us are, and they actively face the current challenges that emerge in Israeli society and its politics; they are concerned with the social and political ethos in the United States as well. But predicting how the Holocaust will be remembered, even in a family such as ours where commitment to transmit the Holocaust is paramount, would be an empty exercise. Who can know what any of our children may have taken in and absorbed during their growing-up years? One thing is sure: the experiences that Gitta and I felt so strongly about are but fragments in Dan and Ari's minds, and even more fragmented in Sasha and Isabel's. Therefore, we cannot begin to presume to know how things will turn out in the future.

While prediction about transmission may be impossible, it seems likely, based on our experience with family, that the Holocaust can be meaningfully transmitted to children at an early age. Ruedenberg-Wright[14] speaks about survivor families where the children heard too much, too soon, or too often, which can prevent the children from attending to their own developmental needs. This may have been the case for the children in our family: I believe that my emphasis on the Holocaust occurred too soon and too often and served my needs more than the children's. But not telling, or only telling half stories, can rob children of feeling that they are vital participants in their family's ongoing present, past and future.

In sum, it seems to me, whether one withholds the memories

or tells them as one would an epic story, it is impossible to predict what may happen to these memories as time moves on. Finally, there is the unconscious transmission to contend with. Who can say what has been transmitted unknowingly or in disguise?

My experience with these interviews has led to a number of impressions. First, it has raised the question of "what are good ways to transmit memories and experiences of the Holocaust?" As discussed earlier, telling stories clearly and correctly, keeping diaries and sharing what can be shared, maintaining dialogues and open communication, allowing the children to ask questions (sometimes questions that are difficult to answer); attending meaningful commemorations (but not too frequently); and reading good literature by writers who were killed during the Holocaust, is a powerful model for becoming acquainted with the great scholars we lost. But when parents overdo the telling of the Holocaust, or make it seem like a duty to be involved in the past (a duty that usually benefits the parents), and when they do not attend to the children's genuine interests, communication about the Holocaust between parent and child becomes unproductive with unfortunate results: the children repeat what the parents want to hear or turn away altogether.

Bar-On and Gilad,[15] and Chaitin[16] underscore that intergenerational studies of the Holocaust should be conducted with nonclinical populations, and that the children of survivors need to be understood not only "as children of their parents but also as parents of their own children." Understanding children of survivors who are now parents of their own children yields doubly rich results. To wit, while the second generation carries their parents' past, they are also sifting through what aspects of that past they mean to transmit to their children, what they intend to expand upon in relation to currently ongoing social and political injustices, and what they intend to stay away from altogether with the intent to never transmit. Of course, much of what gets transmitted happens unconsciously; which means that parents reenact in the present their painful past and therefore, with the best of intentions they may find themselves transmitting attitudes, feelings, and behaviors they thought they had long forgotten. (See the compulsion to repeat in e.g., Roth and Kulb.[17]) However, unconscious processes carry both negative and positive inclinations. One cannot underestimate the force of the spoken word that affects the listener (the descendant) as much as it does the teller. In fact, telling one's children about one's past helps the elder generations reframe and clarify their past and offers the opportunity for self-healing and self-definition. As Benedek[18] noted in 1959, the parenthood condition can help the parent to redo for himself and heal the harm that he or she experienced in the past.

The Holocaust, transmitted orally, framed in ideals, values, and beliefs and clearly articulated, leaves deep and meaningful tracks in the children's minds. These overriding ideas help individuals put into words how life situations are understood, why people take certain actions in times of stress; they help people speak about hope and define hope based on real life situations. In other words, ideals, beliefs, and values impose on people who abide by these ideas, the burden of finding the words to define what they say. In the process of developing definitions, the human mind harnesses the emotions, thereby yielding strong and convincing explanations that explain what is important in making life livable. Hannah and her daughters, who rebuilt their lives during and after the Holocaust, could not have transmitted what they did were it not for their deeply held beliefs.

CHAPTER EIGHT

AFTER THE INTERVIEWS, 2003–2004

Many stories based on real-life experiences were handed down in our extended and multigenerational family. The process began early in Hannah's life and ours, her daughters. But the handing down of memories was not planned. Memories were told in bits and pieces in the midst of life ongoing, unlike in 1982, when transmission was done with considerable forethought. What Wally and I wanted our children to see were the places and experiences that had shaped our early lives and we wanted to instill in them the historical contexts of World War II in the parts of Western Europe we had known. We hoped that together we would share thoughts, feelings, reactions, and questions. And this we did.

Eighteen years after the summer of 1982, in the year 2000, the questions about legacy took on a new intensity. I was curious to see how our children, now adults and parents in their own right, had integrated the Holocaust into their current life. A sabbatical from the university made it possible to engage a trained journalist to interview every older adult family member, namely my sister Gitta, Wally, and me, about our experiences before and during the war and about the legacy we thought we had handed down. In addition, those children and grandchildren who felt comfortable doing so were also interviewed. The very act of being interviewed had a powerful impact. None of the younger generations had ever sat for so long, never had been asked to think about what they remembered being told, nor had they been asked what they thought about the Holocaust. Some seemed startled, others expressed surprise.

In writing the previous chapter I summarized the individual interviews and proposed some principles that have informed my thinking about the process of transmitting our experiences during the *Shoah* and about the children's understanding of what they have been taught about the *Shoah*. In the years after the interviews, we and our children continued to explore this history, and our children became further involved in teaching the next generation.

June 2003

In June 2003 our daughter Gefen initiated and organized another voyage to Europe. She wanted to visit two places in Europe: the area of northern Italy where in 1943–1944 my family and I, her mother, hid in the mountains, and the town in Germany where her father Wally was born. Together with her husband Steve, Gefen felt it important to share the family history with her two lively children, Miko who was eight, and Tema who was three years old. Their presence was electric for they asked questions, Miko kept a diary, and Tema drew pictures; their questions and responses to explanations enriched our voyage immensely and set off a series of events that became significant markers in the family clan. That Miko and Tema lived in New York City when 9/11 occurred added a subtext to this journey. Gefen reasoned that the subtext for the trip was: "How does one instill hope and the capacity to trust human beings in light of such terror and destruction?" She thought that the Holocaust, as experienced in her family, provides meaningful markers to 9/11: "Life must go on and trust in the future may not be lost."

What the children and their parents experienced during that journey has yet to be unraveled fully, but I noticed that I was changing in anticipation of that journey. I was treading more carefully now on my wartime stories. I no longer felt that I "owned" my stories. Having told them to the children often, I felt less responsible for what the grandchildren made of them. How they saw that past lay largely in their parents' hands. In a sense, I felt that these stories of the war belonged to them now.

My experiences in the Italian Alps of 1943–1944 were no exception. The children would make their own meaning of my tales. I was achieving a certain distance from that past, a past that for a long time had preoccupied me greatly. Looking back, I recognized, without being fully aware, that I was letting go. Our adult children were now at the helm, firmly deciding what had to be heard, seen, talked about, read, and explained. And I took on a new function now: I began to think of myself as the "translator" of our experiences. As translator I could describe and identify situations without necessarily explaining them. How, I wondered, would I prepare for this upcoming voyage? I would not bring a tape recorder this time, but instead a journal would suffice.

I took up studying Italian again along with the history of Italy between the years 1940 and 1945, and I listened to my mother's tape-recorded interviews of that period. These tapes, recorded periodically from 1978 to 1986, were a large source for this manuscript.

One day, listening to a short segment of tape, I heard my mother say: "In March 1944, I began to despair. The children were cold even though spring was arriving. Soon the shepherds would be returning to graze their cattle and they would need to take their *cava* and barn back. I told Andreina, please find me someone who will help us leave this place, because if we don't run now we will be caught either by the Nazis or the Fascists."

Andreina brought a priest who came to help. Susan Zuccotti's[1] and Alberto Cavaglion's[2] books, both covering the war in northern Italy, were helpful. In my readings I found references to the priest who had brought winter clothes and the urgently needed forged papers that would allow us to leave our Alpine hideout. This hideout was beginning to look barren with the melting snows on the mountain slopes. Fascists and Nazis, who were forcefully hunting down Jews and members of the Italian Resistance, had overrun these, now dangerous, slopes. The priest who came to our rescue was Don Francesco Brondello, a twenty-four-year-old assistant priest to the parish of Valdieri. Don Brondello was a member of a group of priests resisting the Fascists and the Nazis. Their leader was Don Viale, who was later recognized by Yad Vashem as a Righteous Among the Nations.[3] Don Brondello, the young red-haired priest, flew on his skis from *cava* to *cava* bringing necessities for living, such as food, winter clothes, financial assistance, and forged papers. He helped save our family and a number of other Jewish people hiding in the mountains during that fall and winter of 1943–1944. If not for him we could have been caught in any of the numerous roundups that took place during that fatal year of 1943–1944.

Don Giordanengo, the priest in charge of the parish of Valdieri, left a daily log of the parish's activities that verified Don Francesco Brondello's deeds. It was thanks to this log, and to Alberto Cavaglion, the Italian historian and archivist of northern Italy who discovered the log, that we were able to document to Yad Vashem that Don Brondello was indeed the priest who helped our family. "It could have been none other at that time and in that place," declared Cavaglion.

Don Francesco Brondello was eighty-four years old in 2003. Eager to find our family's rescuer, Gefen, Steve, Miko, and Tema went on a search for Don Brondello. And find him they did. Now living in retirement near his church, he greeted us warmly in his simple quarters. We spent an afternoon together and he told us his tale:

Brondello was twenty-four when he became assistant priest to the Valdieri parish. The Resistance in northern Italy included a number of priests. Under the leadership of Don Viale, Don Brondello trudged in the snows helping those Jews and Italian Resistance fighters who were hiding in the mountains. He was caught by the Nazis on a mission to deliver to the Jewish families still living in

Nice some seventy-six letters from their family members who were incarcerated at the camp of Borgo San Dalmazzo in northern Italy. These letters were written in Yiddish with Greek characters! Arrested, he was tortured and beaten, and asked to reveal the names of those he swore to protect. His scars were still visible on his hands and neck. The irony was that when he was caught again on another mission, this time by Italian Fascists, his own countrymen, they interrogated and tortured him as brutally and sadistically as the Nazis had.

Don Brondello told the family his story and I translated as best I could. Then I told him our family story. I showed him our family picture that included all fifteen family members. Sitting around his table, a strong bond developed between Don Brondello, the little children, Gefen and her husband, Wally and me. Gefen and Steve took turns videotaping; Miko, sitting close to the priest, was writing in his journal and little Tema felt perfectly secure sitting on her parents' laps until her comfort zone spread, and she allowed herself to leave us, exploring the living room and sucking on the candy that Don Brondello had given her. When time came to take our leave we all knew that we soon would return.

The trip to Germany was equally meaningful. The family visited the cemetery; we saw Wally's old house and the synagogue. German friends who had helped rebuild the old synagogue and cared for it prepared a musical program. Many stories were told and people who remembered Wally's family spoke. The next day, a local newspaper published the event of our family visit. Leaving was hard, but returning the keys of the cemetery and the synagogue to their current caretakers was harder still, Gefen observed.

Back in the United States, I contacted the Department of the Righteous at Yad Vashem in Israel, which collects survivor testimony and documentation in its ongoing program to recognize non-Jews who risked their lives, freedom, and safety to rescue Jews from the threat of deportation or death during the Holocaust. Together with my sister Gitta, I submitted Don Brondello's name to be nominated by Yad Vashem as a Righteous Among the Nations for his courageous deeds in helping Jews and non-Jews during the war.

Photo 8.1 Don Francesco Brondello is named a Righteous Among the Nations by a representative from the State of Israel and Yad Vashem, September 2004

May 23, 2004

Almost a year after this meeting, Yad Vashem in Jerusalem elected Don Francesco Brondello a Righteous Among the Nations for his selfless deeds, and declared that he would be awarded the Medal and Certificate of Honor among Jews and Gentiles of his community in Cuneo, Italy, in the state of Piemonte on September 2, 2004. He was unable to receive the honor in Israel because he was physically unable to undertake the voyage to Israel.

June 16, 2004

Our younger daughter Miriam, her husband Mark, and their three children, Jonah, Emma, and Talia, had planned a summer sabbatical in Israel. Together they would stay in Israel for two months. They asked Wally and me to join them for two weeks, requesting specifically to visit the places where I, as a ten-year-old child, had been sent after the war in 1945. While they planned on visiting many sights together, they particularly wanted to visit three places that had captured their imagination: Atlit, the detention camp, where Gitta and I were detained when we first came to Palestine; Ben Shemen, the Youth Aliyah children's village that had opened its doors to orphans and child survivors; and Kibbutz Ma'aleh Hahamisha, where courageous members of the Palmach had fought for survival and the independence of the state of Israel, and where their grandfather Wally had lived and worked in 1952 to 1953.

Visiting Israel with young children for the first time is an arousing experience. Biblical, post-biblical, and historical events assume an exciting reality. So much so that upon ending their visit, all three grandchildren beginning with the oldest, Jonah followed by Emma, and including the youngest, Talia, who was then two years old, decided to interview each other as well as the adults to discover what were the most meaningful experiences during their visit! No one had told them to conduct these interviews; it seemed that they wanted to hear what each thought about what they had just lived through. It was only natural to do so because asking questions had become a natural part of our family's lives. And now it was the grandchildren's turn to probe and explore; even Talia, who at first had turned her back on this family scene, when asked if she too wanted to ask questions, smiled broadly and enthusiastically climbed into the interviewer's chair and had her questions all ready to go!

Photo 8.2 The entire family revisits the stone *cava* (in the background) above Valdieri, Italy, September 2004

September 2, 2004

We are now in the Cuneo Synagogue. Gefen and her family met us earlier and helped prepare us for the family reunion and Don Brondello's award. Present in the synagogue are Don Francesco Brondello, Andreina Blua's daughter Anna Marabotto and her family, and many dignitaries: Jesuit priests, Resistance fighters who had been incarcerated in Dachau, mayors of several towns in northern Italy, including Valdieri, Cuneo, and Saluzzo, the Rabbi of Turin, the emissary of the Israeli embassy in Rome, the head of the Jewish community in Turin, members of leading Italian families, the historian Alberto Cavaglion, the head of the Cuneo Jewish community Enzo Cavaglion, who organized the event, and members of the Jewish and non-Jewish Italian press, radio, and television.

In this ancient and beautiful Cuneo synagogue built in the 1700s, thirty-two members of our joint extended family are gathered from various corners of the United States, Israel, and Germany; including all the children, grandchildren, and spouses, as well as four extended family members. A total of over 120 participants are gathered here. All are present and ready to participate in honoring Don Francesco Brondello as a Righteous Among the Nations.

We knew why we were here: to honor courageous Italian Gentiles, including the family of Andreina, who lent her *cava* to help save us from the looming *razzias* (raids by German soldiers to plunder and pick up Jews), and others who never looked down on us because we were Jews and who staked their own lives to save ours. When asked why they did these generous and heroic acts, they merely replied in historians Samuel and Pearl Oliners' words: "What we did was not remarkable. It was what anyone would have done in the face of such human need."[4]

And the cycle keeps on going. It is sufficiently strong to make us believe that memory of the *Shoah* spawns ideals that encompass all the people on earth who have suffered at the hands of barbaric persecutors.

Three years earlier Ari, our son, returned to Germany and Wally's birthplace to interview the people of the village who had helped rebuild the tiny old synagogue that had been broken up and neglected for these many decades. Herb (Wally's brother) and his family had been there by this time and initiated the reconstruction of the synagogue that would now become a center of historical significance: a place where people get together to hear music, drama, and reflections, and where children come with their teachers to commemorate the *Shoah*. Ari was securing material for a new play dealing with the German people and their relationship with their children during and after the war.

Later, Gitta took her family to visit the places in Europe that contained her travails during the war; that visit, too, left significant markers and memories.

Gefen, Steve, Miko, and Tema joined us on September 6, 2005; we participated in the annual Remembrance March across the Alps from Saint-Martin-Vésubie to Valdieri. The climb was difficult for me, but Miko and Tema climbed that mountain in hail and storm; Tema was freezing, tired, and soaked from the rain, Miko was climbing vigorously in spite of the storm, and when they both got to the top they exclaimed triumphantly, "We made it!" And indeed they did. They made it and will no doubt remember the effort and courage they put into this Remembrance March of 2005.

I have come to the end of this tale of transmission. But I have never stopped thinking, and neither have my children. In spite of my age, I feel that I am still in midstream. When our third generation says that the Holocaust cannot be the only thing they need to hand down, they put their muscle to the grindstone and follow various routes. One brings an Arab writer from North Africa to the United States to collaborate on a play; one examines various reactions to terror in Israel and the West Bank; and one finishes a book on learning how to trust what you know in the context of human relationships. And the children of the third and fourth generations now follow the footsteps of their elders to widen the cycles of transmission.

Photo 8.3   Gitta and Chaya hiking near the *cava* in the mountains above Valdieri, Italy, September 2004

IN MEMORY

FISHEL HOROWITZ, 1903–1995

Photo 9.1   Fishel Horowitz with Chaya and Gitta, Antwerp, 1994

In 1942, Fishel Horowitz and his young wife Rosa Reisla, née Offen, were deported to Auschwitz. Fishel survived the camps and returned a sick and broken man. His wife was murdered in Auschwitz. Obsessed by his experiences and the events he had witnessed, Fishel spoke incessantly about the years at Auschwitz, in the slave labor camps surrounding Auschwitz. In listening to his story I hear his emphasis on the personal relationships between the men and those who guarded and harassed them, the enormous physical hardships of the work, and the sadism not only of the Nazis guards, but also of the Jewish *Kapos*. He also developed friendships that he maintained throughout the war. He spoke about the two death marches, and what followed when he and other prisoners arrived in the end-stage camp in Buchenwald.

Fishel was my father's closest cousin; he visited our family often in Berlin in the mid-1930s. And when our father came to Antwerp in 1938 to see if he could bring his family over, as our mother so fervently wished, it was Fishel who showed our father around, introduced him to his family, the large Horowitz clan, and to the diamond cutters and the merchants.

Uncle Fishel returned from the camps a shattered man. He told us how it was for them when he and his wife were apprehended shortly after they were married; what it was like for them when they were interned in the gathering camps of Breendonck[1] and Malines[2] in Belgium, and then about their deportation to Auschwitz. They were separated because a guard in Malines wanted to get even with Fishel for not telling him where his wife had hidden her wedding ring. Therefore, as punishment, Fishel would not be allowed to be together with his wife on the same train.

The way Fishel tells it, he hoped that his wife, who was good with numbers and a competent typist, would receive a decent job in the camp, possibly as a secretary. He could not imagine that anyone looking at his beautiful wife would overlook her handsome and respectable demeanor. And once they saw her, they would want to give her a "good job" at the camp. From the day he arrived in Auschwitz, he never ceased looking for her, as did all the inmates who had been separated from their loved ones when they arrived in Auschwitz. Fishel never saw his wife again.

Gitta and I returned to Belgium from Israel (then Palestine), in 1947. Because we were not Belgian citizens, immigration papers for my sister and me were hard to come by. But our mother, who was persuasive and persistent, wrote incessant letters to Camille Huysmans, then the mayor of Antwerp, and did succeed in receiving the necessary papers for our return. We were relieved and thankful to be reunited with Mother and Uncle Herman, and to embrace the Horowitz family again.

In Belgium, Fishel visited our house daily. He joined us for coffee or dinner at least three or four times a week. I remember greeting him on my return from school. After I had done my homework or looked over some lessons, Fishel would ask me, "Well, are you done with your homework yet?" I would then go over to him, sit next to him, and because he could not do otherwise, he would start telling me about one or another unbelievably painful experience in the camps. When the telling got painful, I'd end up sitting on his lap, a twelve-year-old girl, his only listener. There were many such stories, and Fishel's urge to talk about what happened to him, and what he had done, was unrelenting. His tales were so intense and gripping that my mother, more than once, felt pressed to interrupt, "Oh Fishel, stop already. Talking so much about such terrible things will make you sick!" But Fishel did not hear her. He never cried as his tales pressed forward, but he captivated me and I wept.

In the 1970s, when I began recording our mother's life experiences, Fishel asked that we tape-record his experiences during the war as well. And why not? Weren't we, after all, the only descendants to whom he felt closely connected? He had not remarried after his wife was murdered in Auschwitz, and had no children. Though his parents, brothers and sisters all survived the war in hiding, he felt more of a bond with us than with most of his siblings. Fishel's seven brothers and sisters had escaped the roundups. Tante Roizele and her husband Itsche were saved by their Belgian family physician, Dr. Baeten, who had hospitalized the elderly couple and secretly withheld their identity from the hospital staff from the time the roundups began in 1942 until the end of the war.

Fishel began telling his story on tape after Uncle Herman died of esophageal cancer, on July 17, 1979.

Fishel Speaks

Like my five brothers and two sisters, I was born in Galicia. I am two years younger than your Uncle Herman.

When I was nine years old I remember *de Mama* (our Tante Roizele) took me to the back of the house where she had buried some diamonds. She needed money to get a smuggler for my brother Dudek to bring him over clandestinely to Antwerp, Belgium. What happened then is not so important; I went to *heder* (religious school), I studied; I was an *illui* (a supremely gifted student of the Talmud); I was *Bar Mitzvah;* I put on *tefillin* (phylacteries: two boxes containing biblical verses with leather straps attached to them, put on daily on men's foreheads before reciting the morning prayers).

In 1920, I too had to leave home. My mother and father sent me to Vienna to learn bookkeeping. I received the best grades, but the teacher, who was a convert from Judaism, humiliated and taunted me whenever he could. Here my handwriting was not good enough, there my calculations were incorrect. He was a real anti-Semite even though he once had been a Jew. I got the best grades, but not right away because I only spoke Yiddish. But slowly my marks went up from four to three to all ones. But when it came to the end of the year, after the exams, and you should know we studied hard for these exams, this teacher told me he had lost my exam notes and there was nothing to be done. It was as if I had not been there. So I told him, "I don't need this. I'm going to Antwerp, to my brother Hersch." Hersch had married Fella; she was a Kornreich—they were very wealthy people and they would help me. And they did. They not only helped me but the rest of the boys as well.

Hersch brought me into the diamond profession. I learned *klieven* (to cleave), *schleifen* (to polish), and *zegen* (to cut). I studied only for three or four months and then I was done. When I had learned what I needed to know, I told my patron, I must have been nineteen or twenty years old at the time, "I will work on Sundays to earn more money to help the family in Galicia." And this I did. I was industrious and my workmanship was appreciated.

My mother, *de Mama,* was unbelievably good. She was more than that. She was quiet, smart, and learned. She was my role model. What my mother said, I trusted. First, I earned 60 gulden, later 80 gulden. And then, I sent them everything I earned. Hersch Diller, your father's brother (Uncle Herman) was my cousin from my father's side. We brought him over to Belgium and he immediately understood the diamond business too. And he too sent money home to his family.

In 1940, I became acquainted with a *meidel* (young girl).[3] I met her in a cafe. She was beautiful and her hair was like gold. Her father was a big Talmudic scholar. But in 1940 the Jews in Antwerp were notified that they must go to Limburg to register for work. Her parents decided to move to Brussels instead. Until 1942 we were able to live in the open, more or less, because those people who did not register for work in Limburg were not yet picked up. *De Mama* knew I was very serious about my *meidel*, but at thirty-seven I was still a virgin, so she thought it would be good for me to spend the weekend in a hotel. Then, in May 1942 we married according to Jewish custom, and we also registered our wedding officially in the *Stadthuis* (at city hall) in Antwerp. After the wedding, my wife stayed home with my mother and me and on the weekends we usually went to Brussels to visit her parents.

On *Erev Tishe Buv* (eve of *Tisha B'Av,* a fast day commemorating the destruction of the ancient Temples in Jerusalem) my wife was due to arrive in Antwerp alone. She would be coming into the station at 11 am. There were very few people traveling at that time; but to our great misfortune, a Gestapo agent was walking back and forth on the quay. A woman who apparently knew me saw that I was walking up and down with my star [of David] showing. As I came up the stairs, the Gestapo agent saw me and arrested me. And another Gestapo agent picked up my wife coming down from the train walking toward me. They put us on a train to Malines, a detention and transit camp. At that time we still could have saved ourselves if I had paid off some people, but I didn't know how to go about doing this. Before we went to Malines, a guy in charge came in and said, "Everyone must send a postcard." I said we have family, older people. So we sent postcards: my wife to her parents, I to *de Mama*.

After Malines, they took us to Breendonck, also a transit camp; the guards there were savages. Among the people who were arrested, there were two types: the *Politische* (political prisoners: underground and Resistance fighters) and the Jews. I wish they hadn't taken us to Breendonck. There was a *caserne* (barracks) there. And there, they beat and tortured people. The commandant of the camp, a Nazi, was a harsh and vicious sadist. In Breendonck you could hear horrible screams from people who were being tortured. They took a Resistance man, put a sack over his head.... I can't even tell you how they tortured him. The tortures and the excruciating screams were unbearable.[4]

We got one piece of bread and a little touch of sugar there. The soup was water. They separated the men from the women. And there was a German officer there who took some women to peel potatoes. One woman gave me one piece of bread and I gave it to my wife. All of a sudden my wife tells me that one of the officers she saw here was also the officer we had seen in Malines. This officer wanted to take some of the women into his office. Those who had registered to go to Malines would leave Breendonck. But my wife hadn't registered to go to Malines: "You made a mistake," he said to her. Later when she wanted to register it was too late. There were thousands of people in Breendonck. In the beginning they gave us food. Every day, my father-in-law sent packages with the best of foods, delicacies, and clothes too. Maybe we tasted something once, but we never received the packages.

Imagine, we were picked up before the major deportations began. After us, they took 2,000 people a week in the cattle cars. Ours was the ninth transport; it was already September 1942.[5] In Breendonck there were forty-four women; I received a roll and my wife received a roll and preserves, so we gave some of the food to the person in charge so they'd treat us better. Then, my wife wanted to sit at a table to eat. We gave everything to others. I saw the young girls looking at us. I said to my wife, "Please don't be mad, let's eat a little closer to our bed; we'll have more privacy."

I had three years in concentration camps and I was 99 percent dead, but in Breendonck I was still alive, so I wanted to cry and pray. Once, as I sat down to pray, the door opened and I saw a figure coming in and tears started streaming down my face. As I cried that same figure turned around and went away; there was a light around his head. It is said that if you perform a meaningful act, such as be *teshuva* (be repentant on Yom Kippur), then *Eliahu Hanuveh* (Elijah the Prophet) will appear and help you. And that is what happened to me. (Fishel is apparently telling about a visual hallucination he had, probably as a result of the trauma he endured in Breendonck.) When I told this to my friend and fellow diamond-dealer Shimon Langsam, he didn't believe me. He said don't tell this to the rabbi, he'll think this was a dream, not reality. Then, another Jew who stood behind me asked, "Are you Fishel Horowitz?" This was a fine Jew, a religious and a good man, I told him. So he said to me, "I also have noise in my ears." I said to him, "I think you also saw something."

"You are imagining," he said to me. He wished me a *refieh shleime* (a complete recovery) and I wished him the same, but I didn't tell him what I saw.

Chaya: Did you speak to the *Rav* (rabbi) after the war?

Fishel: No, he usually speaks to people who are *gvierim* (rich folk) who can do something for the community. Once he called me over and asked me, since I wasn't married (I was a widower), would

I marry a Russian woman to enable her to stay in Belgium? I said, "I'm sorry, Rav, I'm still thinking of getting married again, so I cannot do that in good conscience."

Chaya: Can you tell me more what it was like in Breendonck?

Fishel: We stayed in Breendonck six weeks. Then we were taken back to Malines, we were going on a transport. They examined my wife first. When she came out, I knew they would start with me. The Nazi asked me if I knew where my wife hid her ring. I said, "No." So, he slapped me hard across the face. Then he asked me again, so I said, "Yes." There were other officers standing around, but no one said to me, "If you don't give him the ring you will not stay together" or "You will not go on the same transport."

Another officer, making fun of me, said, "I have an idea. We will send the husband back to Breendonck." We stood at *Appell* (roll call) and later we went up to the barracks. We stayed in Malines from Wednesday to Sunday. Then we left. They put us on an express train. There was a guard by the door, but otherwise it was an ordinary train. We "flew" to the German border. And at the border, they told the men aged fifty-five and younger to get off. The women, the older people, and the children went on, *nebich* (a pity), they went to Auschwitz. The men they took to the slave labor camps until they died. I hoped that my wife, who had been the administrative secretary of the Jewish community, would have gotten a job right away.

I returned to my seat and found my old countryman, Fishel Wilk. Then, we were taken to a transit camp, Laurahuette.[6] Once we went by tram to *Oberschlesien* (Upper Silesia, Poland), Schengut.[7] In this camp there were *razzias* (not of people, but of goods that people still had with them; *Kapos* or others who had authority over us took things away from us all the time): this meant you had to give your things up. We had to open our suitcases; I had suits. I said I had already given my things away. My wife had a pair of shoes that she had gotten from a young man, so I gave the shoes to this man who had been with me in Breendonck. He became *Oberkapo* (head *Kapo*) here.

In return he promised me that he'd give me bread and fat, but all he gave me was one piece of bread, yet he received *zu fressen* (to eat) and drink. Finally, I got angry and asked him why didn't he follow up on his promise? He just walked away. But once at night he passed me by and said: "Horowitz, you have a chance to become *Judenälteste* (senior Jewish advisor to the men in the barracks)." At the end of the year, the guards spoke to us and said that we should not be afraid and that we should give up everything we have. They said that they would save it for us, otherwise people would steal what we have.

Later, I went by tram to Katowicze.[8] From there we went to a place called Bismarckhuette[9] where only *goyim* (non-Jews) worked. We went with our striped uniforms, but to keep warm we wore, underneath the striped uniforms, sacks of paper that held the large amounts of sand that we schlepped in the camp. In Katowicze I met a young man who was very *messugal* (capable). His name was Spruch. The guards ran into the work place to warm up and they told us to do the same; they also said we shouldn't be so afraid. This man, Spruch, a friend of Uncle Herman's, decided to stay back; he didn't run. The *Vorarbeiter* (foreman) also stayed back and continued to work. I said to Spruch: "I am curious, here everyone is running to keep warm and you are continuing to work."

He said to me, "If I could drown them with a spoonful of water I would do it now. But you see, if you run to a warm place and then you have to go back out in the cold, then you can get sick. I stay and work so my blood will continue to circulate."

I thanked him and the next time when a similar situation arose, I too continued to work and did not run to keep warm.

When I worked I had a system: I worked slowly but used my eyes and looked to see whether someone was coming. When I saw a guard coming, then I increased the speed of my work.

The Dutch Jews, *nebich*, were not up to the task. At home they had a good life. Physically and morally they were so different from us Polish Jews. We were used to the anti-Semitism and had to work hard just to survive. The Dutch Jews, on the other hand, when they got a little piece of soap for a week or a month, they ran around with the soap asking to trade the soap for soup. The soup was nothing, just water; but when you're hungry, of course, you can eat even grass. But the Dutch gave away their little piece of soap and in doing this they weren't able to wash; so, morally they were beaten and physically they were beaten as well.

I used my eyes more than anything else. When I saw someone coming I first looked for my *Meister* (boss). Later, I had a Ukrainian boss but I'll tell you about that later.

The second day I was there (in Katowicze) I began to cough—it was minus 40 degrees Celsius! How long could I survive? So I said to the *Vorarbeiter* from Sosnowitz, a fine guy, "What should I do? I'm sure I won't survive this." So he went to ask the *Meister* who said that there was a barracks where for fifteen minutes you could warm up and eat whatever there was there.

There were a few Polish and German workers in this camp. The *Oberkapo* realized that he had not behaved properly toward me when he took my shoes and gave me nothing in return but a small ration of bread. That's when he told me that he would help me become *Stubenälteste* (barracks elder). On that day, he also told me that all the people who went to Katowicze would stay in the barracks to live there. Then he left.

All the Jewish men who worked in the barracks were very satisfied with me. The Sosnowitzer asked the *Vorarbeiter* to have me join that new group. This was a miracle because if I had not gone I would have died. Every day they brought back dead people in a wheelbarrow. In a short time so many people died that we remained sixty people.

I have to interrupt here. When we came to the Bismarckhuette, the *Vorarbeiter* stood in line and said 170 people were present. Everyone had a *Kapo* and a *Vorarbeiter*, but the shoemakers and the tailors were like the upper class. I was in barracks number two. The *Judenälteste* was running back and forth, dividing up twenty people per barracks. This *Kapo* appointed Becker, the guy from Breendonck who befriended a Nazi guard, and he knew how to deal with these criminals once we got to Poland too. I did not like him and he did not like me either.

Before we went to Bismarckhuette, I became friends with very religious people. I was with Leibsich Schwann, *z"l* (abbreviation for *zichrono livracha*—may he rest in peace). He was a Hasid. He prayed every day for his eight children and his wife, but none returned. We were in a long barracks. For every twenty people they decided there should be a *Stubenälteste*. What was his job? In the morning he was the first to get up and at night he had to see to it that the barracks should be clean. In the morning he had to get coffee with bread and the margarine. This Schwann, in our barracks, became ill. So he asked me, "Please, Horowitz take my place until I feel better." He thought he would return soon. I told him that I could not replace him as *Stubenälteste*. I could not tell people what to do. That's not for me. I'd have to jump up every morning, make sure they get up, tell them to go wash up, make sure their bunks are straight. No, that is not for me. Unfortunately, he became much sicker. And I took his place.

But I too was not well. I told you I had a bad cough, and I saw that I was getting worse. Being *Stubenälteste*, I was the last person to go to bed. We had the runs every night, so we had to run to the *latrinen* (toilets) because of this shitty food. I was afraid to sleep, but one morning I fell asleep. The *Oberkapo*, his name was Schlaim, gave me a *frask* (huge slap)! I thought I would not survive. A man who left for the toilets had not come back. I was *Stubenälteste*, and this Schlaim knew and he asked me, "Horowitz, where do you stand?" I said, "Please do not make me be a *Stubenälteste*. Herr

Schlaim, you gave me a double room, and I can't do it all." He then yelled at me and said "Stand up, *Achtung!* This is an order." There was someone there, [Benjamin] Brachfeld, a good man, a fellow diamond dealer from Antwerp; he was from the Mizrachi (a religious Zionist organization). This Brachfeld stood next to me and said, "Horowitz, I will help in everything." He wanted to work with me. Schlaim had given me fifty people to watch over, so I took Brachfeld with me to help. Then Schlaim gave me a *Nachschlag* (a bit of food). From then on, every time I received *Nachschlag*, I gave a part of it to Brachfeld. [Brachfeld's son, Sylvain Brachfeld, who survived the *Shoah* as a hidden child, later wrote a book about the Jews of occupied Belgium, see note 4 to chapter three.]

I think that later I got a room of twenty-five people. In my room most of the people were satisfied with me: I kept the room clean, went for coal, there was a cabinet with potatoes. There was a little oven, and I had to watch so none went missing. Every day, I gave everyone a warm baked potato, and then I'd go to get coal. After that I entered the barracks to keep warm.

Once when there was a *Kontrolle* (inspection), I saw a young man who didn't want to go out into the cold. So, I said, "I will watch out for you and tell you if someone is coming." Our *Hauptmeister* (chief supervisor), also did not want to leave the barracks. The less he was outside the less he had to hit, slap, and kick the people here. I saw the inspection officer come over to the barracks. I said to the *Hauptmeister, "Er kommt"* (He is coming) so he got up and opened the door. He was ready! And I had narrowly saved a bit of my skin. This was in February, the worst frost ever.

With all this I felt a weakness take me over, so I stole one or two potatoes every day. I stole a bit of grease. Once the *Meister* came in. "I caught you," he said. "You've been stealing potatoes; I've been counting them!" So, I said, "*Herr Meister*, there are workmen who come here every day; it is quite possible that they felt free to steal. I'm afraid I wouldn't dare to steal."

Now I have to add something I omitted to tell you: when I entered the barracks, after I became the *Stubenälteste* when we were in Bismarckhuette. They taught us to get up and take off our caps, even when the *Judenälteste* came in: you get up, and take off your hats.

The *Judenälteste* told me, "Here is a piece of soap. You should know they will come and check that everyone should wash themselves." When the people in my barracks went to the toilet, I was responsible (this was not the real concentration camp yet) to see that two people go in together at the same time to watch over each other.

I took it seriously. There were some young Polish men who were very slow, so I asked them kindly (I never hit anyone, God forbid) to be faster. Then came these two young Polish men. They were dished out a bowl of soup; it was like water. These fellows said to me that if we gave them one potato in the soup then they would do the work of cleaning the barracks. Since I was *Stubenälteste* I had to make this decision.

There was a Jewish policeman. Why did they (the Nazis) make him into a Jewish policeman? Because he sustained many blows for not giving info about who brought him a little package from home that was still in Poland. In any case, he seemed to be a tough guy so they appointed him as *Polizei* (police). He was in my barracks. And I had to divide up the food, and Leibsich Schwann was also in my barracks. And the *Judenälteste* said I don't have to do *Nachdienst* (night duty). So I went up and down asking about *Nachdienst*. I came to the *Polizei*. He said to me, "You don't have to do *Nachdienst*."

I said to him, "If you can bring a note from the *Judenälteste,* then we'll see."

"Then, I'd like to do guard from nine to ten."

I said, "I am sorry, I take the *Nachdienst* from nine to twelve even though I don't have to."

The two young Polish men, having received more food, were now cleaning up the barracks. Once, I rushed them because we were going to be late for *Appell*. The room was not cleaned yet, so I took the broom and cleaned quickly. At night, the *Judenälteste* spoke severely to everyone. There had been an inspection that day and the barracks were dirty, except the Horowitz barracks saved the situation somewhat. So, after that, everyone wanted to sleep in my barracks. The third night after that inspection, the *Hauptwachende* (head guard) walked in and said, "*Achtung*! There were some sick people here, is everyone washed?"

"*Jawohl* (yes), *Herr Obermeister,*" I say, a real soldier. He took each man and examined him. In barracks three and four you could hear yelling and beating because there the men had not washed themselves. In barracks five and six everyone was beaten. The only barracks that was quiet—and received *Nachschlag*—was ours. Everyone said they would give me bread if I let them come into my barracks.

When we went to the delousing center in Katowicze, there was a commission and they decided that the only barracks that was clean was my group. From 174 men, within a few weeks, we were reduced to sixty-five: people were being sent away. The *Judenälteste* saw that he was running short of men, so they decided we should go to Blechhammer,[10] a slave labor camp. Some of the detainees stayed in the old camp, but I went to Blechhammer.

When I entered the new barracks at Blechhammer, there was a *Judenälteste* who was a fine man and did not allow beatings. The *Kapos* had to beat the inmates and some of them behaved like animals. One day, on our way back from work, I was pushing a wheelbarrow filled with coal with another guy, Lifschitz. He was a strong man and had a pair of boots. He wanted to show off before the guards, so he gave me a kick with a shovel and said, "*Schneller!*" (faster!)

So, I said to him, "Lifschitz, you wanted to show off, but you beat me for nothing. You're a *Myuffisnik* (misfit) just to show off to the guard."

I got my comeuppance from him. Another day, we were supposed to lift iron pieces, and one Dutch boy working with us was weak. He came up to me, and Lifschitz pushed me away. There was an Italian who sat with a gun who witnessed this scene. So, this Lifschitz took a big stick and wanted to hit me, but I took a long iron with tears streaming down my face. The Italian soldier was watching and did not do a thing.

"Well, try," I said, "I'll split your head open." He got scared, this Lifschitz guy. The next day on our way home, I said, "I will tell the *Judenälteste,* and also a second *Oberkapo,* an entire general staff." So Lifschitz went to the Jewish guy in command and complained about me, saying that I didn't want to work. I got punished. I had to stand in a space and shovel and split stones and was watched all the time.

How can one bear this? The first day went by *be schulem* (in peace). I came home, and before me were some Jewish boys and they begin to kiss me. Every fourteen days there was a change in watch guards. This Italian soldier must have told the *Oberkapo.* I was in *Strafcamp* (punishment camp). In the morning, the *Oberkapo* came to me and Lifschitz and said to him, "You beat a blameless man, I will show you how one works."

He tore off Lifschitz's *Kapo* armband and sent him off to work. In the evening, after we came back from work that was extra hard, he gave Lifschitz back his armband and said, "Let this be a lesson."

After the day I was beaten, I was weak like a child. I told the *Oberkapo*, "I can't stand it anymore." "I'm glad you told me," said the man. The next morning I had to stand by the *Oberkapo* to tell him what I wanted. So I told him that the *Judenälteste* wanted me to tell him about what happened to me. "Is that true?" he asked. "Yeah, it's true," I said. In the meantime, everyone wanted to have me in their barracks. This *Strafcamp* was really awful; all the *Commandanten* (commandants) used to stand and beat the prisoners. I told Lifschitz, "You should remember this was commanded by God, so you shouldn't beat anybody." After that he died. (Fishel doesn't say how Lifschitz died.)

A *Calefactor* is a little heater. When you clean a barracks in which there is a little stove and the workers hurry in to eat, another guard enters immediately to watch us. This guard didn't know me and he looked at me with hatred in his eyes. "You have a good life here, yes?"

So, I said to the first guard, when we were outside, "Please, say a good word about me to him, I think he wants to kill me." The next day, when the vicious guard came in, he said to me, "You can go and do your work." I stayed in that place for a very long time.

For the next two years, life was really at its worst. We had to go to the toilet in the middle of the night, and we'd run through the snow, but one night I couldn't hold it anymore, so I went then and there on the snow. A Jewish man, a *Kapo*, came up to me, it looked like he wanted to beat me, but there was no one there, so he didn't. But this *Kapo* had appointed another Jewish man as *Vorarbeiter*. That one immediately began to push people around. Sometimes, there was nothing to do, but we weren't allowed to be idle, so that Jew put us in a forest and we had to push sand from one part the woods to the other for no reason at all, just so we wouldn't stand idle. Another Jew started to work but I decided to stand still. The young Jew was afraid to tackle with me. The next day a German soldier kept an eye on me. I cleaned the wagon and then I jumped down. He said to me, *"Nu Yah?"* (implying "what gives here?")

So I asked the *Kapo*, "Excuse me please, how would you have reacted if one of your men were to beat you for nothing?" "I beat the *Vorarbeiter* because he behaved badly," he said. Impulsively, I gave him a *gesinten klop* (a strong blow). The *Kapo* gave me a *patsch* (slap).

The first week, one guy, Bloch from Brussels, a baker by profession, was able to carry a sack on his back with little effort, so he asked me to carry some sacks too. Impulsively I said to him, "He beat me and I beat him, and the German saw me. Aren't we beaten sufficiently? How would you respond in this situation?" He didn't answer.

Once, on a Sunday, I heard someone say, "Where is Horowitz?"

I said, "Here I am. Do you want some more beatings from me?" He then became quiet. I didn't like to let myself be humiliated.

In Blechhammer, the conditions were a little better. Once, in the beginning, you received a so-called ration card that they punched daily to pick up the soup. I was so weak and the food was awful, but the hunger was worse than anything. I lost the ration card so I went to the office, and told the officer that I didn't know if I lost the card or if someone stole it from me. "Here, have a bowl of soup," he said.

I looked at him, "What will be tomorrow?"

He asked me into the office; there sat a pretty girl, a secretary. I thanked him because, first, he gave me the soup and second, he invited me to come in. I wished we could stay together until the end. The officer took out a new ration card and gave it to me. I went back into to the barracks; they called the soup *Mallorca,* a black soup.

In the beginning when I first came to the camp, I couldn't eat it, but later I got used to it. The guys were able to manage; they organized bread and worked for food. Once I came back from the office, I saw that they put all the plates of soup of *Mallorca* on my bed. They were making fun of me. They didn't eat this soup any more: they had managed to get different food. I ate the soup, but a little soup spilled on the bed. So, I went up to the *Stubenälteste,* he was a Parisian fellow, a partner of a coiffeur in Antwerp. I said to him, "This is all very well and good, but my bed is dirty now." He ate bread and eggs and pork. I looked and said to myself, "This won't do. I too have to organize myself, so I can get better food."

Next to me lay a Romanian Jew who told me "if you want to earn bread, take these papers to roll cigarettes, and exchange it for margarine or whatever." So I went around and tried to exchange the papers for whatever I could find. One man wanted to give me margarine but I refused. I earned money with my cigarettes and was able to buy a ration of bread. Then came some guys from Antwerp, they had gold pieces. One had been a *Kapo,* he had a lot of bread.

"How much for the gold pieces?" I asked.

In Blechhammer, you could buy bread, as much as you want. Once I found out that they were doing business. The *Vorarbeiter,* they called him Rothchild, he didn't beat people. "Do you know where you can sell fifty marks?" he asked me. "Yes," I said. I earned fifty marks then because I had connections. And I was able to buy about three rolls. I bought the fifty marks, but I didn't use it all for bread. Once, two young men from Antwerp lay in the hospital. So, I brought three rations of bread and three margarine slices into the hospital barracks. One was named Gottlieb, and the other ones I knew as well. The next day someone told me there was soup from where the prisoners had been and now had left. I had some soup and brought the rest to the other fellows in the hospital. I ran around finding a place, I gave someone fifty marks, I brought him eggs and bread; in some concentration camps you couldn't do that. For the most expensive diamond you couldn't get a piece of bread. And if they caught you, you'd have lost the diamonds and be beaten too.

Now, every day we had to watch ourselves to remain healthy; if not we'd go on the transport. On the way to the camp and leaving the camp there were many toilets, very primitive. Once, one of the young men came up to me and said, "Fishel, I need advice, what am I to do?" I was walking with another fellow who liked me very much because he had already spent two years in this camp. So, the fellow tells me that when he arrived in the camp he hid some small *brillianten* (cut diamonds) in a condom in his belt. When he got used to the camp he saw that he could use the same toilet every time, and he found a little hole there, and since then he had hidden his *doseke* (a small packet of diamonds used for trading) in there whenever he was deloused. Afterwards, he got his belt back out of the hole with the condom still intact. But his luck ran out. Once he went to the toilet and someone else was also there, and the young man saw him. On the way home he no longer found his *lottl* (same as *doseke)*. He was sure that the guy had stolen it. I wasn't so sure that he had even a *Sicherheitsnadel* (safety pin). "Listen," I said, "if we survive this, then this man who stole the diamonds, you'll talk to him and you will surely get the diamonds back."

On the Death March[11]

The first two days we received some kind of food. The following days, we received less and less until we were totally without food. No water, nothing. Some of the German peasants left water outside, sometimes a carrot. People fell like flies. This was the first death march. I also went through the second death march. When a person fell they shot him, that's it. We stood an entire day in *Appellplatz.* We received maybe one ration of bread. I asked God whatever happens should happen, but it should happen in train cars because I just didn't have the strength to walk any more. We got some train cars and I was with my countryman Wilk again. Once, we were pushed together so much in the car that one could die just from not being able to breathe. People were dying around us. But just then, I felt a huge draft of cold air. I lay against someone, and I felt cold, ice cold, I look up and see that I was leaning against a dead man. So, I turned around and lay against someone else. When we came to Weimar, before we went to Buchenwald, there were a hundred or more cars with people, open cars.

Standing there I saw from far away a white airplane. It must have been an American: first there was one plane, then another, then a third, and they began bombing. They didn't know we were concentration camp people. Then, another set of planes came and they began bombing. The guards jumped down, and I did too and I went under the train. The young men were so hungry they found some food. They cut some lettuce, and I looked for Wilk and I found him but he was so weak he stood by a wagon, and one young man cut a piece of lettuce and gave it to him to eat. The hunger was so awful, no one cared if the guards would shoot or not.

Finally, we went on and arrived at another concentration camp. There were 80,000 people, but those of us who came now had to stand outside. Then, we received clothes: one would get a shirt that was too small; the other got one that was huge. At night it was minus 30 or 40 degrees Celsius, freezing cold. So we slept outside, holding on to each other, Jews and non-Jews; our feet were freezing and uncovered. In the morning, they woke us up; we stood in line and received the bread ration with the shit soup.

I forgot to tell you: when we arrived in Buchenwald they gave us a bread to share, but there were Poles and Ukrainians, and as we cut the bread, the *goyim* stole the bread and we had nothing. In the morning, they brought us to a disinfection barracks; it was very primitive; they dunked us, and everyone got soap and we were supposed to shower, after which we were supposed to return to the new barracks. However, there was one big *Unglick* (misfortune): the showers didn't work. We lay totally naked waiting; more days without bread or water. If someone had to go to relieve himself, you can imagine what it was like, because it was so crowded it was as if we were glued to each other.

Eventually after a few days, the showers were fixed, so everyone wanted to be first. Everyone was pushing and these strong guys, communists, *goyim* and *shkutzim* (uneducated combative non-Jewish men) began to push the weaker ones such as us. I took Wilk's hand, once, twice, until we arrived to the showers. On the grass you saw people who had fallen before the disinfection. People went to steal other people's shoes, pants, shirts, because they were too weak to defend themselves. I and others yelled, "Murderers, thieves, what are you doing?"

That was some hell there. And after that I don't remember; I thought Wilk was dead. I simply became crazy; I lost my mind. People told me later, those who came back, that they couldn't understand how I came back to my senses, that it was a miracle. I went around, I don't know for how many days. While walking around, I found a piece of gold, so I wanted to go first in line for bread and soup, but I was beaten. I didn't know what came over me. I was abnormal; I don't know how many days I was like this—one or two days. Later, I told one of the guards that I had a treasure. One of the guards took me to a place and on the table there was an axe. The guard said to me, "Where is the treasure? Between four eyes, between you and me, are you afraid?"

So he pulled me and began beating me. I didn't feel a thing because I was not normal. At night it was freezing. In the morning they woke us to stand in line to receive the bread with the soup. As I stood up I felt a terrible headache. I became conscious again and replayed the scene with the guard in my mind, the axe, his question about the treasure, and what I told him. He was afraid and he beat me, and standing in line for bread he could have been a socialist, and standing there I saw a broken barracks and against the barracks stood Wilk, more dead than alive. I recognized the guard who hit me. He recognized me, and he knew I was conscious, and said "Tell me, what happened yesterday?" I didn't answer. With sympathy he said to me, "Tell me what happened." I was afraid he would hit me. So I asked him, "Aren't you ashamed you hit a person who was not normal?" He said, "I was afraid—there was an axe and I was afraid that you would kill me!" Yes, now I remember. Then he saw that I was looking toward someone, Wilk, I said, he was one of the men with whom I lay on the grass. "I thought he was dead," I said. "Is he your brother?" the guard gently asked. "He is like my brother," I said. "Believe me," said the guard, "today is his turn, tomorrow will be yours. And the day after tomorrow, will be mine."

Still in the soup line, I saw that my turn was almost there. I ran to Wilk and took him by the hand. I thought he should also get his bread and soup. He said, "Oy, Oy, Oy, Fishel, I already feel better seeing you." I gave him his bread; he didn't want to eat it. I fed him the soup and he wanted to give me his bread. I didn't want to take it. I brought him back to the barracks and the guard carried this stretcher like a bed with a couple of other fellows. I wanted to help, but the guard pushed my hand aside, as if to say we don't need your help.

In Buchenwald, I finally arrived at a barracks. Also, a *ness* (miracle): there were two *lagers* (camps), a small *lager* and a large *lager.* In the small *lager* there were only Jews, they had to stand in *Appell* for hours on end. My luck was that I came to the large camp with both non-Jews and Jews. Here there were Yugoslavians who played chess. They said to me, "We are looking for a good chess player." I thought with the chess game the time would go by faster. One said I was a strong player, and so we played together. As we played we both said we had to stop because we were getting too tired.

In front of the barracks a doctor examined us. I was very thin like a skeleton. Those people who had some meat on them had a stick put up their rear end because they looked better fed and that's also where their diamonds were hidden. But me, I was paper thin, and had nothing inside me, so they kept me in Buchenwald.

A few days later I saw people were kissing. The Red Cross sent packages of approximately six kilograms each, and I received a package. I lay with another guy from Antwerp in the diamond business, Zwirn; he covered me with a blanket. I ate slowly from the food from the package and didn't want to eat too much because I didn't want to get diarrhea. I tried to enter the hospital, for blankets, tea with saccharine, and to avoid *Appell.* Then soon after my luck was that I received a "rose" on my cheek (a rose is an infection that is very contagious). The *Stubenälteste* called me and said, "You have to go to hospital." But I was afraid. I knew that if one went into this hospital sick one left the hospital only one way: dead.

I had given Zwirn this gold piece, my treasure, that I had found on the grass before I lost my mind. Zwirn was a fine man and he sensed my fear. He promised me that he would bring me my portion of bread every day. I remembered that I had with me a can of sardines. I opened it with a few things, the saccharine I ate at once. At the hospital, they gave me a blanket, so I took another blanket. That was some hospital. It was a death hospital. There, people were almost dead. There were these little beds, one next to the other. I saw how they took out the sick people, one was naked, and the other was swollen. Every day they took out the dead people. On my one side they took one, then the other. And every day I saw doctors and also political prisoners. The political prisoners were not treated like us. One of them came to me, took my temperature. I was feeling better. But I was worried, what should I do? Should I say I'm better and ask to leave the hospital, or should I take advantage of the little peace I had in this hospital? Well, I needed not to worry—the decision was out of my hands. The second day, after my fever broke, they called my name. I had to go. I didn't know how I'd survive out there. One day they took everyone out, the entire camp, and everyone got a shovel or a pickaxe to dig trenches. The young SS were walking around and beat the inmates to death if they did not work fast enough. And I went with the shovel and forced myself to work, because if I didn't I'd be done for. But there was a miracle: every few minutes the SS changed guard; there were enormous numbers of SS guards, they were in a hurry to evacuate, they knew the end had come. One SS man came up to me and yelled, "Why are you working so slowly?" I was afraid to answer, but I did and I said, "I'm doing the best I can."

He was about to beat me, but just at that moment there was a whistle, which meant that his turn to change off had come. The next day we had to go back to work. The *goyim*—the Poles and the Ukrainians—said they were not going. So they took only Germans. When they came back they said not only were they not beaten, but they received bread and soup.

Then I hear, *"Juden raus!"* (Jews out!) They put us in a large barracks. The guards said, "Don't worry, we will not kill you." The SS, who were dressed to kill, they gave us bread. They did not shoot anymore. At the same time they evacuated the Germans. The Germans looked at us with hatred. In line we were watched every two meters by an SS with rifle. Those who couldn't walk were put on a wheelbarrow. As we walked I went with a young man, I was like his father. At one point he asked me to carry his potatoes. A guard yelled, "Here Jews, put the potatoes away!" Once at night some people hid in hay along the road, but they were counted again in the morning. The guards went looking for the people and had iron pokers with which they forayed in the hay. And they found people and put them in the wheelbarrows. I was afraid that something would happen to the young man. No water, no food.

We were walking by a farm and a woman was throwing out refuse. The guards shot in the air. The woman ran back in, but she was angry. We ran to the side of the house, and I found what she had thrown out, a beet, a carrot, and whatnot: I got a beating on my head but I shared what I had with those around me. But I couldn't go on like this. I knew I wouldn't make it. A voice spoke to me, my own voice, for about two hours, I said to myself "Fishel, when you come to a place where the road curves and you're either up or down a hill, go out of the line and jump away." I said to the young man "Go with me. We'll try to get away." I fell behind and I got kicked, and then I was the last in the row. There were four SS, three Ukrainians, and a dog. I see a scene ahead in line, a man fell and the SS beat him and yelled "Stand up!" while the dog bit him in the leg. He wanted to stand but as he tried to stand up they beat him to the ground and put him in the wheelbarrow. I saw that with my own eyes. Then I hear,

"Go escape from the front not from the back, go up," but I couldn't any more. I couldn't and fell behind even more. At that point I wanted to be shot. But my voice said, "Go out of the line with all your might. Remember you should try even if there's a one percent chance of success."

We were going by a house, and there was a hill ahead. At the house as the road curved, we were walking on the *trottoire* (sidewalk). I see the house; I want to go to the door. I see the boy, but I couldn't help him. Another man wanted to join me but the guards came and the man did not run to me. I ran. I wanted to go up the ladder on the house, but I couldn't. I said to myself, be careful don't faint. "Try again," I said to myself: and the *passuk* (verse from the Psalms) came to me—*Me'ayin yavoh ezri*? (From where will my help come?) I try again to go up the ladder. I went up and saw little windows. I was afraid that if anyone saw me they'd be frightened at the sight. I saw some hay in one of the windows and a black cat jumped out. I climb in from the ladder and in the hay I lay down, and slept, totally unconscious. I woke up to the sound of voices, and I saw men with the wheelbarrow, one person with a shovel, and I recognized the four SS with the three Ukrainians walking below. I lay down in the hay again and lost consciousness. How long did I lay there I don't know. But when I tried to get up I fell. My ears were ringing. I wanted to look for some food. I was afraid to go down to the ground, but I went to look for an egg. I didn't find any. I saw a hen sitting on eggs. I couldn't push her away, she was just like a mother. I put my hand under her and got two eggs. One egg was fresh, the other was nearly a chick. "Fishel," I said to myself, "go down put the fresh egg back, lest the farmer find you if he discovers that there are no eggs." I went down the ladder and arrived at a doorway. I take a step, I hear a woman's voice: "Who's there?" She passes me by, closes the door, she doesn't see me. The woman says to a man, "I could swear that I heard someone go by."

In the morning I see French prisoners. I hear a man and a

woman speaking German. I open the doorway to the house. I see a cow and potatoes; Frenchmen had come to the house. I ask for something to drink. They brought me coffee and milk. It didn't take long, the American soldiers arrived. Another Jew had come around and the American soldiers wanted to shoot him because he had no striped clothes on.

I said, "Don't shoot us, we are from the concentration camp." They took us to the hospital; a colonel—a Jew—came by. I was in the hospital six weeks. Then a Jewish girl came to help. I knew I shouldn't eat too much, and I didn't.

◆◆◆◆◆

Fishel came back from the camps where, after the liberation, he received humane and caring medical attention. I don't know when he returned, or how he was when he came back home. Because, by the time my sister and I were back in Belgium, Fishel had already been back for about a year.

For most camp survivors the homecoming came as a shock. Despite the devastating blows they had suffered in the camps, the homecoming was the heaviest blow of all. In coming back home, they were hit with the reality of their losses. Not only with the loss of their loved ones but also because they had lost their former selves. Coming home to his intact family, Fishel's human dignity in tatters, came as another blow. Toward what end home? To remain alive and daily face what he no longer possessed? Without his beloved bride or the person he had been, who had been ripped apart?

But he did come home to his mother and father, and to all his siblings and their families; and he came back to us, to Hannah and Herman, and Gitta and me; and finding his close ones, he slowly recaptured some slivers of hope with which to refurbish the flesh that had been ripped and torn from him.

Fishel had a deep belief in God. And God was no scrap or sliver. His belief in God to which he clung, which stood by him even in madness, would never abandon him in the ordinariness of every-day life. Fishel's life came to an end when he was eighty. He never remarried. He worked in the diamond business as a diamond pro-ducer, buying one type of merchandise, such as industrial diamonds, and giving part of the lot he bought to convert into luxury diamonds. He continued to be a sought after chess player in the diamond bourse; he studied scriptures, and stayed in close touch with his fam-ily and ours.

In the Jewish retirement home to which he eventually moved, in his bright and comfortable room, hung a large picture of his mother, *de Mama*: a wise and loving woman with a serious mien, big black, intelligent eyes staring at him, a velvet hat perched on her head, and a fashionable feather set to the side.

NOTES

Introduction

1.   In the literature survivors are seen as those individuals who survived the Holocaust and World War II. It is important to distinguish, whenever we speak of survivors, between those who survived the labor and extermination camps and those who survived on false papers, lived on the run, were sheltered in convents, boarding schools, and lived with non-Jewish families; and those who hid out in forests, caves, mountains, and many other dangerous environments: these survivors did not experience the brutality and dehumanization of the concentration camps.

2.   Hayim Nachman Bialik, *Shirim* (Poems), vol. 1 (Tel-Aviv: Dvir, 1926), 179–180. Republished in 1966, trans. Chaya H. Roth, August 2007.

3.   *Shoah* is the Hebrew term for the Holocaust.

4.   When in the text I use the first person plural, I am including either Hannah and Gitta or Wally and myself, or my children.

5.   Gary Kenyon, "Holocaust Stories and Narrative Gerontology," *International Journal of Aging and Human Development* 60.3 (2005): 249–254.

6.   Mark L. Howe, *The Fate of Early Memories* (Washington, DC: American Psychological Association, 2000), 3–17.

7.   Sarah Moskovitz and Robert Krell, "Child Survivors of the Holocaust: Psychological Adaptations to Survival," *Israel Journal of Psychiatry and Related Services* 27.2 (1990): 81–91.

8.   Jane Marks, *The Hidden Children: The Secret Survivors of the Holocaust* (New York: Ballantine, 1993), 188.

9.   Robert Krell, "Child Survivors of the Holocaust: Strategies of Adaptation," *Canadian Journal of Psychiatry* 38.6 (1993): 384–389.

10.   Katherine Borland, "'That's Not What I Said': Interpretive Conflict in Oral Narrative Research," in *Women's Words: The Feminist Practice of Oral History*, ed. Sherna Berger Gluck and Daphne Patai (New York: Routledge, 1991), 63–76.

11.   Alan Baddeley, "What Is Autobiographical Memory?" in *Theoretical Perspectives on Autobiographical Memory*, ed. M.A. Conway, D.C. Rubin,

H. Spinnler, and W.A. Wagenaar (Dordrecht, Netherlands: Kluwer Academic, 1992), 26.

12. Natan Kellermann, "Psychopathology in Children of Holocaust Survivors: A Review of the Research Literature," *Israel Journal of Psychiatry and Related Services* 38.1 (2001): 36–46.

13. Julia Chaitin, "Intergenerational Transmission in Families of Holocaust Survivors: The Relationship of Working Through the Holocaust to Values and Social Perception," accessed November 30, 2004 at http://complex.fiz.huji.ac.il/~mult2020/chaitin.html.

14. Family transmission of unconscious fears, hopes and unacceptable thoughts, mistrust, feelings, desires, and the like surely do occur. This family's story, however, does not focus explicitly on unconscious processes. The emphasis here is on manifest content and communication.

15. Not all children of generations two and three participated in the interviews or allowed their interviews to be used, once taped. This being an ongoing project, they may still do so at a later time. As of this writing, however, the current interviews represent seven participants, including Hannah, Gitta, Chaya, Ari, Dan, Isabel, and Sasha.

16. Susan Rubin Suleiman, "The 1.5 Generation: Thinking about Child Survivors and the Holocaust," *American Imago* 59.3 (2002): 277–296.

17. Marianne Hirsch, "Surviving Images: Holocaust Photographs and the Work of Postmemory," *Yale Journal of Criticism* 14.1 (2001): 5–38.

One   Hannah's Memoir

1. Sachsenhausen was a concentration camp in the vicinity of Berlin on the outskirts of Oranienburg. It was built by prisoners in 1936. Following *Kristallnacht* in November 1938, 1,800 Jews were sent to Sachsenhausen; some 450 were killed after their arrival. The total number of persons imprisoned at Sachsenhausen was 200,000; 30,000 perished there. See Falk Pingel, "Sachsenhausen," in *Encyclopedia of the Holocaust*, vol. 4, ed. Israel Gutman (New York: Macmillan, 1990), 1321–1322.

2. With a stateless passport, our father's cousin was let go; however, the same was not true for Jakob Horowitz because with a Polish passport he was an undesirable alien who would be either sent back to Poland or interned in the concentration camp at Sachsenhausen.

3. *Appellplatz* was the gathering place in concentration camps where inmates were made to stand for long periods of time at the will and whim of the Nazis. They were counted, at first by last name, and later by their tattooed numbers. There too, announcements and punishments were dealt.

4. There was another version of the episode of how our father was beaten to death. And that I told my children first. As told by our mother Hannah, "Papa was standing at *Appell* together with all the other prisoners and they stood for a long time. Then a young boy who stood next to our father fell to the ground and fainted; he was maybe sixteen. Father said the *Shema* out loud, and because of that a guard came up to him and beat him to death. I don't know what happened to the boy."

5. The death certificate issued later gives September 21 as the date of our father's death.

6. In the early days of the Third Reich the Nazis incinerated the bodies of the victims they killed. This was done to undesirables such as the mentally disabled, children, homosexuals, communists, and Jews. Their ashes were poured into small wooden boxes and sent on to the families.

7. The Talmud is the multi-volume compendium of rabbinic Jewish law; traditional Jews would set aside time daily or weekly to study Talmud.

8. Moabit was the Gestapo headquarters and prison in Berlin.

Two   Hannah's Family

1. This conversation took place between Hannah and me in 1982.

2. Hannah did not know much about the battle of Tannenberg. What follows is my translation of Gerald Bocian's first-hand account and Gitta's granddaughter Arielle Bier's discoveries in the Berlin Archives about her great-great-great-grandfather, Rav Itsche Kupferstock.

3. Paul von Hindenburg, *Out of My Life* (New York and London: Harper and Brothers, 1920), 6.

4. Dennis Showalter, *Tannenberg: Clash of Empires* (Hamden, CT: Archon Books, 1991).

5. Personal communication with Gerald Bocian, 2000.

6. Letter to Maren Krueger from Paul Bocian, 1992, courtesy of Gerald Bocian.

7. Personal communication with Gerald Bocian, 2000.

8. Ibid.

Three   Hannah and Her Children, 1940–1942

1. This chapter was adapted from tape-recorded conversations with Hannah, Gitta, and me in 1979 and 1982. I indicate in italics who is speaking when.

2. Tape #1 and #2 (July 1, 1979 and October 27, 1982).

3. Around May 26, 1940.

4. In 1941, about 3,284 persons were ordered to report to the province of Limburg, in Belgium. They were mostly émigrés from Germany and Austria. They stayed in barracks, huts and some with local families in different towns. They had to report daily to the local police station. This situation lasted only a few months and finally they were able to go home on condition that the men would not live in Antwerp. Sylvain Brachfeld, *A Gift of Life: The Deportation and Rescue of the Jews in Occupied Belgium (1940–1944)* (Jerusalem: Hemed Press: Institute for the Research on Belgian Judaism, 2007).

5. Malines (Mechelen) is a city in Belgium between Antwerp and Brussels. In 1942 the Germans took over the city to serve as an assembly camp, from which Jews were deported to concentration and extermination camps in the East. Dan Michman, "Mechelen," in *Encyclopedia of the Holocaust*, vol. 3, ed. Israel Gutman (New York: Macmillan, 1990), 956–957.

6. Breendonck was an internment camp in Belgium, south of Antwerp. It was a fortress surrounded by a moat built in early 1900. Toward the end of 1940, foreign Jews were brought to the camp to work side by side with political prisoners. Later the situation changed; Jews and Christians were separated and brutally mistreated, and tortured by sadistic Gestapo agents. By the end of 1942 all Jews were sent to Malines, and from there to the East. Dan Michman, "Breendonck," in *Encyclopedia of the Holocaust*, vol. 1, 241–243.

7. Official documents state that the donning of the Jewish star was decreed and enacted by May 27, 1942. Hannah had received these badges from representatives of the Jewish community earlier, around March or April. She never did sew the stars on the outer garments, and we never wore any such badges. What mattered to us was that we saw her rebellion and resistance against the Nazis; she refused to identify us as Jews.

8. Hannah, Gitta, Chaya (Tape #5, 1979).

9. Hannah, Gitta, Chaya (Tape #6, 1980).

10. I discovered many years later that the gathering place for Jews caught in the roundup of August 26, 1942, was the caserne Auvare. The Vichy police in Nice had expected to arrest 2,200 Jews. It is believed that many Jews were helped by Frenchmen to find hiding places for them, so that the number of arrests in Nice and its surroundings was 655. The Nazis and Vichy were frustrated by this "low" number. See Serge Klarsfeld, *La Shoah en France* (vol.2): *Le Calendrier de la Persécution des Juifs de France 1940–1942* (Paris: Fayard, 2001), 873–905.

11. "The camp Rosdzien-Schoppinitz appears on a list of forced labor camps for Jews on the territories annexed by the Reich.... It is located in Upper Silesia, within the province of Slask in Poland, where a number of slave labor camps were located in the surroundings of Auschwitz.... Schoppinitz is first mentioned in existing documents on Oct. 9, 1942, and closed down in Nov. 1943. The employer was Firma Haage, that built the railroads... [among others]." Yad Vashem Reference and Information Services (Israel: International Tracing Service Archives [Arolsen], 2006).

12. Willy Toronczyk was a member of a special political commission that was formed by the Jewish social institutions to systematically organize the reception of a large number of Jews who came from all parts of France and Western Europe to save themselves. He had some information about the activities of the local Vichy police, and was able to alert the Jewish community of impending danger. See Leon Poliakov and Jacques Sabille, *Jews Under the Italian Occupation* (New York: Howard Fertig, 1983), 27.

13. Drancy was an assembly camp outside Paris. Some 70,000 Jews passed through there on their way to the camps in the East. The organization of the camp was modeled after the Nazi camps. In 1942 the first transport left Drancy for Auschwitz.

14. Historian Serge Klarsfeld's records indicate that Luzer Dafner was deported in Convoy 29 on September 7, 1942 to Auschwitz. He probably never arrived at Auschwitz, but died of typhoid fever in Schoppinitz, a slave labor camp in the surrounds of Auschwitz. There is no birth date or birthplace in Klarsfeld's book. See Klarsfeld, *Le Mémorial de la Déportation des Juifs de France* (Paris: Klarsfeld, 1978). But after the war, our mother received Luzer's death certificate from the Belgian government.

Four   The Italian Occupation, 1942–1943

1. Hannah, Gitta, Chaya (Tape #8, July 12, 1980).

2. In November 1942, the Italians occupied eight departments east of the Rhone: Drome, Isere, Hautes-Alpes, Basses-Alpes, Alpes-Maritimes, Savoie, Hautes-Savoie, and Var. See Michael R. Marrus and Robert O. Paxton, *Vichy France and the Jews* (New York: Basic Books, 1981), 315.

3. On September 8, 1943 Eisenhower announced Italy's capitulation to the Allies.

4. Our experiences in Italy, including the escape across the mountains, and our rescue by an Italian woman who hid us for months and a young priest who helped us escape, are described in greater detail in chapters six and eight of this book.

5. There were two summits, the Colle delle Finestre (the summit of the windows) and the Colle delle Ciriegia (the summit of the cherries), with the Gesso valley in between. With nearly 1000 Jews trying to escape, people took the path they could, with some going towards one summit and the rest towards the other.

6. Jewish refugees waited for World War II to end before attempting to return to their countries of residence when the war broke out, but none could predict when the war would end. In Rome, World War II ended on June 4, 1944. In northern Italy, Milan was liberated by the end of April, 1945. Mussolini was executed on April 28, 1945. German forces in Berlin surrendered the city to Soviet troops on May 2, 1945. German forces in northern Germany, Denmark, and the Netherlands surrendered on May 4, 1945. Alfred Jodl surrendered unconditionally all remaining German forces on May 7 in Reims, France. The Western Allies celebrated "V-E Day" on May 8, 1945. The Soviet Union celebrated "Victory Day" on May 9. Some remnants of German army groups continued their resistance until May 11 or 12, 1945.

Five   Eretz-Israel, 1945–1946

1. The Jewish Brigade arrived in Italy in November 1944; its members stood at about 10,000. Yoav Gelber, "The Meeting between the Jewish Soldiers from Palestine Serving in the British Army and *She'erit Hapletah*," in *She'erit Hapletah, 1944–1948*, ed. Israel Gutman and Avital Saf (Jerusalem: Yad Vashem, 1990), 60–79. See also Yoav Gelber, "Jewish Brigade Group," in *Encyclopedia of the Holocaust*, vol. 2, 745–747.

2. In the army the acquisition of necessary food or other items is called to "commandeer," while in the camps they called it to "organize." Both words have the same meaning, referring to the obtaining of necessary goods for survival through barter and bribery, although the circumstances in the army and those in the camps were totally different.

3. Youth Aliyah was a project of the Jewish Agency, initiated by Henrietta Szold in 1933, enabling the Jewish Agency to transport Jewish children who had survived the Holocaust to Palestine.

4. From the Jewish soldiers who befriended us we received legal documents identifying us as orphans. We left our mother and Uncle Herman, and were driven to the Italian port of Bari. From there we sailed on March 22, 1945 on the ship *Princess Kathleen*, arriving at Atlit on March 25. It was reported in the local Hebrew press that all immigrants on board the ship had official documents, to ensure that our entry into Palestine was legal. "900 Jews came to Eretz-Israel [trans]," *Davar*, March 26, 1945.

5. The *Struma* was an illegal boat of refugees that exploded at sea in February 1942. 769 lives were lost, leaving only one survivor. The children in Ben Shemen participated in the national commemoration by observing a fast day.

Six   The Summer of 1982: Revisiting the Past

1. Based on my diary and family conversations tape-recorded during the summer of 1982.

2. Gerald Reitlinger, *The Final Solution: The Attempt to Exterminate the Jews of Europe 1939–1945* (New York: A.S. Barnes, 1961, c.1953).

3. Elie Wiesel, *Night* (New York: Bantam, 1960), 45, 50.

4. Leonard Gross, *The Last Jews in Berlin* (New York: Simon and Schuster, 1982).

5. Rabbi Leo Baeck was one of the outstanding German-Jewish scholars of the twentieth century. After the World War II, he became chairman of the World Union of Progressive Judaism. During the war he was interned in Theresienstadt and was the leader of the Jewish community in this "model" camp. He was criticized both for not telling the Jewish community in Berlin what he knew about Nazi plans for the Final Solution and for not telling his compatriots in Theresienstadt what he expected the plight of the Jews to be when they were transported from there to the East.

6. Adapted from Israel Gutman, "Barasz," in *Encyclopedia of the Holocaust*, vol. 1, 148–149.

7. According to historian Stephen Whitfield, Arendt claimed in Jerusalem that fewer Jews "would have died had the Jewish councils not collaborated to varying degrees with Nazis like Eichmann." She argued that even anarchy and noncooperation would have been better than submitting to the decrees, as they would have shown open resistance. "Her attribution of some responsibility for the catastrophe to the councils (*Judenräte*) not only met sharp criticism, but also provoked a considerable historical literature that investigated the behavior of Jewish communities under Nazi occupation. The subsequent debate has often reinforced the picture of venality, delusion, fear, and selfishness that Arendt briefly presented." Stephen J. Whitfield, "Hannah Arendt," in *Jewish Women in America,* vol. 1, ed. Paula Hyman and Deborah Dash Moore (New York: Routledge, 1997), 63. Used with permission of the American Jewish Historical Society (AIHS).

See also Hannah Arendt, *Eichmann in Jerusalem: a Report on the Banality of Evil* (New York: Viking Press, 1963).

8. "With the war in Europe coming to a close, heads of the governments

of the United States, the United Kingdom, and the Union of Soviet Socialist Republics, met in the Crimea during the first weeks of 1945, to finalize wartime military strategy and plan for the postwar world.... The 'Big Three,' consisting of Josef Stalin, Winston Churchill and Franklin Roosevelt, were present at this conference known as Yalta. The first order of business at Yalta dealt with a proposed United Nations conference...." [The second dealt with the Declaration on Liberated Europe and the Atlantic Charter that was discussed at length between Churchill and Roosevelt only in Potsdam.... The third, in Yalta again, was the dismemberment of Germany and Reparations to compensate Germany's enemies during the war and to destroy the war potential of Germany.] Adapted from Brennan R. Collins, "The Yalta and Potsdam Agreements," May 3, 2001, http://sunnycv.com/steve/WW2Timeline/yalta3.html.

9. The Vélodrome d'Hiver was a sports stadium into which over ten thousand Jews were arrested and crammed by Vichy police (headed by a Nazi commandant) in a massive roundup in 1942. The stadium had insufficient toilet facilities, food, and water; prisoners were held for days, resulting in much sickness, and some deaths including suicides. Those who survived were transported to the East.

10. For an informed overview of the changes in regimes and policies toward the Jews, see Susan Zuccotti, *The Holocaust, the French, and the Jews* (New York: Basic Books, 1993), chapter 1.

11. On January 20, 1942 at Wannsee, the Nazis decreed the systematic annihilation of the European Jewry. From that time on, a system was set in place to programmatically speed up transports with a final destination going to the East.

12. The Germans occupied southern France after the Allies landed in North Africa. At that time, Mussolini occupied the eight departments of the Rhone. See Susan Zuccotti, *The Holocaust, the French and the Jews*.

13. Re. Guido Lospinoso and Angelo Donati, see Zuccotti, ibid.

14. See also Leon Poliakov and Jacques Sabille, *The Jews Under the Italian Occupation* (New York: Howard Fertig, 1983).

15. Alberto Cavaglion, *Les Juifs de Saint-Martin-Vésubie, Septembre–Novembre 1943*, trans. from 1981 Italian edition, Charles Arnould (Nice, France: Serre Editeur, 1995).

16. Susan Zuccotti, *The Italians and the Holocaust: Persecution, Rescue and Survival* (Lincoln: University of Nebraska Press, 1996), 89. "The Nazis entered Nice on September 9, angry and determined to take revenge for the ten months of Italian interference with their Final Solution.... The Jews of Nice, French and foreign alike, were caught in the most ruthless man-

hunt of the war in Western Europe."

17. Rebecca Weiner, "Venice" from The Jewish Virtual History Tour website, www.jewishvirtuallibrary.org/jsource/vjw/Venice.html.

18. Stanley Mann, article on the Jewish community of Venice, from the *Zachor* (Remembrance) website of the Holocaust Education Center at Michlalah-Jerusalem College. http://zachor.michlalah.edu/english/khila/khila-6.asp. My own notes from 1982 read that 247 Jews were deported and eight returned.

19. Zuccotti notes that 212 Jews were deported. Of those, fifteen returned. *The Italians and the Holocaust,* 189.

20. See Zuccotti, *The Italians and the Holocaust,* 155–165, for a powerful narration of those brutal roundups, and the courageous individuals who, trying to help others, became victims themselves in Milan, Turin, and Florence, among other cities where roundups took place.

21. Ibid.

Seven   The Family Interviews, 2000

1. The interviews are segments adapted from longer interviews that specifically address open-ended or semistructured questions.

2. Please see discussion in the last section of the introduction on the issue of counting survivor generations.

3. Sam, Gitta's husband, was eight years older than she was. He was already a young adult during the World War, but the family was in hiding in Brussels during the years from 1942 until 1945.

4. Primo Levi, *The Voice of Memory: Interviews 1961–1987,* ed. Marco Belpoliti and Robert Gordon, trans. Robert Gordon (New York: New Press, 2001), 136–147.

5. John K. Roth, "How Is the Holocaust Best Remembered? Reflections on History, Religion, and Morality after the Holocaust," in *Remembering for the Future: The Holocaust in an Age of Genocide,* vol. 3, ed. John K. Roth and Elisabeth Maxwell (New York: Palgrave Macmillan, 2001), 402.

6. "Transactionalism," as defined by Arnold Sameroff, and "Feedback," as defined by James Miller, are but two principles of systems theory that help explain how Holocaust memories might be transmitted by a survivor, received by a descendant, and then provided as feedback to the survivor. Systemic feedback can lead to fresh change in perception in thinking about the Holocaust when the discrepancy of the feedback is optimally discrepant because optimal discrepancy in communication shakes up preexisting

patterns of perception. When the discrepancy in feedback is too small, then what is heard like old news, i.e., uninteresting. When the discrepancy is too large, the information may be too new and difficult to absorb which leads to becoming overwhelmed, then prompting the listener to run away from the information. Arnold Sameroff, "Transactional Models in Early Social Relations," *Human Development* 18 (1975): 65–79; and James Miller, "Toward a General Theory for the Behaviorial Sciences," *American Psychologist* 10.9 (1955): 513–531.

7.   John J. Sigal, "Long-term Effects of the Holocaust: Empirical Evidence for Resilience in the First, Second and Third Generation," *The Psychoanalytic Review* 85 (1998): 579–585.

8.   Anna Ornstein, "The Aging Survivor of the Holocaust. The Effects of the Holocaust on Life-Cycle Experiences: The Creation and Recreation of Families," *Journal of Geriatric Psychiatry* 14 (1981): 135–154.

9.   Dan Bar-On, *Fear and Hope: Three Generations of the Holocaust* (Cambridge, MA: Harvard University Press, 1995).

10.   Terrence Des Pres, *The Survivor: An Anatomy of Life in the Death Camps* (New York: Oxford University Press, 1976).

11.   Eva Fogelman, "Exploding Psychological Myths about Generations of the Holocaust in Israel and North America," in *Remembering for the Future: The Holocaust in an Age of Genocide*, vol. 3, ed. John K. Roth and Elisabeth Maxwell (New York: Palgrave Macmillan, 2001), 93–107.

12.   Yael Danieli, "International Response to Trauma," in *Remembering for the Future: The Holocaust in an Age of Genocide*, vol. 3, ed. John K. Roth and Elisabeth Maxwell (New York: Palgrave Macmillan, 2001), 63–77.

13   Yael Danieli, "Conclusions and Future Directions," in *International Handbook of Multigenerational Legacies of Trauma*, ed. Yael Danieli (New York: Plenum Press, 1998).

14.   Lucia Ruedenberg-Wright, "The Second and Third Generations: Where Do We Go from Here?" Unpublished paper presented at the Association for Jewish Studies, Twenty-ninth Annual Conference, 1997.

15.   Dan Bar-On and Noga Gilad, "To Rebuild Life: A Narrative Analysis of Three Generations of an Israeli Holocaust Survivor's Family," in *The Narrative Study of Lives*, vol. 2, ed. Amia Liblich and Ruthellen Josselson (Thousand Oaks, CA: Sage, 1994), 83–112.

16.   Julia Chaitin, "'Living with' the Past: Coping and Patterns in Families of Holocaust Survivors," *Family Process* 42.2 (2003): 305–322.

17.   Chaya H. Roth and Steven D. Kulb, *The Multiple Facets of Therapeu-*

tic Transactions (Madison, CT: International University Press, 1997), 15, 27, 70. The compulsion to repeat, a term altered from Freud's repetition compulsion (1920), expresses the proactive inclination of the individual to return to those acts that were left unfinished in the past or had a painful outcome. The compulsion to repeat aims to "re-do" for the sake of mastery. When we reenact a painful experience it is in the hopes that this time the effects will not be painful but satisfactory.

18. Therese Benedek, "Parenthood as a Developmental Phase," *Journal of the American Psychoanalytic Association* 7 (1959): 389–417.

Eight   After the Interviews, 2003–2004

1. Susan Zuccotti, *The Italians and the Holocaust* (Lincoln: University of Nebraska Press, 1996).

2. Alberto Cavaglion, *Les Juifs de Saint-Martin-Vésubie: Septembre–Novembre 1943*.

3. Don Raimondo Viale was an enterprising priest and leader of the Resistance in Borgo San Dalmazzo and recognized as a Righteous Among the Nations by Yad Vashem. See Zuccotti, *The Italians and the Holocaust*; Cavaglion, *Les Juifs de Saint-Martin-Vésubie*.

4. Samuel Oliner and Pearl Oliner, *The Altruistic Personality: Rescuers of Jews in Nazi Europe* (New York: Simon and Schuster, 1992). See also Nechama Tec, *When Light Pierced the Darkness: Christian Rescue of Jews in Nazi-Occupied Poland* (New York: Oxford University Press, 1986), 113–150.

In Memory: Fishel Horowitz, 1903–1995

1. Breendonck was one of the brutal detention camps in Western Europe, where inmates were tortured by vicious guards, all Gestapo members. The developers of the criminal policies and those responsible for devising these brutal forms of torture were Bormann and Kaltenbrunner, and Keitel, who ordered the privations and shootings at Breendonck specifically. Bormann, Kaltenbrunner, and Keitel were tried, indicted, and sentenced at the Nuremberg Trials together with the major war criminals.

I cite from these proceedings because Fishel was shocked and traumatized in Breendonck when he heard the gruesome screams coming from the torture chambers; and he probably saw some of the results of these tortures. The trauma he suffered was a visual hallucination of the prophet Elijah making an appearance at a crucial moment, and then Elijah turned his back and walked away from him. He said to me during the taping that the tortures applied to the people interned at Breendonck were too horrendous to speak about. In his memory, and in the memory of his first experienced trauma, I am citing the major methods of torture engaged in Breendonck (and other detention camps in Western Europe).

The methods of torture that were used are cited here from the testimony of The Nuremberg Trial Proceedings, vol. 6, Forty-third day, Friday, January 25, 1946, as cited by the Avalon Project of the Yale Law School. http://avalon.law.yale.edu/imt/01-25-46.asp.

The methods of torture were: 1) The *lash*. 2) The *bath*: The victim was plunged headfirst into a tub full of cold water until he was asphyxiated. Then they applied artificial respiration. If he would not talk they repeated the process several times consecutively. With his clothes soaking, he spent the night in a cold cell. 3) *Electric current*: The terminals were placed on the hands, on the feet, in the ears, and then one in the anus and another on the end of the penis, crushing the testicles in a press specially made for the purpose. Twisting the testicles was frequent. 4) *Hanging:* The patient's hands were handcuffed together behind his back. A hook was slipped through his handcuffs and the victim was lifted by a pulley. At first they jerked him up and down. Later, they left him suspended for varying, fairly long, periods. The arms were often dislocated. 5) *Burning*: with a soldering lamp or with matches. 6) There was a device, a so-called *bracelet*, composed of several balls of hard wood with steel spikes on the inside of the bracelet; this bracelet and the steel spikes were tightened around the victim's wrist as a form of torture.

2. Malines (Mechelen) was a detention and transit camp for transports going to the East. Dan Michman, "Mechelen," in *Encyclopedia of the Holocaust*, vol. 3, ed. Israel Gutman (New York: Macmillan, 1990), 956–957.

3. Fishel's wife, Rosa Reisla Offen, was born on March 16, 1914, in Chrzanow, Poland. She and her parents moved to Antwerp from Berlin in September, 1939. Information from the research department of the Kazerne Dossin Museum, Memorial, and Documentation Centre on Holocaust and Human Rights, in Mechelen, Belgium.

4. Fishel's account of his experiences in Breendonck, where people were savagely tortured and beaten reminded me of the numerous interviews I conducted with over one hundred Holocaust survivors as part of the work of the Holocaust Educational Foundation, Evanston, Illinois, 1983–1995.

5. The transport records show that Fishel and Rosa Reisla were actually on the eighth transport, departing Malines/Mechelen for Auschwitz on September 2, 1942. Information from the research department of the Kazerne Dossin Museum, Memorial, and Documentation Centre on Holocaust and Human Rights, in Mechelen, Belgium.

6. Laurahuette, in Siemianowice, was one of more than forty sub-camps of Auschwitz employing prisoners as slave laborers. The production of antiaircraft artillery in the Laura mill employed 937 prisoners. "Sub-Camps of Auschwitz Concentration Camp." http://en.auschwitz.org /h/index.php?option=com_content&task=view&id=30&Itemid=33. From the website of the Memorial and Museum at Auschwitz-Birkenau.

7. Fishel spoke, during our taping sessions, of being sent to Schengut. I was unable to find a reference to a camp or location called Schengut in my research and inquiries. Yad Vashem Reference and Information Services, reply to inquiry, June 30, 2013.

8. Katowicze was an industrial city (anthracite, iron and coal mining, iron foundries, smelting works, machine shops) in Upper Silesia, southern Poland. "Sub-Camps of Auschwitz Concentration Camp." http://en.auschwitz.org/h/index.php?option=com_content&task=view&id=30&Itemid=33. From the website of the Memorial and Museum at Auschwitz-Birkenau.

9. Bismarckhuette was a slave labor camp using 192 prisoners for production of cannons and armored vehicles in the Bismarck mill. Ibid.

10. Blechhammer was a slave labor camp. The first group of prisoners there was employed in building Oberschlesische Hydriewerke, a chemical products plant. Soon many more prisoners were sent there. It became overcrowded and an epidemic of typhus, diarrhea, and tuberculosis broke out. Shmuel Krakowski, "Blechhammer" in *Encyclopedia of the Holocaust*, vol. 1, 218–219.

11. "On January 21, 1945, four thousand [most of them Jews], left the Blechhammer camp on foot. On February 2 they reached Gross-Rosen.... After five days they left for Buchenwald by train under heinous conditions." Shmuel Krakowski, "Death Marches," in *Encyclopedia of the Holocaust*, vol. 1, 348–354. See also Fishel Horowitz, oral history.

Buchenwald was "one of the largest camps on German soil. The camp was established in 1937 by Heinrich Himmler for political detainees and criminals." Yehoshua Buechler, "Buchenwald" in *Encyclopedia of the Holocaust*, vol. 1, 254–256.

As Fishel described it, the camp was divided in three parts: the large camp for prisoners with some seniority, the small camp where prisoners were quarantined, and the tent camp where the Polish prisoners were sent after the invasion of Poland, and where others, such as Jews, were funneled on the death marches.

BIBLIOGRAPHY

"900 Jews Came to Eretz-Israel [trans]." 1945. March 26 *Davar*.

Arendt, Hannah. 1963. *Eichmann in Jerusalem: a Report on the Banality of Evil*. New York: Viking Press.

Auschwitz-Birkenau Memorial and Museum. 1999–2013. "Sub-Camps of Auschwitz Concentration Camp." http://en.auschwitz.org/h/index.php?option=com_content&task=view&id=30&Itemid=33

Baddeley, Alan. 1992. "What Is Autobiographical Memory?" In *Theoretical Perspectives on Autobiographical Memory*, ed. M.A. Conway, D.C. Rubin, H. Spinnler, and W.A. Wagenaar. Dordrecht, Netherlands: Kluwer Academic. 13–29.

Bar-On, Dan. 1995. *Fear and Hope: Three Generations of the Holocaust*. Cambridge, MA: Harvard University Press. 41–44.

Bar-On, Dan and Noga Gilad. 1994. "To Rebuild Life: A Narrative Analysis of Three Generations of an Israeli Holocaust Survivor's Family." In *The Narrative Study of Lives*, vol. 2, ed. Amia Liblich and Ruthellen Josselson. Thousand Oaks, CA: Sage. 83–112.

Benedek, Therese. 1959. "Parenthood as a Developmental Phase." *Journal of the American Psychoanalytic Association* 7: 389–417.

Bialik, Hayim Nachman. 1926. *Shirim* (Poems), vol. 1. Tel Aviv: Dvir. 179–180.

Borland, Katherine. 1991. "'That's Not What I Said': Interpretive Conflict in Oral Narrative Research." In *The Feminist Practice of Oral History*, ed. Sherna Berger Gluck and Daphne Patai. New York: Routledge. 63–76.

Brachfeld, Sylvain. 2007. *A Gift of Life: The Deportation and Rescue of the Jews in Occupied Belgium (1940–1944)*. Jerusalem: Hemed Press: Institute for the Research on Belgian Judaism.

Buechler, Yehoshua. 1990. "Buchenwald." In *Encyclopedia of the Holocaust*, vol. 1, ed. Israel Gutman. New York: Macmillan. 254–256.

Cavaglion, Alberto. 1981. *Les Juifs de Saint-Martin-Vésubie: Septembre–Novembre 1943*. Trans. from Italian, Charles Arnould, 1995. Nice, France: Serre Editeur. 23–28.

Chaitin, Julia. 2003. "'Living with' the Past: Coping and Patterns in Families of Holocaust Survivors." *Family Process* 42.2: 305–322.

_____. "Intergenerational Transmission in Families of Holocaust Survivors: The Relationship of Working Through the Holocaust to Values and Social Perception." http://complex.fiz.huji.ac.il/~mult2020/chaitin.html, accessed November 30, 2004.

Collins, Brennan R. 2001. "The Yalta and Potsdam Agreements." http://sunnycv.com/steve/WW2Timeline/yalta3.html.

Danieli, Yael. 1998. "Conclusions and Future Directions." In *International Handbook of Multigenerational Legacies of Trauma*, ed. Yael Danieli. New York: Plenum Press. 669–681.

_____. 2001. "International Response to Trauma." In *Remembering for the Future: The Holocaust in an Age of Genocide*, vol. 3, ed. John K. Roth and Elisabeth Maxwell. New York: Palgrave Macmillan. 63–77.

Des Pres, Terrence. 1976. *The Survivor: An Anatomy of Life in the Death Camps*. New York: Oxford University Press.

Fogelman, Eva. 2001. "Exploding Psychological Myths about Generations of the Holocaust in Israel and North America." In *Remembering for the Future: The Holocaust in an Age of Genocide*, vol. 3, ed. John K. Roth and Elisabeth Maxwell. New York: Palgrave Macmillan. 93–107.

Gelber, Yoav. 1990. "Jewish Brigade Group." In *Encyclopedia of the Holocaust*, vol. 2, ed. Israel Gutman. New York: Macmillan. 745–747.

_____. 1990. "The Meeting between the Jewish Soldiers from Palestine Serving in the British Army and *She'erit Hapletah*." In *She'erit Hapletah, 1944–1948,* ed. Israel Gutman and Avital Saf. Jerusalem: Yad Vashem. 60–79.

Gross, Leonard. 1982. *The Last Jews in Berlin*. New York: Simon and Schuster.

Gutman, Israel. 1990. "Barasz." In *Encyclopedia of the Holocaust*, vol.1, ed. Israel Gutman. New York: Macmillan. 148–149.

von Hindenburg, Paul. 1920. *Out of My Life*. New York and London: Harper and Brothers. 6.

Hirsch, Marianne. 2001. "Surviving Images: Holocaust Photographs and the Work of Postmemory." *Yale Journal of Criticism* 14.1: 5–38.

Howe, Mark L. 2000. *The Fate of Early Memories*. Washington, DC: American Psychological Association. 3–17.

International Tracing Service, see Yad Vashem Reference and Information Services.

Kellermann, Natan. 2001. "Psychopathology in Children of Holocaust Survivors: A Review of the Research Literature." *Israel Journal of Psychiatry and Related Services* 38.1: 36–46.

Kenyon, Gary. 2005. "Holocaust Stories and Narrative Gerontology." *International Journal of Aging and Human Development* 60.3: 249–254.

Klarsfeld, Serge. 1978. *Le Mémorial de la Déportation des Juifs de France*. Paris: Klarsfeld.

_____. 2001. *La Shoah en France* (vol. 2) : *Le Calendrier de la Persécution des Juifs de France 1940–1942*. Paris: Fayard. 873–905.

Krakowski, Shmuel. 1990. "Blechhammer." In *Encyclopedia of the Holocaust*, vol. 1, ed. Israel Gutman. New York: Macmillan. 218–219.

_____. 1990. "Death Marches." In *Encyclopedia of the Holocaust*, vol. 1, ed. Israel Gutman. New York: Macmillan. 348–354.

Krell, Robert. 1993. "Child Survivors of the Holocaust: Strategies of Adaptation." *Canadian Journal of Psychiatry* 38.6: 384–389.

Levi, Primo. 2001. *The Voice of Memory: Interviews 1961–1987,* ed. Marco Belpoliti and Robert Gordon, trans. Robert Gordon. New York: New Press.

Mann, Stanley. 2004. "Venice." From the website of the Holocaust Education Center at zachor.michlalah.edu/english/khila/khila-6.asp. Michlalah-Jerusalem College.

Marks, Jane. 1993. The *Hidden Children: The Secret Survivors of the Holocaust.* New York: Ballantine. 188.

Marrus, R. Michael and Robert O. Paxton. 1981. *Vichy France and the Jews.* New York: Basic Books. 315.

Michman, Dan. 1990. "Breendonck." In *Encyclopedia of the Holocaust*, vol. 1, ed. Israel Gutman. New York: Macmillan. 241–243.

_____. 1990. "Mechelen." In *Encyclopedia of the Holocaust*, vol. 3, ed. Israel Gutman. New York: Macmillan. 956–957.

Miller, James. 1955. "Toward a General Theory for the Behaviorial Sciences." *American Psychologist* 10.9: 513–531.

Moskovitz, Sarah and Robert Krell. 1990. "Child Survivors of the Holocaust: Psychological Adaptations to Survival." *Israel Journal of Psychiatry and Related Services* 27.2: 81–91.

Nuremberg Trial Proceedings. 1946. Vol. 6, Forty-third day, Friday, January 25, 1946, as cited by the Avalon Project of the Yale Law School. http://avalon.law.yale.edu/imt/01-25-46.asp

Oliner, Samuel and Pearl Oliner. 1992. *The Altruistic Personality: Rescuers of Jews in Nazi Europe.* New York: Simon and Schuster. 112.

Ornstein, Anna. 1981. "The Aging Survivor of the Holocaust. The Effects of the Holocaust on Life-Cycle Experiences: The Creation and Recreation of Families." *Journal of Geriatric Psychiatry* 14: 135–154.

Pingel, Falk. 1990. "Sachsenhausen." In *Encyclopedia of the Holocaust*, vol. 4, ed. Israel Gutman. New York: Macmillan. 1321–1322.

Poliakov, Leon and Jacques Sabille. 1983. *Jews Under the Italian Occupation.* New York: Howard Fertig. 27.

Reitlinger, Gerald. 1953. *The Final Solution: The Attempt to Exterminate the Jews of Europe 1939–1945*. New York: A.S. Barnes, 1961 edition. 329.

Roth, Chaya H. and Steven D. Kulb. 1997. *The Multiple Facets of Therapeutic Transactions*. Madison, CT: International University Press. 15, 27, 70.

Roth, John K. 2001. "How Is the Holocaust Best Remembered? Reflections on Religion, and Morality after the Holocaust." In *Remembering for the Future: The Holocaust in an Age of Genocide*, ed. John K. Roth and Elisabeth Maxwell. New York: Palgrave Macmillan.

Ruedenberg-Wright, Lucia. 1997. "The Second and Third Generations: Where Do We Go from Here?" Paper presented at the Association for Jewish Studies, Twenty-ninth Annual Conference.

Sameroff, Arnold. 1975. "Transactional Models in Early Social Relations." *Human Development* 18: 65–79.

Showalter, Dennis. 1991. *Tannenberg: Clash of Empires*. Hamden, CT: Archon Books.

Sigal, John J. 1998. "Long-Term Effects of the Holocaust: Empirical Evidence for Resilience in the First, Second and Third Generation." *The Psychoanalytic Review* 85: 579–585.

Suleiman, Susan Rubin. 2002. "The 1.5 Generation: Thinking about Child Survivors and the Holocaust." *American Imago* 59.3: 277–296.

Tec, Nechama. 1986. *When Light Pierced the Darkness: Christian Rescue of Jews in Nazi-Occupied Poland*. New York: Oxford University Press. 113–150.

Weiner, Rebecca. "Venice." From The Jewish Virtual History Tour website, www.jewishvirtuallibrary.org/jsource/vjw/Venice.html.

Whitfield, Stephen J. 1997. "Hannah Arendt." In *Jewish Women in America*, vol. 1, ed. Paula Hyman and Deborah Dash Moore. New York: Routledge. 63.

Wiesel, Elie. 1960. *Night*. New York: Bantam, 45, 50.

Yad Vashem Reference and Information Services. Israel: International Tracing Service Archives (Arolsen).

Zuccotti, Susan. 1993. *The Holocaust, the French, and the Jews*. New York: Basic Books.

———. 1996. *The Italians and the Holocaust*. Lincoln: University of Nebraska Press.

INDEX

ABOUT THE AUTHOR

Chaya H. Roth is a child survivor of the Holocaust. She earned her PhD in psychology from the University of Chicago in 1960. She was Associate Professor of Clinical Psychiatry at the University of Chicago and Clinical Professor of Psychiatry at the University of Illinois over the course of thirty years.

Among Roth's publications are contributions to *Out of Chaos: Hidden Children Remember the Holocaust*, ed. Elaine S. Fox, introd. Phyllis Lassner, Northwestern University Press, 2013; *The Multiple Facets of Therapeutic Transactions,* with co-author Steven Kulb, International Universities Press, 1997; Roth, C.H., and Morrison, M.M. "Infant-Family Psychotherapy: One Approach to the Treatment of Infant and Family Disturbances," in *Development in Jeopardy*, ed. E. Fenichel and S. Provence, International Universities Press, 1993; and Roth, C.H. et al. "Tellers and Listeners: The Impact of Holocaust Narratives," in *Lessons and Legacies: The Meaning of the Holocaust in a Changing World,* ed. Peter Hayes, Northwestern University Press, 1992. *The Fate of Holocaust Memories* was originally published by Palgrave Macmillan in 2008.

"A remarkable achievement, Chaya Roth's *The Fate of Holocaust Memories* shows how family history is profoundly multi-dimensional, especially when that history must be retrieved from the ruins of the Holocaust. Originating in the author's childhood memories of that catastrophe, this significant book not only recovers and preserves a particular family's story but also brings Roth's mature insight to bear on the history of a disaster that we forget at our peril." —John K. Roth, historian, author, *Ethics During and After the Holocaust.*

"Scholarly literature on Holocaust survivors places all survivors—adults and children—in one category. 'To combine these generational functions... into one conceptual category' does not, Roth believes, represent her 'experienced reality' as either a child survivor or an adult who, as a child, lived through the Holocaust. In this regard, Roth makes a conscious departure from past scholarly tradition in *The Fate of Holocaust Memories.*" —Gail Hickey and David Lindquist, *Oral History Review* 37:1.

Photo by Stephen Zeldes

"Unusual for a Holocaust memoir, Roth not only records her family's history, but also examines the process and purpose of transmitting that memory." —*Chicago Jewish Star.*

www.ingramcontent.com/pod-product-compliance
Lightning Source LLC
Chambersburg PA
CBHW060041100426
42742CB00014B/2658